MYTH AND GUILT

MYTH AND GUILT

The Crime and Punishment
of Mankind

by THEODOR REIK

George Braziller, Inc.
New York — 1957

TO MY SISTER MARGARET

MYTH AND GUILT is based on Lectures for the Robert Lindner Foundation in Baltimore, given November 13 and 14, 1956.

CONTENTS

THE STORY OF
THIS BOOK

IT IS difficult to describe what impression Freud's *Totem and Taboo* made upon us, his Vienna circle. I still vividly remember the meeting of our Analytic Association in 1913 in which Freud presented to us the last and most important part of the work about the return of totemism in childhood. We were enthusiastic and we immediately understood that here was an intellectual challenge for generations of psychologists and historians of civilization. Privileged to speak with the author of the great book, we discussed with him the overflow of ideas it had stimulated in most of us. In the following months Otto Rank, Hanns Sachs, and I—they called us the psychoanalytic trio in Berlin—often talked until early morning about plans for future research work each of us hoped to do. We were friends and helped each other wherever we could. There was no petty jealousy, no quarrel about priority of ideas, no fear of plagiarism that sometimes disgraced the discussions of psychoanalysts later on.

Under the deep impression of Freud's theory a new interpretation of the biblical story of the Fall of Man had occurred to me. The ramifications of that new interpretation led to unexpected concepts of the early evolution of civilization. A very ambitious plan of an inquiry into the origin of the sense of guilt in man emerged. The analytic understanding of the unconscious meaning of original sin was followed by the discovery of hidden threads connecting it with the core of the Christ myth. I still remember at which occasion the idea emerged from vague thoughts and hunches and obtained clear, definite shape. On June 30, 1913, we celebrated *Totem and Taboo* by a dinner we gave on the Konstantinhügel in the Prater (a nice restaurant on a little hill overlooking the chestnut trees of the old park in which we had played as children). We jokingly spoke of that dinner as of a totemistic meal. Freud was in a very good mood. He sometimes looked thoughtfully at an ancient Egyptian animal figure, which an ex-patient had given him on that occasion. We were, I am sure, more than twelve at the table, but something must have reminded me of Christ and His apostles at the Last Supper. I still remember that this thought was one of the connecting links between the two parts of the building of ideas whose blueprint I clearly saw when I walked home through the dark alleys of the Prater on that June evening. (While I am writing this, a familiar tune resounds in me: "Im Prater blühn wieder die Bäume.")

I already knew that I would devote my life to psychologic research, especially to the trail that Freud had blazed, and I passionately felt that "holy curiosity" of which Einstein often spoke. With the conceit of a young man, I daydreamed that I had discovered something valuable and imagined that it would have revolutionary effects in the field of comparative religion. I have never since known the urge and grip of the creative impulse as intensively.

I have often wondered why I never spoke of my discovery with Freud, with whom I freely discussed other research plans. In those long conversations with Otto Rank and Hanns Sachs, all aspects of the new idea were considered. There is even literary evidence of those discussions during the following months: in Rank's *Psychoanalytische Beiträge zur Mythenforschung* the author mentioned twice the plan I had fully presented to him and Sachs.[1] He says there that "Dr. Th. Reik . . . will, in a prepared book, interpret another level of the Fall saga, which will complete its original meaning in another direction," and that I would in that quoted work "discuss the primal form of the myth and the elimination of the feminine element in the Genesis narrative."

After having jotted down its outline in the summer of 1913 I did not write a single line of that book. In a not uninteresting fragment of self-analysis of later years, it became clear to me what unconscious tendencies prevented my writing what had been finished in my thoughts for such a long time. My relationship with Freud played, of course, an important role in that inhibition.

Max Beerbohm did a series of cartoons with dialogues between the Young Self and the Old Self. Such an encounter occurs to all of us at one time or another and in writing this book I imagined it more than once. After conquering the melancholy surprise at the sight of the young man who had been I—"Behold, this dreamer cometh" (Genesis 37:19), I would severely ask him what he meant by postponing an important task for forty-three years. I would remind him of what the Irish say—that a thought, a sword, and a spade should never be allowed to rust. What were his reasons for such an atrocious procrastination? But I am sure he could not give me any satisfactory explanation. He would perhaps become impudent as young men are and say that I, an old

[1] Leipzig and Wien, 1919 (not translated into English), pp. 115, 118.

codger, had no right to make him account for his behavior. He would also remind me how often I had put aside or postponed a research plan in more mature years.

I wrote a number of books in those forty-odd years; yet I was unable to write this one. And then a surprising thing happened, as once before. The plan, postponed for more than four decades, suddenly moved from the fringes into the center of my attention and urgently demanded immediate realization. It was as though an old man returned to a woman he had wooed in vain when he was twenty-five years old, to win her. I again experienced the impatience and the feeling of exhilaration as once in the spring of life. Yet there was some new note in it, some sorrow, and some desperate determination. In writing the book, I felt what Tennyson's Ulysses says:

> Old age hath yet his honour and his toil;
> Death closes all: but something ere the end,
> Some work of noble note, may yet be done,
> Not unbecoming men that strove with gods.

The same task that could not be done because unknown emotional powers had forbidden it had now to be done because other unconscious tendencies ordered it. The inner demand obtained an obsessional character. All was subordinated to the one idea that did not allow other interests to exist beside it. It was despotic and exclusive as Jahveh, the One and Only one.

After forty-three years that old plan had come to the fore and had taken possession of me. The idea to uncover the secret meaning of the Fall story and of its continuation in the Christ myth began to preoccupy my thoughts to such an extent that all other research projects had to be put aside. With full sincerity I could have recited the lines a Scotch

poet, Thomas Campbell, wrote into the album of a young
lady one hundred and forty years ago:

> An original something, fair maid, you would win me
> To write—but how shall I begin?
> For I fear I have nothing original in me—
> Excepting Original Sin.

New York, January 1957.

PART ONE

THE MOST IMPORTANT PROBLEM IN THE EVOLUTION OF CULTURE

". . . I suspect the reader feels that the discussion about the sense of guilt oversteps its proper boundaries in this essay . . . but it faithfully corresponds to my intention to represent the sense of guilt as the most important problem in the evolution of culture . . ."

SIGMUND FREUD, *Civilization and Its Discontents*

CHAPTER I

THE LITTLE SCIENCE KNOWS
OF CONSCIENCE

PSYCHOLOGICAL research works by fits and starts in some fields and moves at a snail's pace in others. It is conspicuous that it progresses at express-train speed in areas of minor importance while it seems to need all its energy to remain at the same spot in problems of greatest interest to all of us. In one of his last books Freud represents the sense of guilt "as the most important problem in the evolution of culture" and conveys that the price of progress in civilization is paid in forfeiting happiness through the heightening of the sense of guilt."[1] If the sense of guilt is the hallmark of civilized humanity, is it not astonishing that psychological research has scarcely made any progress in this area since Freud characterized it as the most important problem of civilization, more than twenty-seven years ago? Reviews of the literature on the subject, for instance in the books by H. G. Stocker and Max Nachmansohn, will confirm the impression that no research of any significance can be noted since Freud's inquiry. The psychoanalysts also seem to avoid the problem in their

[1] *Civilization and Its Discontents* (London, 1930), p. 123.

3

publications. It is as though they hope it will go away when they do not mention it.[2] Yet the validity of Freud's statement cannot be contested. Ours is an "age of anxiety"— and what is guilt feeling but social anxiety?—and more than that of 1930. The Danish prince resurrected from his grave at Elsinore would say, "Thus conscience doth make cowards of us all!"

The fact that the discussion of the problem came to a standstill gives me courage to pick up a certain thread after thirty-five years. In August, 1922, I sent Freud some notes I had jotted down copying a casual conversation with my son Arthur, then seven years old. In his acknowledging letter Freud said:[3] "The contribution of your little son is very beautiful; deserves a commentary." The opportunity for such an analytic discussion presented itself when I gave a course at the Institute of the Vienna Psychoanalytic Society in 1924. The lectures then delivered were published in *Geständniszwang und Strafbedürfnis*,[4] which Freud called a "thoughtful and extremely important book." He considered the attempt made therein to demonstrate the role of the superego "as legitimate as it is fruitful." The contribution of my little son (which Freud considered illuminating) appeared under the title, "On the Origin of Conscience," as a chapter of the book. Since it is not translated into English, the following extracts from that chapter will be an appropriate introduction to an inquiry into the origin of the sense of guilt in human civilization.

We believe that certain analytic findings cast a new light

[2] Some commendable exceptions are Herman Nunberg's "The Feeling of Guilt" in *Practice and Theory of Psychoanalysis* (New York, 1948) and Ludwig Jekel's paper "Die Psychologie des Schuldgefühls" in *Psychoanalyt. Bewegung*, IV, 1932. Edmund Bergler's *Battle with the Conscience* (Washington, 1946) presents only rich clinical material.

[3] Quoted in my *The Search Within* (New York, 1956), pp. 642, 643.
[4] Leipzig and Vienna, 1925.

on the history of morality and solve contradictions that seemed not to admit of any solution. The psychological problem of conscience belongs to this category. The long succession of inquiries into the nature of conscience shows that the significance of that psychological phenomenon was highly estimated. It appears not only in monographs such as those of Paul Rée and Theodor Ebbinghans, but in every system of ethics from Socrates to Paulsen and Wundt, in the Catholic as well as in the Protestant and Jewish theology.

I would like to take as our point of departure the expression "conscience" itself and obtain important information about it in Wundt's *Ethics*. The word "conscience" points to the idea of a science or knowledge shared with someone. The prefix "con" is identical with the Latin *com* and conscience is the direct translation of the Latin *conscientia*. According to Wundt, the "voice of conscience" owes its name to a mythological idea: language conceived of that con-science as of a knowledge God shared with man. Wundt says: "The affect and the judgment that are connected with the consciousness of the motives and tendencies of an acting person are not considered his own psychical acts, but processes produced by a foreign power mysteriously affecting his consciousness." But how can such an attribution to the power of gods be explained? Wundt thinks that the idea progresses here, as so often, in a circle. Man at first shapes his own feelings into objects thus brought into existence. It is to be admitted that academic psychology has here said all that it had to say on this subject, but that is still very poor indeed.

We would like to find an opportunity of comparing these results of an obsolete way of psychological observation with insights reached through analytic methods.

Favorable circumstances allow me to start from a concrete instance.

My son Arthur, to whom I owe the following contribution on the psychology of conscience, is at present seven years old.[5] It seems to me that he is a normal child, intellectually well gifted but not extremely gifted. He is impulsive, of cheerful temperament, without particular tendency to introversion. He likes to play and does so with great vivacity; he is sometimes as naughty as other boys and reads only when he has to. He represents, I think, the typical middle-class boy of a big city without any marked peculiarities.

When he once took a walk with me, we met a man I knew, who walked along with us. During our conversation my acquaintance said that an "inner voice" had kept him back at a certain occasion. After the gentleman had left us, Arthur asked me what an "inner voice" was and I, thinking of other things, answered: "A feeling." The next day a conversation was initiated by Arthur that I am rendering literally according to the script written on the evening of that day:

> "Daddy, I know now what the inner voice is."
> "Well, tell me!"
> "I found it. *The inner voice is one's thought.*"
> "What thought?"
> "Well, you know—for instance, I am sometimes often (*sic!*) going to the table without washing my hands. Then there is a feeling as if someone tells me: 'Wash your hands!' and then sometimes when I go to bed in the evening and I am playing with the gambi (he has kept this word for penis since early childhood) and then the inner voice says: 'Don't play with the gambi!' When I still do it, the same voice says again: 'Don't play.' "

[5] The date concerns the year 1922, at which time these notes were written.

"Is that really a voice?"

"No, there is nobody. Memory tells me."

"How is that? Memory?"

Arthur points to his head: "No, the mind, the brain. For instance, when you said the day before, 'The child will run and fall down' and I am running, the next day, the thought tells me. 'Don't run.' (The instance concerns an actual event. The boy who had been warned not to run so wildly had fallen a few days ago and had damaged his knee so that an infected wound resulted and he has now to wear some bandages on it.)

I asked: "But when you run in spite of it?"

"When I then run and fall, that voice says: 'Did I not tell you that you will fall?' Or when I sometimes annoy Mother, also when I annoy you, the feeling says, 'Don't annoy Mother!' "

At this point we were interrupted. When a few minutes later I entered the room again, Arthur spontaneously began:

"Now I really know what the inner voice is. *It is one's own feeling and the language of someone else.*"

"What does that mean: the language of someone else?"

Arthur seemed to consider that and then thoughtfully said:

"No, that's not it." After a short pause he animatedly said:

"But it is true though. *What you have said before.* For instance, Mother once sent me to the grocer's and you had told me: 'Look out for cars!' And if I had not looked around, the voice would have said: 'Look that no car comes!' Has everybody an inner voice?"

"Yes."

"The inner voice does not come to the outer voice? Does it? Perhaps it does. One of the two will be. The inner voice —when one has it—does not come to the outer voice— only when one talks about it."

The next afternoon he started the conversation again:

"Daddy, the inner voice is really when one has done something naughty and then has fear. For instance, when I have touched the gambi, I am afraid. I do not know what fear. Yet I do know fear because I have done that. It is just such a feeling."

About one hour later he asked me: "Daddy, is it not so that thieves have two inner voices?"

"How is that? Why two?"

"Well, the one tells them they should steal and the other tells them they must not steal. But no, only the one which says 'No' is the real inner voice."

Since that conversation about eight months have passed. The boy has mentioned the inner voice only twice. Once he spontaneously said:

"When Mother does not obey Grandmother, she has also an inner voice that tells her she should always do what Grandmother says and when she does not obey the next time she is afraid."

Another time he asked me: "Daddy, one has not always an inner voice. Only when one needs it, isn't that true?"

When I asked him, "When does one need it?" he declared: "When one wants to do something bad."

The special value of these statements of a child is that they provide a splendid confirmation for the correctness of the analytic theories on the origin and development of several functions of the ego. Here can be shown *in statu nascendi* what psychoanalysis had to reconstruct in tracing the psychic processes of adults back to childhood. A considerable part of the emotional processes that will become unconscious later on is here still capable of conscious thought. Another part is already, at this stage, withdrawn from conscious thinking. The separation between conscious and unconscious in the child cannot be as sharply differentiated as with the adult. According to Freud, the conscious could not acquire all its characteristics in the child. It is still in the phase of development and does not yet possess the full faculty of speech presentations. The spontaneity and free naturalness with which the little boy gives us information about his emotional life increases its scientific value as evidence of fortuitously caught self-observation during an important part of infantile ego development.

It is necessary to point out that the psychological use of these statements of the child has certain limitations. They are connected with two factors: the child has no general theoretical interest turned to the understanding and explanation of emotional processes. He accidentally heard an expression puzzling to him ("inner voice") and wants to know what it means. He now compares the emotional situation that the man had discussed and that he could certainly understand only to a limited extent with similar experiences involving emotional processes from which memory traces have been preserved in him. His interest goes beyond this point only as he wants to understand how the "inner voice" operates. His questions show that he wants to compare what he has introspectively found in himself with what I, an adult, can tell him about the subject. This psychological interest is certainly remarkable for his age; his capability for self-observation is superior to the average, but you cannot expect him systematically to follow the threads. He repeatedly returns to the questions that occupied him. The same problems re-emerge after long intervals and his endeavor to clarify his own emotional processes is obvious. But we have to take it for granted that this striving is limited. On the other hand, I thought that I should not artificially turn his attention to questions for which he was not yet sufficiently mature and which he had not voiced himself. I thus restricted my speaking—in a way similar to the analytical situation—to cautious questions and to re-

quests to explain only that which he had himself said. This
was also the only possibility of excluding all suggestion.
We have thus to evaluate the statements of the little boy
with regard to the range and to the depth of the problem
solution according to the given situation.

The second factor to be considered is that of language.
The boy struggles here with a material difficult to master.
His vocabulary is restricted and his choice of expressions
can, of course, not fulfill our requirements with regard to
precision and accuracy. As is to be expected, his faculty of
verbalization is not always sufficient to express the issues he
wants to discuss and that are difficult even for adults. We
certainly observe how unsure he is when he tries to denote
what he wants to say, that he conceives the "inner voice"
sometimes as thoughts, sometimes as feeling. But he endeavors to make his expression, "language of another,"
more precise in his definition and to explain it as that which
I had previously said. By the way, it is astonishing how his
need for clarity propels him to find sharper formulation. In
the conquest of the inadequacies of his childhood vocabulary he has been remarkably successful.

Let us now comment on the child's statements and compare them with the insights into the ego development obtained in clinical psychoanalysis. The boy at first explains
to himself the "inner voice," which we conceive as censuring expression of conscience, as being "the thought one
has." It is characteristic that when he searched for instances,
those that occurred to him concerned washing and playing
with the penis. The other instance he mentions shows that
censuring factor in the service of the reality principle. While
he runs, that self-criticizing voice will warningly interfere;
the thought after falling ("Did I not tell you that you will
fall?") shows that he preconsciously expected to fall and

that he now considers it as anticipated self-punishment for his disobedience.

At this point it becomes possible to him to recognize "the inner voice" as something heard, as a warning or admonition of his father. During the few minutes in which he was alone this insight became so clear that it could be shaped into a definition: the inner voice is a feeling of oneself and the language of someone else. This definition is quite correct and can be considered the retranslation of the analytic theories on the origin of conscience and of guilt feelings into child's language. The boy has there reached a respectable psychological achievement. Compare his definition with the analytic theory: In his paper on the *Introduction of Narcism*[6] Freud sketched the origin of a censuring factor that measures the distance between the actual ego and the ego ideal. The incentive for the formation of the superego was provided by the critical influence of the parents transmitted through their voices. Later on, to these the voices of educators, teachers, and other persons joined. In his *The Ego and the Id* Freud had picked up this same thread: the superego formed itself in consequence of the identification of the boy with his father. The child obtains his power for accomplishing repression expected from him by establishing in himself the same inhibitions that previously his father had put into his way. The infantile ego borrowed, so to speak, strength for this task from the father. The superego shows itself as heir of the Oedipus complex. The tension between the demands of the superego and the actual ego is experienced as guilt feeling.

In Arthur's case we can observe this process still in its first phases. We see the primary results of the identification with the father. We follow the development in which the

[6] *Collected Papers*, IV.

contrast of the continued demands of the father with the
actual accomplishments of the child manifests itself as guilt
feeling. We can observe that the veto of the superego originates in the father's admonitions and forbiddings. The
categorical imperative of the superego in its genesis from
the relationship with the father is here still transparent. The
child who traces the guilt feeling back to a feeling of oneself and the language of another has gone the right way.
The "feeling of oneself" developed from the echo of the
critical, warning, and forbidding voice of the father within
the self—"what you previously said." It is tempting to compare the genesis of religious emotions of the masses with
the formation of individual conscience. "God," says Kant in
his lectures on philosophy of religion, "is, so to speak, the
moral law itself, but conceived as personalized." The church
declares that conscience—which amounts to the same as
Arthur's "inner voice"—is "God's voice in man"; that
means the continuously sounding and efficient voice of the
elevated father within the individual.

   We learned to understand the significance of the voice
hallucinations that play a distinct role in the symptomatology of certain psychotic disturbances. Those patients
hear voices that speak of them in the third person and
incessantly comment on and criticize their actions and
failures to act. Freud traces those voices back to parental
criticism. The development of conscience is regressively
reproduced by those patients, who reproject the voices into
the outer world from which they originally came. It is characteristic that the voices that the patients mean to hear
speak of them in the third person. It is not difficult to guess
whose voices are here originally reproduced: those of the
persons who talked together about the child, of parents and
nurses who were later replaced by other persons, and finally

by society ("public opinion"). These features present a kind of circumstantial evidence for determining the time when those factors of observation developed from the primary identification with the father. It must have been at the time when the child still spoke of himself as of a third person. Yet it was an age in which the ego already could recognize to a degree the contrast between its own impulses and the demands of instinctual suppression working upon it from outside.

Arthur asked whether "the inner voice" can come to the "outer voice" or not. That can only mean whether or not the inner voice can become an external voice. After some doubts he comes to the conclusion that this is the case only "when one talks of it." The voices that psychotic patients imagine themselves hearing present another instance of such an externalization of the inner voice that was once an outer one. It is significant that conscience is conceived as a speaking agency. The royal villain in Shakespeare's *King Richard III* says:

> My conscience hath a thousand several tongues,
> And every tongue brings in a several tale,
> And every tale condemns me for a villain.
> (ACT V, SCENE 3)

Freud's insights made possible the pursuit of the significance of preconscious word presentations for the superego. Those word presentations are memory traces of old perceptions and are sometimes, in isolated form, accessible to conscious thinking. We know how often men remember sayings and proverbs of their parents ("My father used to say") without being aware of the pattern value of those views for their own lives.

The part of these word presentations seems to transcend this narrow area and to extend to the beginnings of thought processes. The importance of parental patterns is also obvious here. Some remarks of Ludwig Feuerbach in his *Essence of Christianity* point in the same direction:[7] "Originally two persons were necessary for thinking. Only at the phase of higher civilization man doubles so that he can now also take the part of the other. Thinking and speaking are therefore with all ancient and sensuous people the same. Their thinking is only conversation. Common people (by which I mean individuals not educated in abstractions) do not understand even today what is written if they do not read it aloud, if they do not vocalize what they are reading. How correct is it that Hobbes assumes that human intelligence has its origin in the ears." Some puzzling inner commands and forbiddings in compulsion neurosis, many seemingly absurd or bizarre obsession thoughts, and some strange hysterical symptoms can be traced back to related sayings of father or mother not consciously remembered. The respect and the high esteem we have for certain moral views are not to be attributed to their absolute values, but rather to those first identifications with important objects, that is, to the aftereffects of the early love we had felt for the persons who transmitted those views to us. Yes, I would venture to state that the tenacity of certain moral ideas that have become obsolete depends on the immortality of such identifications with objects of our early affection.

Freud has made us understand that the original conflicts of childhood are those between the demands of our drives and the claims of civilization expressed by the educators of the child. Those early conflicts will be continued at a later phase as clashes between the power of the drives and the demands of the superego. I reported at another place a little

---

[7] *Das Wesen des Christentums* (3d ed., Leipzig, 1849), p. 75. (My translation.)

scene from Arthur's life when he was three years old. It
shows these conflicts at that age. In spite of many admonitions he had been naughty and was punished by his mother.
When she reproached him, he sobbed and said: "Boy wants
to be good, but boy cannot be good." The apostle Paul
means the same early-felt conflict when he complains:
"What I would, that do I not; but what I hate, that do I"
(Romans 7:15). Sixteen centuries ago the Carthaginian
Augustine, whom the Church calls The Saint, wrote in his
Confessions the remarkable lines: "The mind commands
the body and it immediately obeys. The mind orders itself
and meets resistance. . . . The mind gives itself orders to
want, that mind which could not command at all, if it did
not want to; yet it does not what it is told to. But it does
not want it wholeheartedly, therefore it does not wholeheartedly order. . . . It was I who wanted, I who did not
want." The same Augustine as a young man had prayed to
the Lord: "Give me chastity and continency, but do not give
it yet."

The role of identification with the father, upon which the
superego is established, can often be observed in children's
play. Arthur tried to train a dog and used, in his attempts
at educating and teaching the animal, the expressions of
praise and reprimand, of encouragement and admonition
that had been used in his own education. Several indications
reveal the introjection of the object and its connection with
guilt feelings at an earlier phase. When he was not yet five
years old, the boy had once been too vivacious in kindergarten and had been punished: he had to stand in the
corner of the schoolroom. When we heard about it, we
teased him and jokingly called him "Arthur Stand-in-the-
Corner." He was very annoyed by that and vigorously pro-
tested against the nickname. Yet we heard him use the

same mocking name toward imagined children in his plays. It was as though he had projected his naughtiness in that play upon other imagined objects, which he now humiliated through this nickname. It was obvious that the boy had in his play identified with father or a father-representative person and had thus tried to conquer the weaknesses and inadequacies of the ego.

From the same period some notes on Arthur are preserved: after returning from kindergarten he once pretended that he was a policeman. His governess was in the room when, acting this part, he grilled some imagined miscreants. He severely asked such a juvenile delinquent: "What did you do?" and another "What did you commit?" and so on. Finally he turned to the last criminal present in his imagination, addressing him in words that made the governess attentive: "And you, Arthur-Stand-in-the-Corner? Ah, I already know. You have stolen a revolver. You will be put into jail!" The astonished girl then interrupted him: "But, Arthur, you did not steal any revolver!" "Oh yes, there it is!" The boy animatedly answered and took from his pocket a little tin pistol, brought home from kindergarten. We have not observed any inclinations of this kind in Arthur since. But the emotional aftereffect of that early experience reveals itself when he now wants to know if thieves have two voices.

We can, in that little scene, study the operation of the agencies that have contributed to the establishment of the superego. It corresponds to the theory of the origin of the superego in the identification with father when we see Arthur acting the part of a policeman, of a representative of auhority, and accusing himself. Here the transition from identification with the object to the formation of the censuring superego is observable. As the policeman, whom Arthur acts, is contrasted with the self that is in the play projected upon an imagined object, thus the superego will later behave toward the ego. It is clear that the reported play scene anticipates the dreaded punishment and that it is inspired by an unconscious need of self-punishment. The boy acts out the scene of grilling in order to alleviate his anxiety. The guilt feeling originated in the fear of loss of love. The confession, implied in the play, should prevent that loss, even restore love if lost.

We realize in the analysis of this child scene that confession satisfies to some extent the need of punishment and reduces its urgency. It is not doubtful that the effect of the play allows for a conclusion to some of its motives: the play became a substitute for confession, which later on in reality follows. It seems to me that this latent significance of play cannot be restricted to this single case. Observation of children would certainly lead to the conclusion that the play of many a child presents unconscious confessions. The played or acted-out confession deserves the attention of psychologists and pedagogues.

The book from which these extracts are taken introduced the unconscious compulsion to confess as expression of guilt feelings into psychological literature. We shall meet again the problems that emerged in the discussion of that childhood scene. The conflict of the same emotional forces as in a child's play reappears in the battle of the giants that determines the destiny of man.

CHAPTER II

ORIGIN AND NATURE OF
GUILT FEELINGS

TWO HUNDRED years ago Jean Jacques Rousseau, who often said very silly things in very beautiful language, addressed conscience: "Thou infallible judge of good and evil, who maketh man to resemble the Deity."[1] Later on, the phenomenon of conscience was seen less enthusiastically, but more realistically. Research in the realm of the so-called "social instincts" was for a long time reserved to biologists and philosophers. The first group searched for roots of those feelings in the social life of animals. Here is a sample of the treatment of those subjects by one of the greatest naturalists. Charles Darwin discussed certain characteristic features of the swallows.[2] At a proper season these birds "seem all day to be impressed with the desire to migrate; their habits change, they become restless, are noisy, and congregate in flocks. Whilst the mother-bird is feeding, or brooding over her nestlings, the maternal is probably stronger than the migratory, but the instinct which

[1] *Profession of Faith of a Savoyard Vicar* (New York, 1889), p. 64: "*Conscience! Conscience! instinct divin, immortelle et celeste voix . . . Juge infaillible du bien et du mal, qui rends l'homme semblable a Dieu!*"
[2] *The Descent of Man* (New York, 1936), p. 486.

is the more persistent gains the victory, and at last, at a moment when her young ones are not in sight, she takes flight and deserts them. When arrived at the end of her long journey, and the migratory instinct has ceased to act, what an agony of remorse the bird would feel, if from being endowed with great mental activity, she could not prevail against the image constantly passing through her mind, of her young ones perishing in the bleak north from cold and hunger."

Paul Rée, a now unjustly forgotten philosopher and physician, intimate friend of Nietzsche, who owed him most of the leading thoughts of his *Genealogy of Morals,* took occasion to discuss this passage of Darwin, whose contemporary he was. He thought Darwin was mistaken: that swallow would feel regret, but no remorse. The consciousness of having acted badly, wickedly, or sinfully would be lacking. Rée, who was very interested in the genesis of conscience, asked[3] what events would have to precede if that swallow should feel not only sympathy, but also moral regret? The following events: among the swallow people a swallow prophet has to come forth and announce: "Ye swallows, hear! The swallow god whose wings reach from sunrise to sunset, and whose nest is in the clouds, reveals to ye through my mouth: 'I condemn the swallows who desert their youth before they can fly. Woe to the mothers whom the picture of the Nile and of its beautiful shores takes away from their children! They will be stricken by eternal punishment.' " Rée imagines that a swallow mother, seduced by the drive of migration, would desert her fledglings in spite of that revelation. She would feel then not only regret from pity, but also moral regret, the consciousness of

[3] *Philosophie: Die Entstehung des Gewissens* (Berlin, 1903), p. 49 (My translation).

the wrath of God and of eternal penalty. How, Rée asked,
did Darwin arrive at attributing also moral regret or remorse
to his swallow mother? As everyone educated by civilization, Darwin has learned from early childhood on to conceive of pitiless actions as evil and deserving punishment.
He thus assumed that the swallow also would think in the
same way. He attributed his own moral judgments to the
animals.

This interesting sample of a philosophical discussion of
the problem of conscience and guilt feelings is characteristic
of the spirit in which questions of this kind were dealt with
not more than sixty years ago. It does not differ much from
the way psychologists after the turn of the century discussed
the nature and psychogenesis of guilt feelings. Psychoanalysis found a new approach to these old problems.

Freud's papers, which introduced the new agency of the
superego into analytic theory, had turned our attention to
the part of unconscious guilt feeling in individual life as
well as in the formations of social institutions. The new insight in the area of ego psychology helped to deal with
some of those problems. It left others unsolved and created
new ones. Questions concerning the role of unconscious
guilt feelings in the development of the neurosis and in the
genesis of certain forms of masochism remained unanswered. Many attempts at solution undertaken by psychoanalysts were unsuccessful, among them my own, in *Der
Schrecken,* published in 1929.[4] Freud wrote in a letter to
me[5] with regard to this contribution: "The darkness which
still covers the unconscious guilt feelings does not seem to
be lighted by one of the discussions about it. The complica-
tion only increases."

[4] Leipzig and Vienna, 1929. (Not translated into English.)
[5] Dated February 26, 1928; quoted in *The Search Within,* p. 645.

The dawn for this central problem came in 1930, when Freud himself resumed the discussion in *Civilization and Its Discontents*. In the second part of this book, which presents an analysis of the structure of our civilization, Freud now acknowledged a special independent instinct of aggression and admitted that he had not given the universal non-erotic tendencies of mankind their due significance in the analytic interpretation of life. He now asserts that this innate instinctual disposition constitutes the most powerful obstacle to culture. One of the most important measures of civilization to make that aggressiveness harmless can be studied in the evolution of the individual. It will be turned inside, introjected, and taken over by that part of the ego called the superego that now in the form of "conscience" exercises aggressiveness against the ego. The tension between the strict superego and the subordinate ego is called "sense of guilt" and it manifests itself as need for punishment.

Whence does the sense of guilt come? Its first stage can be best designated as dread of losing love. A bad deed is one that, when discovered, would be followed by the loss of love (and of protection) for the child. At this state the sense of guilt is still "social anxiety." It will remain that in its core: that means anxiety that the father or mother and later the community will disapprove of and punish the misdoer. (Freud would have enjoyed H. L. Mencken's definition: "Conscience is the inner voice that warns us somebody may be looking.")

Things change only after the dreaded authority has been internalized; that means after the superego is established. The new authority of the superego does not seem to differentiate between forbidden deed and evil wishes. It seems to know everything that goes on in the depths of the self. It is omniscient as God. Exactly as He it tortures just those peo-

ple who are virtuous. Like God the superego is more severe
toward those who renounce many instinctual gratifications
than toward those who are lenient and allow themselves
some satisfaction of this kind. The superego develops a
special severity toward persons who do not yield to temptations. Since it treats certain wishes as though they were
real transgressions, renouncement is no help and does not
protect the ego against the severity of the inner authority.
The superego increases its strictness in persons who exercise
a great instinctual restraint in their life. There is less inner
absolution for the saint than for the sinner. The dreaded
loss of love and dread of external punishment are thus replaced by the tension produced by the sense of guilt feeling
and by a lingering unhappiness.

Feelings of guilt occur first after one has committed a
forbidden deed and relate to this one act. Freud would
prefer to call these original emotions remorse. Their early
emergence presupposes that the capacity for feeling guilty
was already existent before the deed. That means that feelings of guilt were there in a more or less distinct way before
the agency of conscience had come into being. Remorse is
the reaction to a forbidden deed of aggression. It is in general conscious. The sense of guilt that is later developed is
often unconscious and is sometimes perceived only as some
vague kind of anxiety or uneasiness, for instance in many
obsessional cases. It is in its later phases anxiety toward the
superego: so to speak, dread of the superego. We analysts
had been inclined to assume that any kind of thwarted instinctual gratification results in a heightening of the sense
of guilt. Freud's newest insights convinced him that this is
valid only for the aggressive instincts. In other words, the
origin of guilt feelings is in the area of the aggressive instincts. The general premise of the emergence of guilt

feelings is, of course, the repression of instinctual trends. But only the part of aggressive elements in it will be later transformed into a sense of guilt.

We only hesitatingly accepted the new and narrower concept of guilt feelings. But by and by, it became obvious that it has fundamental impact in practical as well as in theoretical direction. It has a special significance for the problems of civilization. Although we knew—the passage quoted from his letter to me proves it—that Freud was not satisfied with our research into the character of guilt feelings, his new concept came to us his co-workers as a surprise. In contrast with previous assumptions, the origin of the sense of guilt now appeared restricted to the aggressive instincts. We had often observed that suppressed sexual desires were accompanied by intensive unconscious guilt feelings. In the symptomatology of the neurosis as well as in that of perversions, especially of masochism, we had found the undisputed fact that guilt feelings in all cases concern the repressed sexual tendencies. The threads between those two kinds of acts, repressed sensual strivings and feelings of guilt, were so obvious to us that we took their operating for granted.

We had great difficulty in adjusting ourselves to some newer observations of Freud. There is, for instance, the fact that compulsive extensive sexual restraint or abstinence intensifies the sense of guilt. That seems to confirm the origin of the sense of guilt from repressed sexual drives. I myself had, at a Vienna seminar, presented the case of a neurotic patient who showed almost no guilt feeling or anxiety during a long period of masturbation, but who developed increasing guilt feeling in the time when he gave up this sexual activity and lived a chaste life. Could this paradoxical attitude be explained with the help of Freud's new insights? Guilt feeling is the result of unconscious temptation. It can even be defined as that special kind of anxiety awakened by the pressure of rejected drives; that means it is temptation anxiety. I had occasionally pointed out that those pent-up desires obtain the character of something special, dangerous, and urgent when they are repressed. To Saint Hieronymus, whose imagination called up a thousand voluptuous pictures, the arms of women appear as fangs of Satan. To the habitué of Moulin Rouge, they are only the slightly perfumed limbs of a girl. All these impressions are to a certain extent justified. Yet they do not invalidate Freud's concept of the origin of guilt feelings from the home of aggressive trends. Clinical material is here not sufficient to decide because the "sexual" drives whose operation we observe are also of a mixed character, containing aggressive and destructive elements.

A deeper understanding of Freud's considerations led also to the regretful conclusion that our impressions had not been conclusive. The observation that sexual repression awakens or intensifies guilt feelings is valid, but that is not identical with the role of the cause which we had attributed to sexual desires. The suppression intensified only the urgency of their power and the emergence of temptation. Guilt feeling does not result from unfulfilled erotic desire, but from another side. The pent-up sexual drives provoke intensified aggression by prevention of sexual gratification. But those persons are loved or admired and respected and the aggressive tendencies that had been awakened by protest against them were repressed just on account of this love. It is repressed aggressiveness whose energy is transformed into guilt feelings. The aggression that is transmitted to the superego turns its punishing power against the person himself.

Let us for a minute return to the case of my patient mentioned before and examine the emotional situation again. As long as he indulged in daily masturbation, he was almost free from guilt feelings and complained only that this kind of sexual activity kept him away from the company of women. The paradoxical emergence of guilt feelings, which increased the longer he lived abstinent at a later phase of his neurosis, cannot be explained by referring to the power of the repressed sexual drives. The patient was, of course, very aware of their effects and fought desperately against their pressure. But he was himself puzzled by the lack of anxiety during the previous period of excessive masturbation. The character of this anxiety was at first not clear, but it revealed itself as unconscious guilt feeling in the analysis of the patient's fantasies. The images he called up in them pressed him to return to masturbation, but whenever he was on the verge of yielding, he had to think of a certain counselor in a camp who had once caught him masturbating when he was twelve years old and had warned him severely. He then suppressed the sexual desire. He attributed the anxiety he felt afterward to the fact that he now considered the sexual trends as expression of moral weakness. It was, however, obvious that that emotion was his reaction to the unconscious rage against the admired teacher. The upwelling fury that his reproach had once awakened in the boy and that re-emerged whenever he now, as a man, was tempted to masturbate had been repressed since it came in conflict with the conscious respect and affection he still felt for that counselor. The true nature of that anxiety as disguised guilt feeling became obvious at the following occasions: shortly after he had again suppressed the urge to masturbate, he committed within two hours a large number of self-damaging acts such as spraining an ankle, burning his fingers on a match, and losing his wallet. Unconscious guilt feeling manifested itself here, as so often, as self-punishment. That guilt feeling did not concern the repressed sexual desires but the aggressive tendencies against that counselor, which had returned and which he had disavowed in himself.

Our observations had been careful and correct, but the conclusions we drew from them were careless and errone-ous—a case not uncommon in research. Re-examining the situation, we wondered how we could have jumped the abyss between the one group of drives and the other. Did we not recognize that we stretched a cobweb filament between the repression of sexual trends and the origin of guilt feelings? Were we not perceptive enough to feel that the sexual drives are not akin to the emotions we connected in our theory with the idea of guilt? Yet expressions such as remorse (which means to bite again), pangs of conscience, and similar ones, as well as the similes of the poets, refer clearly enough to the aggressive, particularly to the oral realm, as the one in which guilt feeling originates. (Shake-speare calls the guilty mind "full of scorpions" and says great guilt "will bite the spirit fiercely.") Sexual drives be-long, so to speak, to another family, are not cut from the same cloth. A comparison suggests itself by this very expres-sion: A woman who wants to buy material for a dress examines the different cloths the saleslady shows her with three fingers of her right hand and judges their quality and texture. She "feels" whether they are coarse or fine, firm or flimsy, and so on. Does she know anything of manufac-ture of fabrics, has she any scientific knowledge of thread arrangement and other factors? No, yet her opinion is al-most always correct. When we attributed the origin of guilt feelings to repressed erotic desires, we had shown a regrettable lack of psychological sensitiveness. We had no discerning feeling in the tips of our fingers.

To find an explanation for the wrong conclusion we had drawn is perhaps more illuminating than self-recriminations. There had been several reasons for the mistake in our score. First, we followed in that allotment the line of least psychological resistance. It was easier to attribute the birth of guilt feelings to sexual trends than to aggression, especially since those assaulting, hateful, and murderous drives are directed against admired or loved persons—the same persons from whom the sexual prohibitions came. Secondly, so many phenomena observable to the psychologist speak, superficially considered, in favor of the concept that sexual transgressions produce guilt feelings.

Such a surface view made the acceptance of Freud's opinion difficult even with analysts. Gerhart Piers and Milton B. Singer, for instance, seriously doubt that Freud is correct in his assumption that guilt proper is generated exclusively by aggressive and not by any other drive.[6] They say: "I would like to question this standpoint. It would seem to me that in our Christian culture, whether under St. Paul's or Calvin's protectorate, a specific sense of guilt connected with seeking sensual-sexual pleasure is clearly discernible, particularly in women." This purely phenomenological point of view takes into account only what can be observed, neglecting depth psychology and renouncing all advantages of analytic penetration. Otherwise the authors would have recognized that a specific conscious sense of guilt "particularly in women" in "our Christian culture" or any other does not invalidate Freud's concept. They did not understand the emotional dynamic determining the detour in the development of guilt feeling. That "specific

[6] *Shame and Guilt* (Springfield, Ill.), 1953, p. 19.

sense of guilt connected with seeking sensual pleasure"
originates when these drives seeking pleasure are thwarted
and have awakened protest and aggression against parents
or educators who obstructed and frustrated them. The guilt
feeling is here too rooted in the repression of those aggressive trends and presents itself as the reaction of attack upon
loved persons to energetic suppression of those strivings.
The mistake we made in our previous conception of the
sense of guilt was facilitated by a third factor: there are
some elements of aggressiveness in the sexual drives as
there are some sexual (this means here sadistic) qualities
in aggressiveness. It is almost impossible in our clinical
material to find trends that belong unequivocally to the one
or the other group of drives.

Yet there was plenty of circumstantial evidence for the
kinship of aggressiveness and guilt feelings. Was it not, for
instance, remarkable that heightening of guilt feeling under
certain conditions again leads to aggressive breakthroughs—
as though it were retransformed into the original material
from which it was taken? In *The Unknown Murderer*,[7] I
described the return of repressed aggressive and murderous
impulses out of the middle of heightened guilt feelings with
some groups of criminals. It seems that an extraordinarily
intensified guilt feeling favors the emergence of such repressed strivings. A certain type of neurotic criminal whose
dynamics were described by Freud belongs to this category
of individuals whom the pressure of a pre-existent guilt
feeling propels to commit a crime. Guilt feeling acts here
in its propelling and provoking function as though it were
a drive itself. But it proves itself as a descendant of the
innate aggression with which it has a decided family resemblance in spite of all differences.

[7] New York, 1945.

Here are two instances of such retransformation of intensified guilt feeling into anger and ensuing attack: a young
woman who felt wronged by her boss in the office decided
to give him "a piece of her mind" and told him in sharp
language "all" she had against his unfairness. On the evening of this day she felt very remorseful and wished to
apologize to him. When she came to the office the next
morning, she was still feeling guilty. The scene between
her and her boss that followed started with her apology,
but it was continued in a surprising direction in still more
accusations from her side. They reached finally such a
sharpness that she was dismissed from her job. A similar
psychological character can be ascribed to an everyday
occurrence in marital life. A husband regrets that he has
hurt the feelings of his wife in a tiff starting from the discussion of trifling things. The more repentant he becomes, the
more urgent becomes his wish to be reconciled and to admit that he had been unfair and inconsiderate. With this
intention, he begins to speak to her apologetically but,
discussing his own injustice, he begins to criticize her attitude and to accuse her until he is again in the middle of
an argument, this one worse than the one for which he
wished to apologize, and one in which he hurts his wife's
feelings more than before. The emotional process in these
cases is comparable to a tug of war in which sometimes
the superior strength of one party is asserted, followed by
a surprising effort of the other that succeeds in pulling the
rope to its side. The objection that can be raised at this
point is, of course, that such a contest between guilt feeling
and drives is also common in the area of sexuality and frequently with the result that the sexual desires surprisingly
get the upper hand just after a supreme effort of the
repressing forces. Rodin's picture of the temptation of Saint

Anthony shows a similar situation of the return of the repressed: the saint overwhelmed by the sinful sexual fantasies finds his refuge in remorseful prayers while kneeling at the foot of a big crucifix. In the place where the Saviour hangs with nailed-down arms emerges the vision of a nude woman.

But the argument that such instances of a sudden overpowering of repression speak for the possibility of a sexual origin of guilt feeling is not conclusive. The returning of the repressed is the defiant and rebellious tendency against the authorities prohibiting sexual gratification. The power that is victorious in that emotional tug of war is the aggressive energy that is responsible for the breakthrough. There are other instances from clinical material that are in favor of the concept of the genesis of guilt feelings from repressed aggression. Many cases of mixed formation such as the symptoms of defiant obedience and of self-harming rebelliousness obviously, although not always tangibly, indicate the effect of a latent compound of aggression within the feeling of being guilty.

The final and, to my view, most convincing argument for the consanguinity of guilt feelings and aggression and against the hypothesis of their generation from other instinctual sources is the form in which unconscious guilt feelings manifest themselves. One of the most interesting and puzzling signs is an unconscious need for punishment that finds means to express itself in acts of self-harming, self-sabotaging, and self-frustrating. It is as though this need for self-punishment were the executive and representative of the mute sense of guilt. Since my *Geständniszwang und Strafbedürfnis*, published in 1926, is not translated into English, I have to point out here that I had been on the same track as Freud in the discussion of the unconscious need for punishment, which is the most characteristic expression of guilt feeling, four years before Freud's concept. On page 84 I asserted that *"the unconscious need for punishment* that originates in the superego has to be recognized as one of *the most powerful, destiny-forming forces of human life."* It gives me satisfaction that Freud acknowledged this contribution in *The Problem of Anxiety*[8] and called it *"something especially valuable"* in his letter of January 13, 1925.

Why did we enter this extensive discussion of Freud's new thoughts? We remind the reader that the sense of guilt appeared to the old master "as the most important problem of our culture." If Freud's assertion is correct, is this not of greatest significance for the progress in civilization and for the human situation of today and of tomorrow? And is his statement that this progress "is paid in forfeiting happiness through the heightening of guilt" not of greatest interest to each of us? If we trust Freud's assertion, we would have to consider individual happiness as the sacrifice human evolution demands from us. Happiness would play the role of a missing person in the battle. No one knows where it is and it is not unlikely that we have to put it finally on the casualty list in the war civilization wages against the instinctual drives. Can Freud's definite prediction of the future of civilization leave us unaffected? He declared that civilization can reach its aim only in fomenting an increasing sense of guilt. This intensification is inevitably bound up with the development of civilization and may swell to a magnitude individuals can hardly bear.

The main part of this book is dedicated to the attempt to find where the sense of guilt that pervades our culture

---

[8] *Hemmung, Symptom und Angst* (Vienna, 1926). English translation in *Collected Papers* (New York, 1936), VI, p. 57.

originated and what are its causes. We emphasized in the foregoing paragraphs that the analytic exploration of the individual emotional life made it necessary to change our original theory. We were led to the assumption that guilt feeling is generated exclusively by aggression and not by any other drives. If this is correct, we can expect that the same origin and character will be found in the sense of guilt met in the evolution of mankind. Religion, particularly Christianity, traces the guilt feeling of man back to an "original sin," which is conceived as sexual transgression, to the "weakness of the flesh," or to sensual desire. Our whole civilization, including our education, is under the spell of this view. It is common to the moralists, theologians, and philosophers who regard sexuality as the root of man's criminality and sinfulness, as well as to the educators and psychologists (including psychoanalysts) who hope that freedom from sexual suppression will change man and remove the greatest obstacle in our civilization. This writer is of the opinion that both groups are mistaken and believes that also the guilt feelings of mankind have their roots in aggression and violence; in other words, that theology and philosophy were taken in by the same fallacy of which we analysts were guilty when we conceived of guilt feeling as determined by thwarted erotic desires. The narrower concept of the consanguinity of aggression and guilt feeling is bound to lead to a different view of civilization and of the human situation. The last consideration was decisive for the task undertaken here. The following exploration takes us from the ground on which it started, namely from the development of individual guilt feeling, to the process of cultural evolution in which the sense of guilt plays a most important and still unrecognized role.

Freud maintained that "the community, too, develops a

superego, under whose influence cultural evolution proceeds," and adds that it "would be an enticing task for an authority on human systems of culture to work out his analogy in specific cases." Without any claim to be such an authority, I will attempt to pursue this analogy with regard to the "anxiety of conscience" that pervades our Western culture. This presupposes that the evolution of civilization has a far-reaching similarity with the development of an individual, which means that one can speak of a conscience of mankind, of a guilt feeling of all men. In other words, it is legitimate to subject the universal sense of guilt to analytic investigation. Freud warned that the discovery of analogies should not be pushed to extremes, but he thought that "an attempt to apply psychoanalysis to civilized society would not be fanciful or doomed to fruitlessness." He recognized the difficulties, but expected that "one day someone will venture upon this research into the pathology of civilized communities." If I may so conclude from memories of conversations with him, he would have welcomed an attempt such as the one here presented.

The following research into the origin of collective guilt feeling will not proceed from Freud's assumptions. We have to find our own independent way into that virgin territory.

CHAPTER III

THERE IS A WORLD SENSE OF GUILT

DURING the aftermath of the last World War, the question of war guilt was frequently and sometimes passionately discussed. How far were the German people responsible for mass murders and tortures inflicted on men, women, and children, for the atrocities in concentration camps and gas chambers, for the sacrificed lives of millions of people whose only crime was that they did not belong to the Aryan race, which does not exist? In the Nürnberg trials and at other courts, a new kind of offense was judged and sentenced: crime against humanity. It seems to be an innovation not to make a single individual responsible for that crime, but a nation, a people of seventy millons. But was it new? Was it not rather a return to a very old state, to one of the oldest concepts of society, to a basic idea of primitive communities? The historians of civilization agree that crime was originally not considered a merely individual matter. The burden of guilt is often carried by an innocent community within which a single individual has committed a crime, but the punishment falls on all. The community is visited by plague or famine as penalty for the deed of one person. The Scripture recounts such a case: "There was a famine in the days of David three years, year after year; and David enquired of the Lord. And the Lord answered, It is for Saul, and for his bloody house, because he slew the Gibeonites" (II Samuel 21:1).

The affliction that falls upon a nation or a city is interpreted as the judgment of the wrath of the gods. The community first becomes thus aware of the guilt; attention is called to it by the very punishment from an angry heaven. It is then inferred that a crime or sin has been committed and an oracle is consulted as to its nature. Oedipus slays his own father in ignorance and the city is visited with plague and bareness of earth, beast, and men. The affliction is caused by the deed of an unknown murderer. The community shares his guilt and is punished for it as if it were its own. From the earliest times the social group has collective responsibilities. The members participate in one another's merits and misdeeds.

Only very late was the guilt transferred from the community to an individual in a solemn rite of purification whose essential features are similar in ancient Israel and Greece; compare Deuteronomy 21:1 ff. and Plato, Laws 874. The Greek literature is full of instances of unconscious communal sin that is discovered when the city is visited by famine or some other calamity. Primitive civilizations as well as half-civilized peoples share the view that crime is committed by the community and that it has to bear the burden of penalty as long as it is polluted by the misdeed of one of its members. A prominent historian, L. R. Farnell, writes[1] about Greece and Babylon that they "reveal the

---

[1]*Greece and Babylon* (Edinburgh, 1911), p. 152. Hans von Hentig, *Die Strafe* (Berlin, 1954), Vol. I, deals with the problem of collective responsibility in other culture patterns.

phenomenon that marks an early stage of social moral: as
the tribe of the family are one flesh, one corporate unit of
life, the members are collectively responsible. . . . This was
the familiar law of old Hellas, and we may say of the ancient
Mediterranean society." The books of Westermarck, Durk-
heim, Robertson, Smith and other scholars present an abundance of instances from ancient history and primitive tribes
which prove that the solidarity of family or of the clan
implies also responsibility for the crime of the individual.

The concept of war crime shared by a whole people is
thus not a recent one, but the renewal of one of the oldest
social ideas. It does not make any essential difference that
in early historic times the unwritten law was valid only for
a people of a few thousand while it is now applied to a
nation of many millions. The same progress of civilization
that has brought about the formation of wider social groups,
the evolution from families to greater units, has also led to
unheard-of horrors of cruelty and violence against masses.
Only a part of the German people accepted the responsibility for the acts of murder, torture, and brutality of which
they were accused. Many Germans claim ignorance of or
innocence for those crimes—some certainly with some justification; others found many mitigating circumstances. A
great part of the German people acknowledged that they
had failed when they submitted to the madness of their
leaders and pleaded guilty. More important than voluntary
self-accusations and confessions of individuals was the
silent but eloquent expression of the sense of guilt pervading
the German nation. The acknowledgment of common guilt,
professed by the President and the representatives of the
nation, their declaration of willingness to make amends—
as far as amends can be made—is only an official manifestation of the emotional crisis that started long before, even

before the defeat of the army and before the Götterdäm-
merung, the breakdown of the false idols.

But let us look at the reverse of the coin. The imprints
there are not as clear and immediately discernible as on
the other side. It is not likely that there is a guilt feeling of
the victors whose intensity corresponds to that of the van-
quished.

One can expect that the nations or groups that take
vengeance for bloody deeds of aggression would feel only
the supreme satisfaction that revenge gives to the victor.
The triumph for victory is there combined with exultation
of justified punishment for crimes inflicted on their own
people, their relatives and friends. Yet the observation of
primitive tribes shows that the situation is not as simple.
Frazer gives an impressive picture of the extent and number
of atoning and purifying rituals to which the victorious
armies returning from the battlefield are subjected in primitive tribes. Not only the murderers, it seems, but also the
avengers feel guilt.

Here are a few instances from the war customs of primitive tribes: when in the island of Timor a victorious expedition returns, with the heads of the foe, sacrifices are offered
to appease the souls of the killed enemies. If such offerings
were omitted, the victors would be afflicted with some misfortune. Among the ceremonies of appeasement, a dance
is performed during which the people address the slain
men in a song: "Be not angry because your head is here
with us; had we been less lucky, our heads might now have
been exposed in your village. We have offered the sacrifice
to appease you. Your spirit may now rest and leave us in
peace. Why were you our enemy? Would it not have been
better had we remained friends? Then your blood would
not have been spilt and your head would not have been

cut off." The Gollas of East Africa returning from war sacrifice to the spirits of their slain foe before they will re-enter
their houses.

Some people try to change their former enemies into
friends after death. The savage tribes of Borneo treat the
severed heads with affection. The Sea Dyaks of Sarawak
address the heads they bring home from an expedition with
very endearing names and give them delicate morsels of
food. The heads are asked to hate their former friends and
to love their present hosts. The savage tribes of North
America used to go into mourning of many months over
the enemies they had killed and scalped. When the Osages
have mourned over their own dead "they will mourn for the
foe just as if he was a friend."[2]

Freud quoting such instances points out[3] that those savages express, besides their hostile impulses toward the
enemy, also admiration, remorse, and bad conscience for
having killed him. It seems that they "were in possession of
a living commandment, 'Thou shalt not kill,' a violation of
which would not go unpunished."

We are impressed by a significant difference between the
savage tribe and us. They kill their enemies and love them
afterwards while according to Western religion we are supposed to love our enemies before we kill them. It is not
known that the Germans, the Italians, the Americans, and
the French showed any real mourning over their slain
enemies. No mass was sung nor any prayer said for them.
There seems not the slightest remaining trace of guilt feelings toward enemies in our progressed civilization. Not the
faintest echo of those emotions the savages manifest is

[2] J. G. Frazer, *Taboo and the Perils of the Soul* (London, *The Golden Bough,* 3d ed., 1911).

[3] Freud, *Totem and Taboo* (New York, 1930), p. 39.

audible after our armies victoriously returned from the war.

Are we justified in speaking of a world sense of guilt? Is there such a thing as guilt feeling shared by all mankind? A very perceptive French writer, Denis de Rougemont, has observed and described the reaction of individuals and groups after that horror of destruction unleashed on Hiroshima.[4] One would have expected that the death-dealing explosion which, in a flash, killed many thousands and brought the great war to an end, would be followed by an exultation of the masses. Should the Americans, the English, and their allies not have given expression to their joy on that glorious day? But there was no dance on the streets nor jubilant or joyful celebrations. When the news of that hell broken loose on men, women, and children in a faraway land reached our country, when we heard that science had now reached the point where it could blow up a world of enemies, there was no triumph on the faces of the citizens of New York, London, and Paris. Denis de Rougemont reported from Lake George that someone said, "They have hit the mystery right in the solar plexus," and that another man answered: "It will take its revenge." No joy, no exultation, when the Atomic Age began on that August 16, 1945. In his letters the French writer reports that a gloomy mood was prevalent on that day as though that triumph marked the failure of civilization, as if mankind had been declared bankrupt. Some Americans said on that wonderful day: "Morally, we have lost the war." That depression was caused not only by the planetary threat, or by the fear of retaliation in the foreseeable future.

The possibility that the war could have ended with the victory of the others was at the time scarcely imaginable, but a few months later it emerged as a grim fantasy. When

---

[4] *Lettres sur la Bombe Atomique* (New York, Brentano), 1946.

a newsman after the postwar trials in which the crime
against humanity was punished, once asked General Eisenhower whether he believed he would have been hanged,
had the war gone the other way, Eisenhower smilingly answered: "Such thoughts you have!" The commander of the
allied armies showed already then the charming naïveté of
which he has given so many proofs later on as President of
our country. "Such thoughts" were by no means beyond
all imagination. As a literary wag in *Time* Magazine reported in October, 1946, on October 16, 1946, eleven top
U.S. war criminals were hanged in the yard of Moyamsing
prison in Philadelphia. According to the six German,
Japanese and Italian newspapermen, all met their fate
calmly except J. Edgar Hoover, who was drunk and dis-
orderly. Among the eleven men convicted on one or both
counts of waging aggressive war or spreading equalitarian
doctrines were Bernard Baruch, close collaborator of the
late Franklin D. Roosevelt, General George C. Marshall,
Charles A. Beard, democratic philosopher, and others. Not
more than eleven years have passed since this time. We
have almost forgotten how easily such a political fantasy
that strikes us today as unlikely could have become reality.

Emotions we once deeply experienced are almost immortal as far as our unconscious goes, but our conscious
recollection of them is rather weak. We scarcely remember
that we, who belonged to the party of the victors, also
sometimes felt guilty for the war as if we were responsible
for all its horrors. In this streamlined Atomic Age, we
scarcely remember that nightmare of October 8, when a
rather primitive bomb killed 18,000 city dwellers in an
instant. We do not feel guilty any more, if we ever felt
consciously guilty. We arrive here at a decisive point of
the problem: the guilt feeling of a group, of a nation, or of

all nations need not be conscious to unfold tremendous effects. Here is perhaps an emotional power operating whether its presence and effects are consciously perceived or not. That quality of consciousness can be absent, or can be only sometimes present.

Is it conceivable that there is a free-floating guilt feeling in all men beyond the frontiers of races and nations, a collective sense of guilt of mankind that only occasionally reaches the threshold of conscious feeling? Is it possible that beneath the self-assurance, complacency, and smugness of our civilization an unconscious sense of guilt is operating, shared by all? The analogy with the emotional life of the individual would make us assume that the existence and effects of that pressure of guilt could be there although they are not recognized as such. But is there any area of human thought in which such a shared guilt feeling is clearly perceived? It must occasionally emerge at the surface of civilization as it does in the individual, must sometimes ascend from unconscious depths and reveal its subterranean activity. Certain facets of it in our civilization would then appear as manifestations of this common guilt feeling and perceptive men would acknowledge them.

There are such occasions in different areas. In the domain of criminology, some enlightened men such as Professor Franz von Liszt spoke of the "collective guilt of society." In the field of social organization, many voices since that of Jean Jacques Rousseau have been heard claiming that there was some sense of injustice immanent within that civilization. In the books of socialistic writers, an appeal is frequently made to that sense of guilt, but here as in the works of many social critics—and not only of those of the Marxian school of thought—the feeling of guilt is attributed to the privileged classes and excludes the major part of men and women. The reason why we do not dwell on the discussion of their views is just the fact that these critics restrict their arguments to certain forms of society. We are searching for observers who have understood that there is something rotten not only in the State of Denmark, but in the human situation, in the state of our civilization. In other words, that the guilt feeling is common to mankind, however diverse the expressions of this deep-rooted sense may be. We shall find views of this or similar kinds rather in the works of those philosophers who encompass all sides of the human situation in their Weltanschauung. As representative philosophers of this character we would like to mention Schopenhauer, Nietzsche, Kierkegaard, Heidegger, and some of their modern successors. It is not difficult to name the features common to those men, so different in their characters and viewpoints. Common to them is that they focus their critical attention on the unsurmountable abyss between the drives of the individual and the supraindividual demands of society. The second common feature is the fundamentally tragic sense of their philosophy.

In the survey of the situation of mankind, the glib and easy-going optimism of previous generations is nowhere to be felt. It is as extinct as the dinosaur. Nietzsche, here as in so many directions the predecessor of Freud, heralds the onset of psychoanalytic insights into the latent connection of the universal sense of guilt and of aggressive and cruel drives. He came also very close to the assumption of an innate disposition of mankind to aggression. In his *Genealogie der Moral* he speaks of an "attack of mankind against itself" and numerous paragraphs of his writings show that he recognized that sense of guilt as operating in men for many millennia. Kierkegaard's profound and perceptive insights make him reject the conventional and superficial view of the nature and origin of the universal guilt feelings. He once compares the "conventional" and "external" idea of guilt with banknotes without any value of their own and searches for the original guilt. We already discussed the psychological assumptions about the sense of guilt at which Freud in his old age arrived. He was the first who acknowledged that here is the fatal flaw inherent within our civilization itself. We should not forget that flashes of recognition of that universal sense of guilt emerge in the works of our great writers. They are to be found in Shakespeare and Goethe, in Dostoevski and Tolstoi. Occasionally, psychological insights pointing in this direction emerge also in the books of contemporary writers such as Franz Kafka (*The Trial*)[5] and Sartre, O'Neill, and Faulkner.

Our search for expressions of that universal sense of guilt was only partly successful. We could show that its presence and effects were clearly recognized and acknowledged by several individuals, philosophers, psychologists, and writers. Can we be content with so poor a result of our search? Is it possible, is it conceivable that the significance of that powerful and fateful tension that determines the character of our whole civilization, that gave its imprint to the past and will decide what is the future of this planet was understood only by so few? It is not likely that the particular force that someone has justly called "the nemesis of civilization"[5] was always neglected in the evaluation of the human situation. Yet we cannot discover any area in which the impact of the shared guilt was appreciated by the masses.

But how could we be careless enough to overlook that this sense of universal or common guilt has a central position in religion! Our mistake can be explained but not

[5] Lewis Samuel Feuer, *Psychoanalysis and Ethics* (New York, 1956), p. 72.

excused by the fact that this shared guilt feeling does not appear there under its proper name, but in a theological term, namely as sin. As such it permeates the religions from the time of early Babylonian hymns and Egyptian prayers to this day. It is almost as alive in religious people of our age as in the prophets of ancient Israel and in the Christians at the time of Saint Paul. J. Wesley asked:

> And can it be that I should gain
> An interest in the Saviour's blood,
> Died He for me who caused His pain
> For me who Him to death pursued?

and a modern theologian answers:[6] "If there is such a thing as the shared guilt of mankind, then I had a share in the sin that crucified the Lord of glory." Here is even the wording "shared guilt," identical with ours.

But many hundred of years before the Lord arrived in human shape on this earth, the religious leaders proclaimed the doctrine that we are altogether sinners, left no doubt that we have to believe in a universal guilt. It is true that the religions trace this common guilt to a transgression of God's laws, but we are at the moment merely interested that they acknowledged that a sense of guilt lives in all men. Bridging for a minute the abyss that separates religious belief and scientific psychological research and neglecting the difference of the terms guilt and sin—what's in a name?— we are astonished to find ourselves in agreement with a fundamental assumption of religion. Such a common ground has to be acknowledged also when we realize that we as psychologists arrived there from a different point of departure and when we foresee that our ways will soon separate.

Soon, I said? Immediately, it seems, because at this point

---

[6] F. W. Dillingstone, *Jesus Christ and His Cross* (Philadelphia, 1956), p. 133.

the question of the origin of that common guilt feeling
emerges. The theologians are to be envied because they
have an answer ready. We are not as fortunate and have to
toil and search for it. They answer: the origin of mankind's
guilt feeling is, of course, the "original sin" as it is told in
the story of the Fall of Man in the Holy Scripture. We consider that story a myth and are determined to find the beginnings of that common guilt feeling in the emotional
evolution of men. We have to assume that there is such a
beginning on account of the enveloping analogy between
the cultural process of the masses and the development of
the individual. Depth psychology could observe and describe how and why the sense of guilt in the child emerged
and slowly developed. We will, of course, take into account
the incisive differences between the individual process and
the collective phenomena; also, in the evolution of mankind a series of events must have taken place resulting in
the emergence of that guilt feeling now permeating and
endangering our whole civilization. We want to discover
and explore this evolution and to penetrate to the sources of
collective guilt feelings. No paved road leads to that home
of the sources. We are aware that many obstacles will block
our way. The very sense of guilt is wrapped in mystery and
seems to forbid research into its origin, as Lohengrin says:

Nie sollst du mich befragen	These questions ask me
Noch Wissens Sorge tragen,	never,
Woher ich kam der Fahrt	Brood not upon them ever,
Noch wie mein Nam' und	From whence I hither came
Art.	Or what my race and name.

As is Josef K in Kafka's *Trial,* all mankind is arrested
and does not know why, is fighting a charge of whose terms
it remains ignorant. We all are accused of some crime by
an invisible judge and we are not told what it is.

CHAPTER IV
MYTHS AND MEMORIES

WE ARRIVED at the hypothesis that man acquired a guilt feeling at a certain phase of his evolution. The emergence of an intense guilt feeling becomes conspicuous among the Greeks, the Hebrews, and other Mediterranean peoples, five or six hundred years before Christ. The rise of a collective sense of guilt at this period marks one of its peaks rather than its first appearance. It became articulate only then and obtained a distinct voice, but it had been active and operating many thousands of years before this time. It had been latent, and innumerable generations had unconsciously felt its effects without being aware of its nature. That primeval guilt feeling had been invisible and nameless. It needed many millennia to dig its way up to the threshold of conscious thinking. Its unconscious activity must have preceded the earliest social and religious organizations. We have no means of dating the first appearance of that primitive sense of guilt. When we assume that civilization began in the Neolithic Age, we must conceive that the primal guilt feeling was already present and effective many thousands of years before.

To what does this earliest sense of guilt refer? What was its content? Whatever was its origin, however different it may have been from what we understand by the name, it must have been akin to the character we attribute to that emotion. Its frame of reference was perhaps very different from ours, but guilt feeling was for the Paleolithic man, as for the primitive Australian native, a reaction to an action or to a conduct that he considered wrong or evil. In order to penetrate to the sources of primal guilt feeling, we have to study its earliest traces in the unwritten laws that control the behavior of primitive social organizations and religions. Law, religion, and morality are, for the man of the Old Stone Age as for the savage of our time, identical. Students of prehistory have to acknowledge that religion and law at primitive stages cannot be differentiated, that the delinquent is identical with the breaker of a taboo, and that the criminal and the sinner appear the same to the primitive mind. We are accustomed to make a clear distinction between acts that offend the Supreme Being we call God and those that are condemned by the State or by laws formulated by society. No such demarcation line exists in early social organizations. Crime, vice, sin, and pollution are all embraced by the category of evil. It is thus indifferent whether we begin our search or research in the area of early religious beliefs or in that of moral and social ideas.

But did we not assume that the genesis of primal guilt feelings must have taken place in a phase preceding that in which the first social and religious organizations were formed? That part of evolution that gave birth to a primitive sense of guilt is not accessible to historical research and cannot be reached with the methods of prehistory. We know less about the emotional life of those remote ancestors who felt the first sense of guilt than the archaeologist who has discovered a prehistoric flint ax knows about the daily life of the Paleolithic man who shaped a stone into a weapon.

Let us freely admit that the situation is really difficult. It can be compared to one we often face in psychoanalytic practice where it seems almost impossible to penetrate to early childhood memories, especially to those of traumatic experiences before the third year. Dreams and fantasies of a much later period sometimes provide material whose interpretation can lead to a reconstruction of those early events. In such reconstructions fragments or remnants of those early experiences can be lifted from the deep well of oblivion. Certain features of late fantasies, analytically interpreted, often cast thus a surprising light on the origin and nature of puzzling symptoms, fears, and inhibitions.

In the situation in which we find ourselves, unable to discover any clues for the origin of that primal guilt feeling of man, we search in vain for productions comparable to the fantasies of our patients. Is there no way to unearth traces of those lost memories, remnants from the infancy of mankind? There is at least one kind of collective production that can be compared to those individual fantasies. They contain, distorted and transformed by changes during thousands of years, memories from an early phase of human evolution: I mean the myths. As primitive flint axes and other relics excavated together with bones of extinct animals are witnesses of a Paleolithic existence of man, thus early myths bring us information of a past to which no human memory can reach. Snatches of truth emerge from such tales and talks. "Memories believe before knowing remembers, believes longer than recollects, longer than knowing even wonders," says William Faulkner in *Light in August*.

When we speak of myths we generally mean something opposite to history. We call something mythical as synonymous with imaginary or fictitious and contrast it with reality. But not all in myths is mythical. Myth was once not separated from history, but its early shape was the only form in which the oral tradition of man was conveyed from generation to generation. The early historians, for instance Herodotus, report mythical stories together with their records of historical events. Myths often bring to us knowledge of forgotten happenings in a fantastic form. The biblical story of Noah preserves thus the memory of the Ice Age and of the Flood resulting from the melting of the glaciers. In many of the Australian and African myths recollections of the migrations of certain peoples are found. Wrapped in mythical garb, interspersed with animistic beliefs and primitive superstitions, many myths contain historic recollections.

During the last century the etiologic concept of myths was accepted by most scientists. It maintains that the purpose of myths was to explain certain phenomena of nature and of tribal customs and beliefs. This concept is certainly justified for a very progressed phase of myth formation. The allegoric and symbolic interpretation also has its place in the later development of many myths. Yet the assumption of numerous scholars of the nineteenth century that this kind of interpretation could enable us to discover the original meaning of myths appears disarmingly naïve to us today. Not so long ago mythologists saw in each bit of folklore and each legend reflections of events in the sky, changes in the phases of the moon, and in the constellations. Let me present some samples of such interpretations of that school of thought: according to Genesis, Abraham stayed for some time in the city of Kiriath-arba. Now the Hebrew word "arba" means four. In the view of the Pan-Babylonists, Kiriath-arba is not a city at all, but means the four phases of the moon. The three hundred eighteen men with whom the patriarch pursued the captors of Lot represent the three hundred eighteen days of the year when the moon is visible. Since sheba means seven, the name of Beersheba means the seven days in each phase of the moon. The four wives of Jacob represent the four phases of the moon, and so on. That period of mythological research in which so many scholars were, to use B. Malinowsky's expression, "moonstruck" has passed. We now recognize that the ancient people of a certain period projected conflicts of their own lives into the sky, but we are interested rather in the nature of those conflicts than in the process of projection.

Within psychoanalysis a new evaluation of myths has also taken place. They appeared to us at first as collective daydreams, as wish fulfillments of the masses. Such a characterization is still psychologically valid, but we apply today the interpretation of myths in the hope of discovering at their depths precipitations or sediments of real prehistoric events or situations. The new analytic research arrived thus at a new assessment of the function of myths within the prehistoric or savage society. What we psychoanalysts search for is the matter in the myths, the fact in the fable. That means the kernel of historical truth. Analytic interpretation can often reveal that core after cautiously removing layer after layer of distortions and transformations. The interpretation and reconstruction of the concealed mythical core might almost result in a reversal of Napoleon's famous saying that history is a fable agreed upon: a fable agreed upon is an immanent part of history. In this sense a myth is not the tale of some fictitious past, but memory of the past told in a fictitious way: not a story told as history, but history told as a story.

When we choose myths as sources for the study of Paleolithic man, we can appeal to two representative contemporary investigators, the one a prominent historian, the other a distinguished anthropologist. Arnold J. Toynbee points out that history grew out of mythology in which the line between fact and fiction is left undrawn.[1] It has been said of the Iliad that "anyone who starts reading it as history will find it is full of fiction, but equally, anyone who starts reading it as fiction will find it is full of history." After careful consideration of the factors of race and environment, Toynbee comes to the conclusion that neither of them, taken by itself, has offered "any clue" as to what has "shaken part of mankind out of the integrational custom into the differentiation of civilization within the last six thousand years." In search of such a positive factor, the historian arrives at the "mythological clue" and expects some insight into the nature of the challenges and responses from the light mythology casts upon the problem of the genesis of civilizations.

Bronislaw Malinowski emphasizes in his last book the place myths have in primitive society.[2] He rejects the concept that myth is a savage speculation about the origin of things. It is rather a sacred tale, "a living reality believed to have once happened in primeval times and continuing ever since to influence the world and human destinies." To the savage myth is the same as the biblical stories of Creation, of the Fall, of the Redemption are to a believing Christian. As the sacred stories make an integral part of our lives and govern our conduct as well as our faith, so do their myths for the savages. This class of story lives not as fictitious or even as true narrative, but is to the natives "a statement of a primeval, greater and more relevant reality" by which the facts and activities of mankind are determined.

[1] *A Study of History* (New York and London, 1947).
[2] *Magic, Science and Religion and other Essays* (New York, 1948).

So much for the justification of our endeavor to search
in myths for traces of a forgotten past that no history can
unearth. The concepts of representative explorers such as
Toynbee and Malinowski pave our way into that dark
region. Our aim is much more modest than theirs. We do
not strive to discover the beginnings of the civilization nor
do we try to grasp the origins of religion and social organization. We want to find the sources of that sense of guilt
that once emerged in the evolution of mankind and op-
presses man to this day.

Before we descend into that mysterious mine, some self-
admonition not to expect a smooth and quick landing at its
bottom is appropriate. We spoke of myths as of collective
dreams. But the original text of those dreams from the
infancy of mankind is not conveyed to us. They have been
subjected to many and to manifold changes. Numerous
generations have mutilated, distorted, and elaborated even
the primitive myths. Many elements of their original content have been replaced by others; some have been removed
or put into a new context so that their first form has become
unrecognizable. Yet in spite of many and incisive changes
through the millennia a core of the original was preserved.
Also, in the many distortions of individual dreams we can
detect remnants of their original meaning when we apply
the analytic method of interpretation. We are thus forewarned that we will, in myth interpretation, encounter the
same difficulties and, besides them, new ones resulting from
the differences of the material we have to cope with. Dreams
are to a great extent productions of unconscious activity
and not destined to be communicated. In the formation of
myths conscious and preconscious factors play a much
greater part since they are part of a common oral tradition.
Those tendencies try to transform the original myths in the

sense of later religious and social conventions and make them acceptable to the people of the tribes that have arrived at a progressed state of society. The age in which the first myths were produced in the primitive mind is remote from the phase to which they refer. It is as if an adolescent boy would try to remember the time in which he was an infant. His memories will be colored and distorted by tendencies of his present attitude.

Another consideration will slow our descent. Do we not have to account for the different cultural levels on which myths emerge, of the various religious and sociological strata in which they grow? But a long and tedious scientific work of preparation would be needed in order to differentiate this or that piece of folklore from another with regard to the cultural soil and the phase of civilization to which it belongs. It certainly makes a difference whether we deal with an early Sumerian myth or with a saga of a late Hellenic period. The importance of that difference is, it is true, diminished by the fact that even the oldest myths, handed down by tradition, do not reach us in their original form. We have, of course, to take into account the difference of the phases in which the myths originate, but we apply the same method of interpretation as we do in the interpretation of individual dreams, whether they are dreamed yesterday or thirty years ago. Otherwise put: we judge myths without regard to their origin or the phases of civilization from which they emerge, without discrimination, so to speak, without respect of person as if they were equal before the aims of our research. Such a treatment is indicated when primeval myths are conceived as memories from a past in which mankind lived in an animistic perception of the world, from the dawn of civilization in which neither myth nor history was known. Myths preserve the

voices and noises of early man living in hordes, not much
removed in their organization from that of the higher apes.
Mankind had not yet spread over the earth and lived in a
smaller area, in closer and more cohesive units. The primitive form of hordes was given up only much later and replaced by more complex and larger forms of social life, by
the first organizations of clans and tribes.

We are searching in myths for snatches of memories from
the early life of the family of man. Late descendants of
Paleolithic men, who were united in primitive hordes, produced those stories in which fantasy and truth about a past
beyond their memory merged. Those late descendants lived
at places different from the homes of their ancestors and
lived under different sociological circumstances, in a progressed state of civilization, although yet crude and primitive enough. They already had new weapons; they already
used fire and had become articulate. They could express
themselves much better than the members of the primitive
hordes who could utter not much more than their most vital
needs in inarticulate noises. The creators of the first myths
were many thousands of years separated from the events
whose memory continues to live in their stories.

We spoke earlier of memories of the family of man in
the way of comparison. There is a strange thing about comparisons. They almost never correspond to the situation of
living reality. We remain aware of their incongruity and
inconsistency. At the same time comparisons often point to
concealed similarities of which we become aware after we
have thought of them. When we follow that comparison of
primeval men, living in closely knit, smaller units, intimately interconnected, within families, it might help us to
make a certain character of early myths clearer. In continuing our comparison, we assume namely that a family,

let us say, originally at home in Poland, is broken up; for instance, by the invasion of the Nazis. Its members are dispersed and scattered in all parts of the earth. The parents are killed and the children, escaping from the cruelties of the Nazis, emigrate to different countries. An older brother lands after many adventures in England, where he is educated and becomes a lawyer. Another brother arrives after a long detour in Bulgaria, where he makes a living as peddler. A third brother becomes a farmer in Australia, and a fourth succeeds in arriving in the United States, where he settles after many years as a wool merchant. Their parents were uncultured and uneducated and life at home was poor, primitive, and without any comfort. The brothers, separated by thousands of miles, have all founded families. Their new life is determined not only by their individual personalities, but also by their vicissitudes since they left their common home. Not only the external conditions of their new countries, but also the different education they had there, their various opportunities and social experiences, the economic and cultural situations in which they found themselves—all these factors will have marked their characters.

Let us now assume that each of the brothers recalls his childhood, his life with father and mother, remembers important and trivial events of those years at home. Each will remember something different or present the same happenings differently, will select various situations or put the accent differently in his report of the common experiences. Yet each tale, colored by the divergent personalities, influenced by the different states of their educations and positions in life, will have a core of sameness when they speak of their childhood. A common stock of memories, a reservoir of things past will provide material for recollections of illnesses and deaths, of failures and successes, of happy and disastrous events. This common stock of memories has remained relatively unaffected by their later experiences, so different from those of their childhood, and by the views they acquired far from home. It is true that the past will reflect itself differently in each of them. But their stories, however disparate, will have certain features of content in common. Some patterns in these reports will be identical.

Such is the nature of the differences of myths or at least of the memory traces contained in them. They all present reactions to events and situations within the early family of mankind. The comparison helps us to understand that there is a "family resemblance" between them since they reflect the common adventures of mankind of the Old Stone Age. They reveal, to quote Josef Campbell,[3] "such constant features, that innumerable mythologies of the world resemble each other as dialects of a single language." The oneness of mankind is better manifested in myths than in other productions.

When we assume that there is a common sense of guilt, a collective guilt feeling of mankind, our investigation has to start from an obvious premise. It is the following: that guilt feeling must refer to a misdeed, sin, or crime that was committed (or was supposed to have been committed) by all men. We become at this point aware that the subject of our inquiry has almost imperceptibly changed. From the problem of the first emergence of a primeval guilt feeling we were transported to a question as to which sin or crime that common sense of guilt originally referred. We want to know the nature of that offense or bad act for which all mankind once felt responsible. From the inquiry into the genesis of a sharply defined emotional reaction we are led

---

[3] Foreword to Maya Derens, *Divine Horseman* (London, 1953), p. 1.

to a historic or rather prehistoric problem, to a problem of criminology at the dawn of civilization.

It is not any longer a question of genetic psychology that arouses our curiosity, but one of criminal investigation. This means that we shall use the scarce material at our disposal as a kind of circumstantial evidence drawn from early myths. The facts behind the mythical tales appear to us from a point of view similar to that of a criminal investigator or of a detective who examines the rumors of neighbors and the statements of witnesses of a deed. But is the character of an investigation such as we plan not approaching that of a mystery story? There is perhaps the danger of becoming confused with "sleuths of prehistory." Let us stop a minute at this point. What a crime to investigate! It is not only the first one mankind committed, but also one for which all men feel guilty—the universal or ubiquitous crime, since it was committed before all history and since all men feel responsible for it until this day. More than this: if our assumption is correct, the very concept of crime began with it.

But we need not worry. Not every report of the investigation of a puzzling crime belongs to the field of fiction. Not every report of this kind is a whodunit, or a search for the murderer. In applying the psychoanalytic method in the investigation of the nature and the circumstances of that primeval deed the character of scientific exploration will be strictly maintained. We shall have to add a few remarks on the character of the mystery story at the appropriate place.

We emphasized earlier that myths which contain perhaps the only or at least the most important clues can give only uncertain and distorted bits of information, difficult to seize and to recognize, merely scraps and snatches of a prehistoric reality. Can those indefinite traces be used as circum-

stantial evidence? We assumed that the primeval crime was
committed many thousands if not a hundred thousand years
before the dawn of civilization. Is the suspicion not justified that, to use the jargon of the detective story, the track
will be cold after such a long time? It cannot be denied
that we are likely to fail, but we take this calculated risk.
The patterns of psychoanalytic interpretation that so often
succeeded in penetrating the secrets of early childhood in
the analysis of dreams and fantasies give us new heart. We
decide to follow the track. There is a foreboding that it is
the scent of blood.

CHAPTER V

NEVER REMEMBERED,
YET NOT FORGOTTEN

SUFFICIENTLY forewarned, although insufficiently forearmed, we are entering the area of the myths of mankind about its first crime or sin. Where should we begin? The first thought goes, of course, to the biblical narrative in the third chapter of Genesis, but the first choice is not necessarily the best. The road to the Bible is certainly the path of least resistance, but perhaps not the path of greatest advantage to a critical exploration of the subject. We would like to be free from the theological connotations immanent in the biblical story. We would prefer as point of departure myths that belong to an older tradition than that of the Fall of Man. That story is essentially the work of the Jahvist, that is of that author, or of a school of authors, who used without restrictions the name "Jahveh" for God. The scholars have dated the time of the Jahvistic source differently, but they generally agree that it was between the years 8000 and 1000 B.C. The Jahvistic myth of the Fall of Man was traced back to much older sources. It had a long oral tradition before it was shaped into the biblical narrative.

Here is, no doubt, a report of the first crime, at least in

biblical theology, but the very concept of an original crime or sin belongs to a comparatively late phase of religious history. There is the astonishing fact that the first and most important crime a human being ever committed was scarcely conceived as such before Christ. Not before Sirach (200-175 B.C.) is there any allusion found to a primeval sin and not before the Apocalypse of Baruch (A.D. 80-150) is there any hint of the story of the Fall that brought upon man the liability of future punishment. Jesus refers neither to the Garden of Eden nor to the Fall.

Someone has said that the only indispensable person in the history of man is Adam. Yet there was a strange silence about him in antiquity. Almost two hundred years ago Voltaire expressed his astonishment about that lack of attention in his *Dictionnaire Philosophique*. The secrets of Providence, he says, are such that the father and mother of the human race have been totally unknown to their descendants so that the names of Adam and Eve are to be found in no ancient author either of Greece, Rome, Persia, or Syria, or even among the Arabs until the time of Mohammed. He cannot comprehend that God should take pleasure in concealing the origin of the human family and keep silent about the father of all nations "while in the natural course of things his name should have been carried from mouth to mouth to the farthest corner of the earth." It requires a mystery "to shut the eyes and ears of all nations, to destroy every monument, every memory of their first father."

This astonishment is, of course, also justified for the case of the original crime or sin to which no one paid any attention until shortly before Christ. What kind of crime is that which was discovered only many thousands of years after it was committed? Here is an enigma, wrapped in a mystery.

It is the more puzzling since this sin had fallen into oblivion for many millennia and then caused the greatest commotion in the last two thousand years. From a complete oblivion, to be explained only by a conspiracy of silence, the tradition of a Fall of Man stepped into the limelight, blazed into a cosmic display that has not lost much of its bright light for millions of people to this day. This original sin, never mentioned by Christ who took all crimes of mankind on His shoulders, became a sensation only after it was atoned by the Saviour's death on the Cross. It was only after mankind was redeemed from it that that crime, forgotten for ages, became a *cause célèbre*.

Just because of its importance for Western culture and because it cannot be compared with any other myth, we decide to postpone the discussion of the biblical story that will be our main dish. We approach the manifold material we have to present not in the spirit of the scholar who collects folklore of a certain type, but of the explorer who inquires into the meanings of ancient and primitive sagas of this kind.

To the primitive mind all evil comes from outside. Famine, death, and illness are the result of some malicious sorcerer or demon. The world is full of evil demons and the gods have to be propitiated since they too want to harm poor human beings. Their character is not very different from that of malign ghosts who roam over the earth. It seems natural to the primitive myth to attribute all that is evil and terrifying to those superhuman yet all too human wicked beings. When, later on, sin or crime was conceived, those offenses also were traced back to the evil demons. A comparison of II Samuel 24 with I Chronicles 21 is informative in this direction: in one report it is the Lord who moves David to commit a sin, in the other Satan provokes the king to do the forbidden. God is an elevated demon as Satan is a deposed and degraded god. The original united superhuman being is thus divided into two halves. It is the result of a late development when not God but his antagonist, Satan, or one of the other princes of darkness, appears as the author of or tempter to sin. As remnant of an earlier phase a god is present twice in many myths: causing the sin of mortals, but also punishing them for it.

In search for the genesis of civilization, Toynbee arrives at the concept of an encounter between two superhuman personalities in ubiquitous and ever-recurring myths. The superhuman encounters are "a primordial image," to be found in the story of the Fall of Man between Jahveh and the Serpent, in the plot of the Book of Job between the Lord and Satan.[1] The perfect state that is present in the beginning of the plot is disturbed by an impulse or motives coming from outside. Another actor appears on the stage, an adversary of God. Although omnipotent, God is subject to two limitations: he has no opportunity for further activity and when the opportunity for it is offered from outside, for instance by the Devil, "He cannot refuse to take the challenge up." When God's creature is tempted by the adversary, it enables the Lord Himself to resume His creative activity. But this progress has to be paid for and it is God's servant, man, who pays for it. He serves not only by enabling God to renew His creation, but also by triumphantly pointing the way for his fellows to follow him. The encounter of two superhuman beings appears in the fight of Ahriman, the Persian god of darkness and evil, and of Ormazd, the god of light and kindness. The Revolt of the Angels told in connection with the story of creation in Genesis is another example of such an encounter. No doubt,

[1] Toynbee, *A Study of History,* op. cit., p. 60.

here is a report of the rebellion of the "sons of God" against Jahveh. An echo of that early tradition appeared in the tale that the fallen angels, led by Satan, tempt man to disobey God and thus bring misery to mankind. The story of the revolt of those divine beings raises more than one problem: Are there here traces of an original polytheism among the Hebrews? Were the "sons of God" conceived as being just as powerful as Jahveh? When we think of the Genesis story that stimulated Anatole France's great novel, *La Révolte des Anges,* the statement that someone is "on the side of the angels" appears ambiguous. God is made responsible for all kinds of actions, both good and evil. He is a savage, jealous, vengeful deity, striking the guilty and the innocent alike. The adversary in the form of Satan is a late figure, hewed from the original god-demon.

There are good reasons to assume an even older phase of primitive religion in which evil power was not attributed to a male superhuman being, but to a goddess or female demon or rather to several such. A concept of malicious and punishing cruel mother-goddesses whose traces can still be seen in Ishtar, Kali, and Astarte has very likely preceded the emergence of male gods. Those female counterparts of Satan were held accountable for the evils of mankind, including what later on was called "sin." By and by those goddesses changed their characters and became bearers of love and mercy, after a phase in which they appear as mistresses of young gods who have to die young to be resurrected. Later myths in which women were made responsible for the emergence of evil are perhaps reappearances of a much older tradition of malicious or cruel female demons, comparable to a second changed and elaborated edition of a book that had first been published many years ago.

Such a woman is the Greek figure of Pandora, fashioned by the gods: Pandora opened the lid from a vessel or box in which all evils were contained and they were dispersed among men. Only hope remained in the vessel, since Pandora closed the lid again before it too could fly out. Hesiod's account in the *Works* implies that woman is thus made responsible for the evils that befall men. Voltaire, speaking of this early legend, calls it a nice story and adds that one of its advantages was "that you were not burned on a stake when you did not believe in it." The student of the symbolic language that pervades primitive myths will easily guess that the vessel in which all ills and evils are contained represents the female genitals (compare the vulgar English expression, 'box" for vagina). Pandora is, so to speak, the Greek Eve. Intensive misogynous tendencies that dominated a certain late phase of Greek civilization transformed the lure of the female body into an organ of danger and terror and turned the sexual attraction of women into a malicious temptation. Eve appears as such a dangerous temptress in the Genesis story and the Christian Fathers enlarged the theme until woman was called "instrumentum diaboli."

Man took only hesitatingly and reluctantly the responsibility for his fall, for sin or crime as source of all evils upon himself. The scholars have collected an abundance of material, gathered from myths of all nations of antiquity and from folklore of primitive and half-civilized tribes about the Fall of Man. A survey of this manifold material leads to some questions. For instance: was it really man whose primordial sin is reported in those myths and sagas? Was it not rather a god, a half-god, a superman? Consider that the rigid logic of modern man was alien to the prehistoric mind as it is still to primitive people of today. The frontiers between gods and men fluctuate. A god can be sometimes a man and a man sometimes a god. Traces of such a concept are still present in the Christ myth. The nature of man is by no means always the same. He can be transformed into a demon or a totem animal at the drop of a hat. Something similar can be observed in the thoughts of children. I saw a little boy whose playmate pretended to be a bear and approached him with threatening grunts. The frightened child ran to his mother and glanced, thus protected, at his friend, of whom he timidly asked: "Johnny, are you still a bear?" There is no doubt that also to the primitive mind gods are almighty, but they are sometimes more and sometimes less almighty.

When the power of gods and of demons was thus only relative, the power of man was not always conceived of as restricted. The superman whom Nietzsche imagined as a possibility of future evolution has his successors in the figures science fiction creates. His predecessors are to be found in early myths, especially in myths about the first man. He often appears there not as an average man, but as a superior being. In the late rabbinical literature Adam is not a simple mortal, but a being of perfect beauty and wisdom, of enormous power, equipped with physical and spiritual perfection. He is presented as a little higher than the angels who worshiped him. He lost this endowment only after that regrettable transgression. Far from being the missing link between man and ape, the first man was a being of godlike nature. That first sinner of ancient Greece, Prometheus, whom Zeus chained to a rock as punishment for his crime, was not a mortal, but a Titan, who stole the fire from the father of the gods. The great sin in the Egyptian, Babylonian, and Phoenician myths as well as in Hindu legends is committed by a god or a demon. In various myths the Fall of Man is the result of a conflict between two superhuman powers, ending in the ruin and banishment of one of them.

The person of the archcriminal of mankind is thus not always—as a matter of fact, he is rather rarely—a man or a human being. God or one of the gods is in many myths not only the tempter, but the originator of the Fall. We easily recognize in the serpent, who tempts Eve to eat the forbidden fruit, the representative of a forgotten totemistic god of the Semitic tribes. God as author or creator of sin is present in the oldest Babylonian and Egyptian mythology (Seth is the evil demon par excellence) and in a number of passages of the Holy Scripture. It sounds like an echo of this old concept when the harpist in Goethe's *Wilhelm Meister* accuses the heavenly powers:

> Ye set our feet on this life's road
> Ye watch our guilty erring courses,
> Then leave us, bowed beneath our load
> For earth its every debt enforces.

But is it important whether the being who first brought sin and the wages of sin, death, into the world appears as a half-god or a king, a demon or a mortal? Yes, it is important even for the comparative history of religion. To present only a single aspect: in their search for sources for the Genesis story of the Fall, the historians of religion, the exegetists and the theologians, have examined many ancient myths, especially those of the North Semitic nations who were neighbors of the Hebrews. In their comparison of those old traditions with the biblical tale they found many similarities of situations and even of individual traits. Very often that first sinner was decidedly not as we imagined our first ancestor. The echo of an old myth is to be found in the description of Ezekiel 28, which reports the fall of the Phoenician king of Tyre who lived in a wonderful garden and was expelled from the divine abode because of his proud self-exaltation in which he strove to be like a god. Some scholars, such as Hermann Gunkel, see in the Ezekiel tale the remnant of a myth older than the Genesis story. In this tradition, still alive at the time of the prophets, the first man was a half-god.[2] Hugo Gressmann doubts[3] that the Genesis story and the tradition in Ezekiel can be traced to a common source outside Israel and assumes that once a cherub or a similar celestial figure must have originally stood in place of Adam.

In the Babylonian Adapa myth whose fragments were found in 1888 in Tell el Amarna, and in which many scholars discovered a similarity with the biblical Fall story, the hero is a superior being, created by the god Ea. He goes hunting and fishing for the natives of Eridu. He sins by breaking the wings of the storm-bird Ju who is the South Wind. Called before the highest god to give an account of his deed, Adapa is punished and loses his immortality. That Babylonian myth has certain resemblances to the Genesis story, but is Adapa the first man? Is he a man at all? According to Hommel[4] he is rather a kind of demon. Heinrich Zimmern[5] considers Adapa an antediluvial wise man or a primeval king. The old Babylonian Gilgamesh fragment was also often compared with the Genesis story. Its hero is the wise king Gilgamesh who built the wall around Urik. He is only one-quarter human being, three-quarters god. He loses his immortality when a snake smells the plant of life and steals it. Within the Gilgamesh epos is an episode in which the vicissitudes of his friend Enkidu are described.

[2] Hermann Gunkel, *Genesis,* 3d ed., (Leipzig, 1902), p. 35.
[3] *Archiv für Religionswissenschaft,* X, p. 366.
[4] *Die altorientalischen Denkmäler und das Alte Testament* (2d ed., Berlin, 1903), p. 61.
[5] *Die Keilinschriften und das Alte Testament* (3d ed., Berlin, 1903).

Some scholars called Enkidu the Babylonian Adam. Created by the highest god, he lives in peace with the animals until he is seduced by a woman. But Enkidu cannot be the first man because the world is already much populated when he is created by Aruru from the dust of the earth. Alfred Jeremias[6] sees in Enkidu a hero or a god of the fields, similar to Pan. (There is not the slightest idea of a "primeval man.") G. C. C. Maspero[7] thinks that Enkidu is conceived as satyr or as a half-animal being who had knowledge of all things past and future, while Jastro is of the opinion that Enkidu was without any knowledge and not higher than an animal. The scholars who discussed the myth do not agree about whether the Enkidu legend is the basis of the Jahvistic story of Adam and Eve. Yet all admit that certain names and mythological ideas of the tale show conspicuous resemblances to the biblical account so that the existence of a similar Babylonian tradition has to be assumed.

In the Egyptian saga Set, the enemy of all gods, kills his brother Osiris, the son of the Earth and of Heaven, and thus makes an end to the Golden Age in which Osiris righteously reigned in both kingdoms of Egypt. With the criminal act of Set death found entrance into the world. The criminal is a god also in the tradition of the Persian Bunchas. Some scholars recognized a kind of fall story in the battle between Ormuzd, the god of light, and Ahriman, god of evil. He gave men forbidden fruit to eat and they lost thus a hundred beatitudes which they had enjoyed until then. In the oldest part of the Iranian Avesta a primeval being Yima, the most magnificent of all, guardian and governor of the earth, is introduced. This representative of the Golden Age,

[6] *Das Alte Testament im Lichte des Orients* (2d ed., Leipzig, 1906).
[7] *Histoire ancienne des peuples de l'Orient classique* (3d ed., Paris, 1895), p. 576.

the Good Shepherd, governed six hundred sixteen years and six months. He became mortal by the ruse of his enemy, the malicious snake Azni Daliaka. Prometheus, the wonderful son of Iapetus, who steals the fire from Zeus and becomes a benefactor of mankind, is cruelly punished by the father of the gods. But Prometheus is not human, he is a Titan or half-god. Is there a fall of man or a divine fall? Was the original sin committed by the gods themselves, by half-gods, angels, or demons?

In many myths the unpardonable sin is committed by divinities; in others in which dualism prevails, the gods are attacked by evil demons. Where the original sinner is a god, a half-god, an angel, or a demon, it is impossible for us to identify with him. There is not the slightest trace of fellow-feeling with him. It was mentioned that the scholars could demonstrate many and conspicuous similarities of the biblical Fall story with the myths of different ancient peoples. There are extended controversies about the dependence, interdependence, and independence of the Genesis tale and those myths. The result of the discussions is in most cases that the Adam story is considered unique in character and content. Since in most of those other myths the leading characters are gods, demons, or Titans, the first human creature could not be compared with them. Nor was it possible to imagine the first sinner as a king or a mighty governor of a province.

Here another difficulty emerged: when was that first sin committed? In many myths of the ancient Mediterranean people the tragic transgression occurs in an age of progressed civilization and city population. The biblical story is dated soon after the creation of the world. Adam appears as a naïve native or as a savage child of nature. He and Eve lived in paradisaic abundance and were naked. The description of their life in the Garden of Eden reminds us of the reports of early missionaries describing primitive couples living in the affluence of the South Sea Islands. After the Fall man had to eat bread earned by the sweat of his brow. Adam and Eve became aware of their nakedness and the Lord made coats of skin and clothed them. Here is the first story from riches to rags.

But it seems that we have forgotten that we are moving in the area of mythology. The mythical way of thinking is entitled to date the first fall of man as arbitrarily as it chooses. It may assume that the first sin was committed a few weeks after the creation of the world although this appears as absurd as to call an infant in the cradle a criminal. It is not less arbitrary to date the primal crime at the time of the Babylonian kings. The tradition deals with the myth as anachronistically as many medieval painters who in their pictures of the nativity group the buildings of their own cities around the stable in Bethlehem where Christ was born.

Let us put those questions aside for the moment and let us return to the more essential problem of crime or sin by which mankind lost the happiness it originally enjoyed. What have the myths of the world to say about it? What kind of crime was it? In a Hindu legend Brahma was seized with a guilty passion for his daughter Sarasoati and he left his body that he had soiled. According to a legend of the Puranas, he was proud of his work and wanted to make himself equal to the Supreme Being and was therefore sucked in by matter, followed by all his creatures. A genuine ancient Mexican myth told that Quetzalcoatl, Tezcatlipea, and their brethren were gods in heaven and passed their time in a rose garden until they began plucking roses from the great rose tree in the middle of the garden. Thereupon

Tonacotecutli in his anger hurled them to earth where they live as mortals.[8] Ancient myths of the Scandinavian Edda, dating perhaps from heathenish times, also tell of a fall of the gods. In one of them the end of the happy state of gods on Idasplain is brought about by the seduction of female giants, in the other by a revolt of Loki against the other gods.

Many myths ascribe the entrance of death and other evils to the breaking of a taboo. In an Australian recording the first pair was forbidden to go near a tree on which lived a bat, which was not to be disturbed. The woman who gathered firewood approached the tree, whereupon the bat flew away and death arrived. The Niugpos of Bengal say that they once were forbidden to bathe in a certain pool. Because some did, men became subject to death.

Among the divine taboos whose breaking is followed by severe punishments appear frequently those concerning forbidden fruits. To mention only a few instances in which the Fall is contained in breaches of such prohibitions of a divine command: an Australian myth reports that when the god Baiame left the earth the flowers withered and died. Three trees alone were left. None dared to touch them because Baiame had put his mark on them. According to a myth in Madagascar the first man was placed in a garden of all delight, but forbidden to taste of its fruits or drink from its limpid streams. His fall was brought about by his great enemy who painted to him the sweetness of the apple, the lusciousness of the date, and the succulence of the orange. At last he ate and thus brought his ruin. The Andamanese whose theology, according to the best authorities, is inde-

[8] Brinton, *American Hero-Myths*, p. 95. Most of the myths mentioned in the text are discussed in the article "Fall" by I. A. MacCulloch in *Encyclopedia of Religion and Ethics*, V, p. 705 f.

pendent of Christian influence, believe that the first man
Tomo was given certain injunctions, especially concerning
certain plants that grew only at one place in the jungle and
that he was not to touch at certain seasons, for instance
during the rains when Puluga himself visits them and par-
takes of them. Later, some descendants of Tomo disobeyed
and were severely punished. The Masai in Africa have preserved a tradition according to which the first man was
brought down from heaven, his wife coming out of the
earth. They were forbidden to eat from a certain tree. The
woman was tempted to eat by a serpent. She and her husband were, as punishment, driven out from the paradise. A
dog-rib Indian myth reports that the first man Tschapiwah
gave his children two kinds of fruits, black and white, but
forbade them to eat the former. They were first obedient,
but disobeyed him when he went away. He was angry with
them and said that henceforth the earth would produce
only bad fruits, and men would be subject to sickness and
death. A Tonga myth reports that certain immortal gods
journeyed from Bolotoo (Hades) and landed on Tonga,
where they ate of its fruits. Some of them were condemned
to live there and people the world with men subject to
decay and death.

Among the Hindu there is a myth of a Brahma, identified with the first man Manu Svayambleva, and of his wife
Satarupa. God Sive dropped from heaven a blossom of the
sacred vata, the Indian tree of knowledge. Ensnared by its
beauty, Brahma gathered it, thinking it would make him
immortal and divine. While still exalting in this thought, he
was punished by being consigned to an abyss of degrada-
tion, from which he could be freed only after a long term
of suffering. His wife had urged him to take the blossom. On
their descendants the curse was entailed. This myth, often

quoted as a parallel to the Genesis story, is certainly independent of the biblical tradition. One of its many variants recounts that the Brahmas were happy and peace reigned everywhere. A peculiar scum arose on the surface of the earth. One of the Brahmas tasted it and ate it. The others followed his example. Then their skins grew coarse and they deteriorated physically and morally. The world became filled with passion and evil. Tibetan men lived, according to a myth, for a period of six thousand years and were invisibly nourished and able at will to go to heaven. But they lost their gift through covetousness and by eating a honey-sweet herb and became vicious. In a Nepal version the world was inhabited by the dwellers of the heavenly mansions who were innocent and androgynous. But the desire to eat arose in their minds, they tasted the earth, lost the power to return to the higher world, and had to eat the fruit of the earth for sustenance. In the Iranian saga the evil spirit Ahriman brought unhappiness to the first couple. He offered them fruit, which they ate and thereby lost all blessings. With the Greek the garden of the Hesperides is a kind of paradise in which beautiful fruits grow. There is a tree with golden apples that provides immortality to the gods. A hundred-headed dragon guards this tree. Heracles overpowered him and stole the fruit.

In other myths the primal disaster is brought about by some mistake. Some tales attribute the origin of all evil for mankind to the wrong delivery of a divine message or to a simple slip.[9] The Batussi say that the Fall was due to Nyinakigwas, who broke the divine prohibition to tell how, being sterile, she had three children, gifts of the god Imana.[10] In

[9] J. G. Frazer has collected the many stories of the perverted message and compared them with the narrative of the Fall in Genesis in his *Folklore In The Old Testament* (New York, 1927), p. 15 ff.

[10] *Anthropos*, III, 1908, 2 ff.

many myths man lost immortality and all other goods he previously enjoyed by a slight mistake, a minor act of negligence or forgetfulness. We have learned from psychoanalysis that such little mistakes or slips have a great psychological significance and are due to the interference of unconscious tendencies that overpower the conscious intentions of the person. It is certainly permissible to transfer the recognition of those emotional trends to the area of ancient and primitive myths. Their psychoanalytic exploration and comparison has not been attempted. It would lead to the identification of the unconscious tendencies and thus enable us to understand the concealed meaning of various myths.

Enough, no more! This sketchy survey of the various myths about the Fall of Man leads to a surprising result: everything is mysterious about that crime before the beginning of civilization. It puzzles us that it is characterized not only as a sin against a god, but in many myths prompted by him or even committed by a god. There is the question of who is the criminal and who is the victim?

The figure of the criminal: he has in most legends a name, but who is he? A god, a half-god, a demon, angel, or a man? When was this primal crime committed? At the beginning of the world or when men were already the type Homo sapiens? At the level of the Neanderthal being or at that of a progressed phase of civilization? Or was it in a pre-existent state as in Hindu belief, according to which men were banished to the earth and to a purgatorial life? And now the question is crucial not only in the sense of being decisive and critical, but also in the theological meaning because its answer marks the road to the Cross: what was the nature of that primal crime? In most cases it is clearly denoted, but we often do not understand why it is considered a crime—more than that, the archcrime, the most atrocious sin or deed of mankind.

We can well conceive that the murder of the little son of Zeus in orphic mythology was marked as the original sin. The killing of Osiris by his brother Set appears certainly as a terrible crime. In Andamanese mythology the high god Puluga lived with men until they tried to kill him. He said that he was "hard as wood" and that if they persisted in disobeying him he would destroy them and the world. The Maipures in Guiana in South America report that Kurru-muman created men, but they became so bad that they tried to kill him, whereupon he took immortality from them and gave them to those animals who changed their skins. Those are indeed crimes against the deity. In the majority of myths the punishment follows an act of violence or of atrocious cruelty, but in many cases death and all evils are attributed to the eating of a certain fruit or to a slight mistake, to forgetting or confusing something. We do not understand why, for instance, the eating of an apple, as in the Holy Scripture, should have such terrible consequences as curse and death and that all future generations should be punished for that childlike act of disobedience. What lamentations and groans through the millennia for an apple! *"Tant de bruit pour une pomme!"*

Added to these problems concerning the identity of the first sinner, the time and evolutional state in which that primeval crime was committed and its nature, comparative science of religion and anthropology find it difficult to answer another question. How is it to be explained that people as remote from each other as Australian, American, and African aborigines and Hindu have myths that bear in their whole character or in their essential traits a striking re-

semblance to the Genesis story? It would be a grave mistake
to assume that it is due to Christian missionary teaching. In
some cases this is undoubtedly true. A gradual diffusion of
the Hebrew story can also be assumed for certain formula-
tions. The experts have tried to judge each myth of this
kind on its merit. While a very few might have been borrowed, many others and many more are undoubtedly original and one has to admit "the possibility of similar
stories arising through similar circumstances, surroundings
and psychic conditions in more places than one."[11] Joseph
Feldmann, to whom we owe a most thorough comparison of
the Fall story with the myths of all races of the earth, comes
to the conclusion that an analogous tale, though in some
very fantastic forms, is to be found not only with all nations
of antiquity, but also with the primitive tribes of our time.[12]

The scholarly investigator comes to the following conclusions: A myth similar in all essential points of form and
content to the biblical story has not been found, but a tale
similar to that of the Genesis ideas or to some of its individual features has been discovered with almost all peoples.
The following factors can be registered as a common mythological tradition:

1. The ancestors of mankind were at the beginning in a
familiar relationship with God and had a happy existence,
free from complaints and suffering.

2. This state had an end by an outrage of men or of one
man against the deity. With some peoples this deed is one
of violence, with others a mistake or negligence.

3. God is indignant about the deed of his creatures and

[11] J. A. MacCulloch, "Fall," in Encyclopedia of Ethics and Religion.
[12] Dr. Joseph Feldmann, Paradies und Sündenfall, Alttestamentliche
Abhandlungen, IV (Bd. Munster. i.W. 1913).

either expels them or leaves them. Work and toil for the daily bread, illness and death belong to the destiny of each human being henceforth.

Accompanying those ideas appearing in different mythological forms, many important individual features common with the biblical tale can also be found in some old oriental myths. Those accidental elements of the tale cannot be discerned in cultures remote from that of the ancient Orient or at least not in the same specific manifestations. This is the considered opinion of an expert after careful examination of the various myths.

Since it is excluded that all peoples took their myths from Genesis, there are three possibilities to explain the fact that with almost all peoples of the globe tales essentially similar to that of the Bible exist. The first is represented by the view that all those myths, including the Hebrew, emerged independently from each other as products of the imagination of the individual people. Yet this theory of the essential identity of the human emotional life is not sufficient to explain the conformity of so many definite ideas. That similarity leads rather to the concept that all related myths of this kind originate in a mother mythology from which they are borrowed, including the biblical story. The Iranian-Indian circle of sagas, the Egyptian and Babylonian treasure of myths, akin to those of the Israelites, have successively been named as sources from which the biblical story, as well as others, has been taken. But none of them has a story so similar to that of Genesis that it can be considered the prototype of a tale that has all earmarks of ancient, Western Semitic work. The new theories of derivation from a common source are also unable to explain how the tale of the Fall of Man could have wandered to the remotest

corners of the earth and to most distant parts that were isolated since the dawn of history from the culture of the
ancient Orient. Neither the theory of an independent origin
of all sagas of this kind on account of a similar fantasy nor
that of borrowing from a certain ancient people explains
the general world-wide circulation and great similarity of
the myths.

There remains only the third possibility: namely, that
their source is to be searched for in those oldest traditions
that mankind possessed before it became differentiated into
distinct groups or nations. This theory would not only
satisfactorily explain the similarity of the old myths of all
peoples, but also their diversity, since the original tradition
during the many millennia in which it was orally transmitted
was individually shaped according to the character and
particularities of various peoples. Joseph Feldmann comes
thus to the conclusion that at the foundation of those oldest
traditions there must have been some historical event that
left deep traces in the memory of all people. But such an
event cannot be reconstructed with the methods of historical
criticism and comparative anthropology, nor with any other
methods at our disposal. Feldmann searches his way out of
the impasse by returning to the belief that the story as it is
contained in the Holy Scriptures has a core of religious
truth. To consider the biblical story as it is reported in
Genesis credible is not possible for us unbelievers. Yet
we see at this time no other way to explain the facts mentioned than to conceive of a primeval tradition whose mythological layers cover some historical reality.

We cannot put off any longer the task waiting for us: to
re-examine the biblical and mythical story of our first
ancestor. Whoever he was, he was a stranger and afraid, in

a world he never made. Is there a way to find out whether there is any reality in that old story

> . . . of Man's first disobedience and the fruit
> Of that forbidden tree, whose mortal taste
> Brought death into the world, and all our woe
> With loss of Eden?

CHAPTER VI

IT IS STILL A MYSTERY TO ME
(INTERLUDE)

THE MYTH of the original sin is perhaps the best known and least understood tale of the Holy Scripture. The decision to search for a still undiscovered meaning of the Fall story has an unpleasant aftermath. There is, let us admit, a moment of hesitancy and doubt. Let us assume that we even succeed in unearthing a significance not yet recognized in that narrative. Imagine the reaction of a person to whom you announce: "I have news for you. About the Original Sin." There is something ludicrous in the situation. The scholar Joseph Feldmann assures us that no part of the Old Testament—with the exception of the Song of Songs—has found as many and as different interpretations as that Genesis chapter.

How can we even for a moment hope to discover a secret in a tale whose every word has been the object of penetrating and painstaking investigation for many hundreds of years? Such a bold venture can be undertaken only with the premise that there is something puzzling or obscure in a situation that has been clear and transparent before. It can happen that an object distinctly seen is after a certain moment perceived only dimly and that our vision is suddenly blurred. There are everyday situations in which a certain combination of circumstances or the behavior pattern of a person is easily understood by other persons while it puzzles us. There is even a colloquial expression denoting such a lack of understanding on our part. We say: "It is still a mystery to me." There have been instances when you rode on a bus and could not help hearing bits of the conversation behind you. You don't remember any longer whether that phrase you heard referred to the present trend of an industry or to the sale of furniture for the law office of Mr. Jones. That expression might remind you that the word "mystery" means not only something beyond human comprehension, but also a secret rite or doctrine, revealed only to the initiates, also a certain type of religious medieval drama. The course of association might lead then to a mystery story. The train of thought ties in at this point with some remarks about the way we would like to deal with the biblical tale of the Fall.

The Genesis narrative is by definition as well as by tradition a crime story, the story of the first crime man committed. But that does not mean it is a mystery story. The culprits try to hide themselves from the presence of the Lord and He uses Adam's awareness of being naked as psychological circumstantial evidence in proving Adam guilty. Still, it would decisively change the plot and the conditions of the case if we were to transform the biblical report into an elementary mystery story. An American writer—if I am not mistaken, it was Elliot Paul—once asserted that the biblical story of Cain and Abel can be conceived as a real whodunit. The Great Detective (and Judge) in the case is Jehovah. Such a concept is, of course, contrived. There are no secrets before the Lord. A detective story is

impossible if the sleuth is omniscient. It is not the ante-
diluvian setting that makes that development unimaginable,
but the absence of any "mystery," the lack of any suspense
in a yarn in which the heavenly detective has infinite knowledge. The concept of the mystery story is unduly stretched
when the Genesis narrative of the murder of Abel is considered a biblical whodunit.

We hasten to add that in our view the realm of the mystery story is on the other hand unduly restricted when you
look at this kind of production only as a part of escape
literature. I cannot be the first (although I know of no
reference in this direction) who states that the plot of some
of the greatest works of world literature are undiluted detective stories: Oedipus, Hamlet, The Brothers Karamazov.
No unbiased reader who visualizes the king of Thebes
standing before his palace ("Where shall we find a clue to
solve that crime after so many years?"), the prince of Denmark ("Murder, though it have no tongue, will speak with
most miraculous organ"), and the four brothers at the
house of Fjodor Mihailovich Karamazov, will deny that
those works belong to detective literature. It cannot be
accidental and would be worthy of a special exploration
that the crime for whose perpetrator we are searching is in
the three cases the murder of father.

Our statement, "It is still a mystery to me . . ." does not
refer to the plot of the Fall story. This plot is thin and transparent. It has a beginning, a middle, and an end. If we
would tentatively conceive of that tale as of a mystery
story, no problem is discernible. The setting is definite: the
Garden of Eden. There are only three suspects: Adam, Eve,
and the Serpent. As in the case of Dostoevski's Raskolnikoff
the identity of the culprit is established from the beginning.

As a matter of fact, he pleads guilty. All three classic factors of the mystery story—motive, means, and opportunity —are obvious. No alibi is possible. The culprit cannot prove that he was elsewhere. The Lord sees all and knows all. No whodunit here.

The mystery is in the eyes of the beholder. It is not the identity of the criminal or sinner. It does not concern motives, means, nor opportunity, but the nature of the crime. But the Genesis text leaves no doubt about that! It is a transgression, a violation of the law of the Lord. Adam ate the fruit of the forbidden tree. And therefore is the Paradise lost, and death the penalty not only for himself, but for all men? Therefore, condemnation also for all future generations? We all share in that original sin: "In Adam's Fall we sinned all." Those of us who do not accept the literal truth of the Genesis text will say, "It is still a mystery to me . . ."

We are facing a singular situation: there is no doubt that a crime was committed. A crime? The crime of all crimes, an act of such gravity that all offenses ever committed pale to insignificance compared with it. Yet what does the report say? The first man was disobedient to the Lord, eating something He had forbidden. Poe's detective C. Auguste Dupin asserts that the more *outré* a crime is in appearance, the easier is its solution. Well, the crime or sin reported in Genesis is nothing extraordinary and happens every day in millions of families. Yet that short account of an everyday event in the infancy of creation is burdening the conscience of a great part of mankind. "In the entire range of the world's writing," says the Interpreter's Bible,[1] "it would be difficult to find any passage so brief which had such an

[1] New York, 1955, Vol. I, p. 501.

immense influence upon common thought. . . ." We cannot
fool ourselves: the solution of that crime will not be easy.

If the conception of the Genesis text as of the outline of
a mystery story were allowed, it would present a new aspect
of that literature. The question is not who is the criminal,
nor who is his victim, nor what are his motives, nor how
was the deed done—in short none of the problems a detective is supposed to solve. But what is the real nature of the
crime that is precisely and definitely described in the divine
police report?

In a literary attempt at the solution of that puzzle the
technique of the detective story would certainly be appropriate. We would (to remain within the framework of the
comparison) come upon the scene as outsiders, as amateur
detectives. The professional investigators would be the
scholars of exegesis and biblical archaeology, the experts
on the literature of the ancient Orient, the historians of
civilization and the mythologists and anthropologists. Decennia of research work of those scholars have cast a light
on many aspects of that primeval crime. None solved the
enigma of what it really was. The inquiry into the mythological premises, the exegetic work, the search for the
sources of the Genesis story, its comparison with the folklore of other people, facilitate the task for us late-comers.

Not all preparatory work of the scholars was valuable
and fruitful. Some of it has the character of empty activity
and of wasted intellectual effort. The research reminds you
occasionally of the investigation of professional detectives
in interpretation of clues. The solution of the Murders of
the Rue Morgue is prevented by the *idée fixe* of the police.
One sometimes has the impression that the same thing is
true of the solution to the crime in the Garden of Eden.
Some scholars dealing with that biblical problem behave

like the Parisian police who, in A. Dupin's view, try "de nier ce qui est, et d'expliquer ce qui n'est pas."

But what warrant have we in approaching the age-old problem? What claim have we to attempt a task that resisted the efforts of numerous investigators? Is it not presumptuous to expect that we would solve the problem after so many men of superior knowledge, experts in the field, among them men of ingenuity and even of genius, have failed in the task? It certainly would be foolish if we had not an advantage that was not at their disposal, a new instrument of exploration. Sherlock Holmes had more gift of original observation, more perceptiveness, and greater power of deduction than hundreds of modern detectives. But they know the fingerprint method and many other criminological tools he never dreamed of and this advantage enables them to solve problems with which he could not deal at all.

The new instrument at our disposal is the psychoanalytic method of research. Applying it, we can find concealed connections and penetrate mysterious formations that have undergone many alterations and have been subjected to various distortions and disguises. The analytic method of observation and psychological evaluation of small and neglected expressions can be transferred to the field of groups and masses. Freud recognized in the analysis of individuals that we are not made to keep secrets for a long time and that self-betrayal oozes from all our pores. That is also valid for races. Groups and nations unconsciously reveal what they would like to suppress. They give away what is concealed, denied, and disavowed in their myths, folklore, religious traditions, customs, and habits. In spite of all efforts of the suppressing powers, the vital and original drives obtain a certain possibility of surreptitious expression. The analytic method provides us with tools to undo distortions of many generations and to unearth the secrets concealed in unconscious recesses of the people.

The Genesis narrative of the Fall has a long history of alterations, distortions, and camouflages, brought about by the influences of progressing civilization upon the original traditions. We have learned in psychoanalysis to find and to interpret the signs of the repressed and forgotten past. When we apply the same methods in the investigation of myths it can be only in analogies with the individual emotional and mental phenomena. In spite of the decisive differences between productions of the individual and of the masses, these psychological insights became fruitful in the exploration of group phenomena.

Therefore that ancient myth of the Fall of Man that has had immense impact upon our civilizations cannot keep its secret, if analytically explored. It will finally give away what was the real nature of the first crime of mankind, of original sin. And now we will in a rapid survey examine what the experts, the professional detectives, have found about the actual facts of that mysterious crime case. Only after having obtained all the information available can we begin our independent work of detection.

PART TWO

THE CRIME

> 'Tis vain
> To think that arid brooding will explain
> The sacred symbols to your ken:
> Ye—Spirits, ye are hovering near,
> O, answer me, if ye can hear!

FAUST, *Study*

CHAPTER VII

THE INTERPRETATIONS

IT CANNOT be our task to give a history of the interpretations of the Fall story. We refer the reader to the detailed reviews that Feldmann, F. R. Tennant,[1] Williams,[2] and other biblical scholars present.[3] We restrict ourselves to a short survey of the various explanations and to following the literature on the subject until the present.

It is easy to divide the explanations of the commentators, according to their basic attitude to the text, into theological and scientific groups. Among those who approach the Genesis tale in the spirit of religious faith, the adherents of a literal concept have priority. Believers of this kind date from the early postexilic age to our own time; today the fundamentalists state that the Bible is literally true and divinely inspired. They insist that God created the universe within a single week in the year 4004 before Christ and really made man from the dust and formed woman from the rib of sleeping Adam. The snake was, according to Josephus and older Jewish commentators, equipped with

[1] *The Sources of the Doctrine of the Fall and Original Sin* (Cambridge, 1903).

[2] *The Ideas of the Fall and of Original Sin* (London, 1907).

[3] Most of the following material is taken from the book by Feldmann and the article in *Encyclopedia of Religion and Ethics* quoted earlier.

human language. Luther says the animal must have "stood erect like a cock." Fundamentalists did not hesitate to make the biblical story more palatable by embroidering it with many details. Luther tells us that the first couple entered the garden at noon and Eve, feeling appetite, ate the apple. The eating of the fruit and the Fall of Man is thus timed as lunch. It was, so to speak, darkness at noon.

Some commentators of this group explain that the paradisaic life of the first parents was of very short duration. In the Book of Jubilees life with the father lasted seven years, but according to Josephus it had the duration of only a few days. Luther limited it to one day. Friedrich Schiller's *Don Carlos* explains:

> A moment, lived in Paradise
> Is not too dearly paid for with life itself.

The literal concept of the Fall story has its counterpart in the allegorical kind of explanation. For this group the biblical narrative is, so to speak, an allegorical rebus whose solution is relatively easy. For the Jewish philosopher Aristobulus who wrote a commentary to the books of Moses around one hundred fifty years before Christ, Adam and Eve signify reason and sensuality; the serpent symbolizes sexual desire. It eats dust because it craves earthly pleasure. Sexual desire is circled as the snake. The first Fathers of the Church, Clement, Origen, Ambrosius, have followed the allegorical interpretations of Aristobulus and of the Alexandrian Philo who lived a few decennia before Christ. Even Augustine explains the four rivers of the Genesis story as the four virtues, the serpent as devil, the seed of the woman as good works. Such allegorical interpretation continues to the threshold of our time. In 1782 Drede taught that the woman signifies the Jewish synagogue, the serpent the devil, and the enmity between the two is that between the Mosaic law and Satan.

The concept of the Fall as a sexual act still was and is prevalent among theologians and even among ethnologists who conceive of the Genesis story as a mythological tale. For example, H. Reinach gave in 1826 the following explanation: men knew at first nothing of the differences of the sexes. But Eve saw lambs sucking at their mother's breast and the maternal urge was awakened in her. Cunningly she spoke (as the snake) to the man: "Should we alone be deprived of the lust of having children? Let us do like the animals."

A school of thought standing between the literal historical and the extreme symbolic concept believes in the essential historical character of the tale, but assumes that it contains expressions and ideas that have to be understood figuratively. Ambrosius among the Church Fathers argues (in De Paradiso, Cap. XIV) that it cannot be asserted that God walked as in the Genesis tale, since He is omnipresent. It was not an external voice that asked Adam, "Where art thou?" but the voice of his bad conscience. Athanasius reported that the Fathers did not agree with regard to the forbidden fruit. Some assumed it was a fig, others said it was a spiritual fruit, while some conceived it as of Eve's attractiveness. Whether they are inclined to the belief in the literal meaning of the story or see in it a symbolic manifestation, the theologians assumed that the Genesis tale depicts the deterioration of mankind as punishment for man's sin. In this sense they thought that there is at least a core of historical truth in the story.

The mythological concept that became victorious after

the end of the eighteenth century even within Protestant theological circles asserts almost the opposite. The Genesis story does not account for the deterioration of the human situation, but explains just the upward moment in the development of mankind, the progress in the evolution from the lower to a higher state. According to this view the story is not the report of a historic event, but a myth or a fairy tale.

As precursor of such mythological concepts the Roman philosopher Celsus (circa 178 after Christ) treated the Genesis stories with contempt and considered them as old wives' tales of the Jews, who were uneducated people without any knowledge of what Hesiod and other writers have to tell. He reported that the Christians give to those stories allegorical explanations which are, if possible, even more absurd than the myths themselves. A century after Celsus' polemics against Christianity another philosopher, Porphyry, speaks of those explanations with bitter sarcasm and irony and accuses Origen, who grew up in Greek culture, of stealing from the Greeks the methods to explain those miserable Jewish myths in a symbolic manner. Julian the Apostate considers those myths as fables and absurd stuff. It is, he asserts, nonsensical to assume that God had forbidden man the knowledge of good and bad. Since such knowledge is a gain for men, the devil could be considered a benefactor of mankind. Gnostics see in the Fall of Man the first step to insights. The modern rationalistic concept of the Fall story can be traced to German philosophers of the end of the eighteenth century, to Herder, Kant, and Schiller. Kant sees in the story the progress from instinct to reason. According to Friedrich Schiller, the story of Adam and Eve is the tale of how man from a purely vege-

table life finds his destiny through reason. The apparent
disobedience against the divine commandment is nothing
else but turning away from instinct. It is the first expression
of man's spontaneous activity, the first daring act of reasoning and undoubtedly the most fortunate and greatest event
of the human history. The philosopher will consider it a
"gigantic step of progress of mankind."[4]

The rationalistic concept of the Fall story had been followed by a majority of exegetists and commentators and
was later on taken over by anthropologists and historians
of culture. J. Wellhausen[5] conceives of the material of the
story as a historic-cultural reflection. With progress in civilization the awe of God is receding. The knowledge of good
and evil does not mean general recognition and does not
concern the moral side. The forbidden knowledge is the insight into the operating of God, especially into what is useful and harmful. The interpretation of Rudolf Smend[6] and
other commentators is that knowledge is the science of the
useful and harmful, a divine prerogative. Such arrogation
of God's privilege threatened Jahveh's position; and thus,
man who wanted to shape his destiny, lost original happiness by his own fault. Herman Gunkel[7] considers the story
of the Fall an etiological myth; it tries to answer the most
vital problems of mankind. The knowledge attained in the
first place is the knowing of the difference of the sexes,
which the grownups possess and children do not. This
knowledge makes man similar or equal to God. According
to Gunkel, the Fall does not have a central place within

[4] *Thalia*, 1790, Part 11.1, Sämtliche Werke, IV (Stuttgart, 1883),
pp. 227-240.
[5] *Prologomena zur Geschichte Israels* (6th ed., 1905), pp. 299-302.
[6] *Lehrbuch der alttest. Religionsgeschichte* 1 (2d ed., 1899), p. 120 f.
[7] *Genesis Commentary* (3d ed., 1910), p. xv.

the story and is only a secondary feature. It should explain why man possesses that knowledge, but lost paradise. E. Sellin[8] thinks that through the eating of the fruit man entered the state of reason and overcame the state of childhood.

The mythological concept of the biblical story as it appears in the books of those scholars is also to be found in the interpretations contributed by anthropologists and ethnologists. They carefully consider the many transformations the primal myth has undergone, but search for its first form and original meaning. The Hebrew story is re-examined under the points of view of modern literary criticism, its sources explored, and its main features compared with the myths of the ancient oriental nations and of primitive peoples. The point of departure for this kind of research is the premise that the ancient Hebrews also passed through a stage of barbarism and savagery and many survivals of such an early phase are to be found in their literature. J. G. Frazer, whom we choose as representative of anthropological exploration, calls the method he applies "comparative anatomy of the mind."[9] Examining the traditions of ancient Israel and comparing them with those of other peoples, he points out that the myth of the Fall of Man and of the lost Golden Age is disseminated all over the world. Frazer delineates what appears to him the common primordial pattern of all the available versions of the myth and calls it the "perverted message." The Creator, using the serpent as His messenger, commanded the first human couple to avoid the fruits of the tree of death and to eat from those of the tree of life. The treacherous serpent reversed the message and gave it to the foolish woman with the intent to rob man of

[8] *Die biblische Urgeschichte* (1904).
[9] *Folklore in the Old Testament* (New York, 1925).

his immortality and to acquire it himself. The symbolic meaning of this original version is that man yields to sexual desire and chooses its gratification instead of eternal bliss in paradise. The biblical narrator transformed this archaic folklore into a story of moral thoughts and warnings. We meet here again the concept of the Fall of Man as of a sexual offense: here in anthropological interpretation as before in the commentaries of the theologians.

The most recent scientific interpretation of the myth is provided by the psychoanalysts. It follows the same general direction, but progresses on a new, well-marked path. Ricklin[10] and Abraham[11] had pointed out that the myth has to be interpreted as a symbolic presentation of impregnation. In his *Psychoanalytische Beiträge zur Mythenforschung* Otto Rank interpreted the Fall story as an analogy to the infantile theory of sexual intercourse and birth.[12] Rank, applying the analytic method of interpretation, explains that here as so often the latent meaning of a production in which the unconscious takes a great part can be found in reversing its manifest content. There are three such reversals in the Genesis myth: (1) Eve is not created out of the rib from Adam's body, but Adam emerges from the opened body of Eve, who appears as the primal mother of man (Mother Earth); (2) Eve does not present the apple to Adam, but the man gives the fruit to the woman, seduces her. This reversal is made under the influence of rationalistic tendencies of a late editor who tries to trace the Fall of Man to woman's malice in the same manner as a late misogynist conceives of Pandora's mission in the Greek myth. The

[10] Franz Ricklin, *Wishfulfillment and Symbolism in Fairy Tales* (New York, 1915).
[11] Karl Abraham, *Dreams and Myths* (New York, 1913).
[12] Leipzig and Vienna, 1919.

third reversal concerns the role of the serpent. In other myths—as, for instance, in that of the Hesperides—the serpent or dragon appears as the guardian of the tree (with golden apples). Rank comes to the conclusion that the core of the original Fall story is incest of Adam with his mother Eve, from which mankind originated.

Neither the figure of Adam nor that of his sin occurs, as far as this writer knows, in any of Freud's collected papers. Freud made no attempt at interpretation of that biblical story. An isolated passage of *Totem and Taboo* refers to the original sin or rather to the Paulinic thesis of an inherited sin. A fragmentary explanation of the myth became posthumously known from Freud's correspondence with C. G. Jung.[13] In a letter of December 7, 1911, Freud objects to Jung's discussing mythological material at its surface value. Thus the woman in Genesis appears as the seductress of the man to whom she gives the apple to eat. Freud thinks that the Genesis myth "is probably a miserable tendentious distortion by priest's apprentice (Priesterlehrbub) who, as we know now, condensed in a quite witless fashion (as in a dream) two independent sources into an account." Freud considers it very possible that this late amateurish editor inserted two sacred trees into his report because he found one tree in each of his sources. With regard to the creation of Eve, Freud refers to Rank's previously mentioned theory of a reversal of the role of male and female. Eve appears thus as the mother of Adam "and we would thus encounter the mother-incest so familiar to us, the punishment and so on." Equally strange, but equally explainable by reversal of the original tradition is the feature of the woman offering the man something to eat of a fertilizing nature. Freud

[13] Quoted in Ernest Jones, *The Life and Work of Sigmund Freud,* Vol. II (New York, 1955).

points to an old marriage ceremony in which the man gives the woman fruit to eat—"i.e. the way Proserpine has to stay in Hades as Pluto's wife." By those considerations Freud is led to the statement that the manifest form of mythological themes "cannot without further investigation be used for purpose of comparison with our psychoanalytical conclusions." Their latent original form has first to be ascertained "by tracing back through historical comparative work so as to eliminate the distortions that have come about in the course of the development of the myth." In this concept of Freud, Adam's sin is incest with his mother. The biblical narrative tries to conceal this original meaning by different measures of distortion. Freud's other reconstruction of the original crime, which will be discussed later, does not refer to the biblical Fall story and does not contribute anything to its interpretation.

To make the picture complete, a few instances of later analytic explanations of the myth will be sketched here. For Ludwig Levy the Fall story is a symbolic presentation of forbidden intercourse.[14] The apple means the female breast and the eating of the fruit is a euphemistic expression for the sexual act. A climax of multiple interpretation, in which the figures of Adam, Eve, and the serpent give rich opportunities for new complications is reached in Geza Roheim's paper, "The Garden of Eden."[15] For this scholar the latent content of the Fall story is that Adam fought a victorious battle against God, had intercourse with Eve, his mother, and then was afflicted with remorse. Roheim points out that the Hebrew tradition itself was aware of the phallic meaning of the serpent, for it is in the shape of the serpent

[14] "Sexualsymbolik in der biblischen Paradiesgeschichte." *Imago,* Vol. 1917-1919, p. 16 f.
[15] The Garden of Eden," *The Psychoanalytic Review,* XXVII (1940).

that Satan had intercourse with Eve. Eating is, of course, a euphemism for coitus, earth a symbol of mother. Roheim adds the interpretation that the crawling of the serpent on its stomach and its eating dust mean sexual intercourse. The biblical sentence about the enmity between the serpent and the seed of women "means not only versus the serpent, but also the serpent (phallus) against the female."

The character of the punishment for Eve is "quite clear." Her pains at childbirth and the desire for the male are "apposite punishments only for one offense, for intercourse." The myth tells us that sexual desire or maturation is disobedience to the father (Oedipus) and therefore "a sin from the point of the invisible view," that is, of the introjected father image or superego. The sin "is punished by sexual life, i.e., by itself." Roheim's ingenuity finds reasons "to identify the fruit of immortality with the nipple" and follows this interpretation to its logical conclusion that "the sin which leads mankind to the Fall or the loss of immortality is the sucking of the human infant." Reminding us of the use of the word "fruit" as a metaphoric expression for "child" in the Old Testament, Roheim feels "bound" to accept Rank's interpretation of the fruit torn or, to put it more cautiously, the trauma of separation (i.e., from the mother's body or from the nipple.) The "fruit of the womb" torn from the tree means mankind ejected from an infantile paradise.

Let me mention two recent analytic interpretations. The first was published by Abraham Kardiner,[16] the second by A. Fodor.[17] According to Kardiner the basis of the saga is

---

[16] In *Changing Concepts in Psychoanalytic Medicine,* Sandor Rado, ed. (New York, 1956).

[17] "The Fall of Man in the Book of Genesis," *Imago,* Vol. 11, 1954.

"the sexual control of the immature" and it contains a "sexual prohibition against children." The point of departure for Fodor's interpretation is the original duality of the mother-goddess and her repression in favor of male deities. The hidden meaning of the myth indicates that incestuous love was entertained between Adam and Eve, but the tale of the couple simultaneously signifies a dual human unity organization, broken up by God. The drive forward, the restitution of this original dual organization means unconsciously incest, actually the desire to return to the maternal womb—not, however, the craving for the possession of the mother as a mere libidinal object. To be readmitted into the motherly womb "offers an unrestricted security and a complete gratification of all one's desire, the veritable Elysium, the idea of the Golden Age." Here is an interesting or rather amusing variation of the recurring incest theme that appears in almost all analytic interpretations as the hidden meaning of the biblical Fall story.

Here is as a final vignette for the survey on the literature on this subject, the most recent interpretation of the Genesis myth: Francis I. Mott speaks in this sample of science fiction of the psychological significance of uterine experiences.[18] Their universality is, according to this author, supported by the manner in which they are recorded in mythology. One of the best known is the myth of the Garden of Eden: "Here in the garden (womb) lives Adam (fetus) with Eve (placenta) and the Serpent (umbilical cord) until the Fall (birth) brings the idyllic life to an end." The reader does not know whether or not this interpretation is supposed to be a joke, but he cannot laugh.

The preceding survey of the exegetic commentaries and

[18] *The Myth of a Chosen People* (London, 1953), p. 41.

of anthropologic and psychoanalytic theories leads to the result that they all basically agree with the theological explanation that the Fall of Man is a sexual offense. The analytic interpretation added two new elements: the first was the explanation of the emotional dynamic, operating in the transformation of the myth, that means identification of those secret tendencies that are responsible for the repression of its original meaning and their ways of reaching their aim. The second new feature provided by the analytic concept is clarification of the character of the sexual crime veiled in the Genesis story. All analytic explanations agree that the nature of the original sin is incest with mother. Adam had sexual intercourse with his mother Eve and was therefore punished by God. When you read the analytic explanations of Rank, Freud, Levy, Roheim, and others, interpreting the Fall as forbidden sexual intercourse, their coincidence with theological interpretation, as it has been given by Jewish and Christian commentators for many centuries, becomes conspicuous. The only difference is that in the psychoanalytic concepts the sexual intercourse to which the myth alludes was incestuous. The impression of such a far-reaching concord is similar to that of poor Gretchen to whom Faust explains his pantheistic creed: "Much the same way the preacher talks of it, only in words that differ a bit."

We shall not deny that certain elements of the theological, anthropological, and analytic interpretations are present in the later forms of the Fall story as it had evolved many hundreds of years from the original tradition. Some analytic explanations could penetrate the sources of the biblical narrative and uncover the hidden meaning of parts of the story as well as the dynamics perceptible in its formations. We most energetically deny that any of those attempts at interpretations reached the primal core of the oldest tradition. Otherwise put, we are convinced that the original Fall myth as it was preserved in oral tradition did not concern the incest between mother and son, Eve and Adam. We acknowledge and admire the ingenuity of many of the analytic explanations and interpretations, but we believe that they are going astray and were misled and misguided by the delusive light of a scientific will-o'-the-wisp.

Persons lost in the woods often find themselves moving in ever-tightening circles; they return for instance to the same tree. In a similar manner some scholars have wandered by many paths to return on long detours to the concept of the sexual character of the original sin. Theology first pointed in this direction. Afterward anthropology and the science of comparative religion found their own way back to the old sexual concept of the first crime. Finally analysis, following its own method of interpretation, landed at the same spot. Yet a circle, though often repeated, does not cease to be a vicious circle.

There is no use in concealing our disappointment. Our impression is that many commentators have transformed the paradise into a wasteland of interpretation. We wondered about the naïveté of the fundamentalists who believe in the literal truth of the story. But are not some of the scientific explanations of exegetists just as naïve? Is the search for a hidden meaning of the Fall story perhaps futile? "If there's no meaning in it," said the King of Hearts to Alice, "that saves a world of trouble." But we have reached a point of no return. We can only march forward.

We used the comparison earlier of the wanderer who lost his way in the woods. It is as if some hidden magic compels him to wander around the same tree. It was only a comparison, but comparisons are never accidental. Is a tree not growing in the middle of the Garden of Eden? This very tree will be the point of departure for our attempt at interpretation. But first we have to remove a lot of the deadwood that has been accumulated around that sacred tree "in the middle of the garden."

CHAPTER VIII

TEXT AND CONTEXT

THE MANY problems of the composition of the Book are beyond the range of this discussion, but we have to remind the reader that the story of the Fall is the result of the work of different editors and that their efforts were many times combined, changed, and distorted. Most biblical critics agree that the Fall narrative appears homogeneous, has a logical sequence and consequence, and makes the impression of well co-ordinated unity. How is that possible? Here are the facts as far as the historical and exegetic critics can ascertain them: the tale of Genesis 2:4 to 3:24 is attributed to the Jehovistic source, which means that the editors use the name "Jahveh" in contrast to the other source, which speaks of God as Elohim.

The time determined for the writing of the tale is perhaps around nine hundred years before Christ. In the opinion of most scholars, the primal traditions upon which the story is founded reach far into the past and had become folklore thousands of years before its fixation in writing. Some historians, for instance F. Hommel,[1] assume that a considerable part of those traditions had already existed in writing

[1] *Die altisraelitische Ueberlieferung in inschriftlicher Beleuchtung* (Munich, 1897), p. 277.

at the time of Moses and were elaborated and distorted
when the land of Western Jordan was conquered. The
sources from which that material was taken are themselves
collections of sagas, often distorted. The biblical tale is thus
a combination of different traditions, frequently changed
before being written down, distorted by various collectors,
and finally transformed by different late editors. Contradictions were bridged, gaps filled, some things arbitrarily
added, others erased. Everything that seemed not in accordance with the religious and moral opinions of the time was
either omitted or altered. The account as it now appears is
an attempt at reaching unity and logical coherence but the
synthesis has the same sequence and unity as the manifest
content of a dream. The harmonization is the artificial result of a secondary elaboration that has tried more or less
successfully to shape one homogeneous form out of several
pieces that had nothing to do with each other. The appearance of the narrative is that of an organic tale. It looks as
though it were a garment of the same cloth, but we know
that it is patchwork, pieced together, often botched and
repaired. In numerous references here and there as well as
in connecting pieces we recognize the seams.

In small deletions and omissions, insertions, replace-
ments, and other distortions the effort of successive compilers and editors was easily proved by biblical criticism.
Our purpose does not justify more than mention of a few
contradictions and inconsistencies, proving that different
levels are superimposed one upon the other and that an
attempt was made to bring them into conformity in the final
report. The forming of the paradise and the planting of man
in it is told twice. According to passage 2:8 the paradise is
situated in the East; according to 3:24 it may be in the
West, and according to 2:10-14 it could be in the North.

The expulsion from paradise is twice told. One source knows only one tree in the middle of the garden, the other speaks of two. The clumsy structure of some sentences reveals revisions and changes of the text to such an extent that it seems sometimes transformed into the opposite of the original.[2]

A feature of special interest within the narrative is the mysterious tree in the middle of the garden. There is first of all the uncertainty whether one tree or two trees are meant in the original report. In Genesis 3:3 the woman speaks of only one tree in the middle of the garden, and in verses 6, 11, 12 only one tree is mentioned. The tree of life appears first in 2:9 in a sentence that is stylistically doubtful. Jahveh forbids in 2:17 to eat from the tree of knowledge and that tree is, according to 2:9 and 3:3, in the middle of the garden. Budde and others assume that the story originally contained only one tree, that of knowledge. Other scholars such as Chayne, Worcester, and Knenen assert that the passage with the tree of life presents the older edition and the Hebrew introduced the tree of knowledge into the story later on. A. Wünsche is of the opinion that there was only the tree of life in the primal source and the tree of knowledge was inserted for the motivation of the Fall. One group of scholars accuses the other of barking up the wrong tree.

It seems to me that the solution of that riddle is provided by the assumption that the tree of life and that of knowledge are originally identical and the division into two trees is secondary and is founded on a tendentious mistake. Ludwig Levy has pointed out that the Hebrew word "waw," which

[2] A good survey of the variances is to be found in the chapter "Le problème des 'doublets'" in Paul Humbert's *Etudes sur le récit du Paradis et de la Chute dans la Genèse.* (Neuchatel, 1940), p. 9.

connects the names of the tree of life and that of the tree of knowledge in the biblical text, may mean "and" as well as "that is." If that "waw" is explicative, the original reading would be: "the tree of life and that is the tree of knowledge of good and evil." Lord Byron's line, "The tree of knowledge is not the tree of life," is profound, but it does not correspond to the primal meaning of the biblical text.

The process by which biblical critics and exegetes try to attribute the verses to different writers and later editors sometimes gives the impression of shuffling a pack of cards in a competent way. You take half the pack in each hand, deftly insert the corners of one half under the corners of the other, and with a slick and bold gesture cascade the cards together. We are not competent to deal with those problems of text criticism; the task of biblical research of this kind transgresses our restricted area.

We heard that the Genesis narrative is a combination of several legends that had lived for thousands of years in tradition, were frequently changed, and finally fixed in writing. In order to reconstruct the primal form of the Fall story we have to rip open the threads that stitched those different tales. Such an operation requires boldness and delicacy at the same time. The radical distortions and transformations by successive compilers and editors left certain residues of the original text intact. Except for a process you can call erosion—a gradual wearing away of the earliest tales—some ancient traditions were faithfully preserved in spite of all the zeal of late editors. Where should we start with that procedure of tearing out the threads? Which is the most conspicuous seam showing that two pieces were sewed together?

Most critics recognize in Genesis the presence of a Creation story and a Fall story, originally independent of each other and welded together at a late phase. The main tear has thus to be made at the line formed by the stitching together of the Creation and the Fall tales. Modern literary critics (for instance C. Clement[3]) think that a Hebrew sin story in a modified form was welded with a creation legend, resulting in the present narrative. The creation and paradise stories, originally independent of each other, had been connected by the Jahvists but not in such a way as to obliterate discrepancies. It is more likely that this blending of materials took place at different ages until the two entities became a continued story. But if we accept this premise, founded on different and detailed stylistic argument, the figure of Adam himself becomes problematical. We need not think of him as the ancestor of mankind and as the first sinner any longer, but may assume that two figures became here one in the oral tradition and late in the final composition of the sagas.

There were two myths: one of the Creation of Man and another of the Fall. The second saga concerned perhaps a man or men at a much later phase of evolution. Many analogous myths of ancient people, such as those of the Babylonians and Egyptians, and also the folklore of primitive tribes of Australia and Africa, were quoted as comparative material by the scholars. They present two stories of a type in which the Creation of Mankind and a legend of a Golden Age and Fall are independent entities. There are, it is true, myths in which the first crime or break of taboo is attributed to the first man or at least to one of his early descendants, for instance one of the second generation of mankind. How can we reconcile those contradictory as-

[3] *Die Lehre von der Sünde,* I, 1897.

sumptions? If the concept of the biblical scholars is correct, namely the original existence of two independent stories, only the second case, that of their welding, has to be explained.

Who is Adam? Except in the Creation and Fall story the name appears only in the genealogies of the Bible (Genesis 4:25, 5:1-5; I Chronicles 1:1) and is never mentioned again in the Old Testament. But Adam is no proper name; the word means earth-man or soil-man because man is made from earth (adamah). Without an article it can be used to say "man," and corresponds generally to the Latin word *homo*. Adam means thus the first human being in the Creation story and, if our premise is accepted, it means another man in the Fall story. We need not worry whether it means Homo sapiens or some subhuman predecessor of the species. We have only to renounce a thought cliché, a pattern of thinking, familiar since childhood—one, or rather two, preconceived ideas we accepted and never questioned when being taught biblical history and when reading the sacred book.

The man who committed the first crime is perhaps many generations remote from Adam, the first man of creation. The Fall story does not deal with a certain individual called Adam, but with a member of the species man. To call this representative of early mankind "Adam" is as arbitrary as to give the name of Peter Rabbit to the representative of the hares in the tales we heard as children. We feel tempted to continue the comparison beyond the arbitrariness of the namegiving of the figure in the Genesis story. The bunny was warned about McGregor's garden and got into trouble eating forbidden food there. The memory of his childhood told me by a patient gives occasion to compare the process of compilation of the Genesis sagas with the tales of Peter

Rabbit. The patient remembered in an analytic session an occasion when he felt very misunderstood and unjustly punished as a little boy. Before bedtime his mother used to tell him stories about Peter Rabbit, to which the child listened with great eagerness. Father usually sat nearby in an easy chair, enjoying the interest of the son. Once the father, who had returned tired from his office, fell asleep on the couch while mother told the little boy new adventures of Peter Rabbit. The child ran to his father and wakened him. Although mother had scolded him and forbade him to arouse the father, the boy called him again and did not rest until the father had reawakened. The child was spanked and felt that mother had badly wronged him. He had been worried that his sleeping father would miss the further adventures of Peter Rabbit and would not know what had finally happened to the bunny in McGregor's garden. Mother's story had only a remote resemblance to the book of Beatrix Potter. Her fertile imagination dwelt on the home life of Peter Rabbit and provided the tale with many colorful anecdotes about Peter Rabbit's food habits and toilet training. These added tales were tied together only by the name of the bunny.

I imagine that the manner in which the Genesis sagas of the Creation and of the Garden of Eden were strung together resembles the fanciful way in which the mother spun yarns about the adventures at Peter Rabbit's home and in McGregor's garden. The Hebrew tribes listening to those old traditions were very likely as eager to hear of the vicissitudes of the first man as was that little boy to hear the adventures of the bunny. There was as little connection between the story of Peter Rabbit's birth, at which the stork was very helpful, and his furtive eating of lettuce and French beans as there was between the creation of Adam and his tasting the fruit of the tree of life. In other words, the Adam of the creation story and the Adam of the original sin have only an arbitrarily chosen name in common. Their alleged identity is secured only by the fancy of an oral tradition, which shaped different stories into a unity by arranging them around a single figure.

Proceeding from the general to the particular, we will endeavor to reach the core of the Fall story, to be considered the independent narrative of a primeval crime. The stage of the play is well known from the description in the second chapter of Genesis and we can concentrate our attention on its figures. There are four: Jahveh, the character we know under the name of Adam, his mate called Eve, and the Serpent. Leaving God outside the discussion, as is seemly, we ask: what kind of part does Eve play? If we can believe the story, she is the seducer. Without her that primal sin would not have been committed. Everything for Eve! Adam's fault was that he yielded to her. It seems that there is nothing left to his descendants but to regret his complacency and to agree with what Thomas Hood voiced more than a hundred years ago:

> When Eve upon the first of Men
> The apple press'd with specious cant,
> Oh! what a thousand pities then
> That Adam was not Adamant!

But Eve was more than an instrument to precipitate the fall. She was really a delegate of the serpent, of the evil spirit. The early church fathers, who identified the serpent with the devil, called her and each daughter of Eve "instrumentum diaboli." Several scholars connect the name "Eve" with the Arab word for serpent and assert that the snake belonged to the oldest form of the Paradise story, while Eve came into it later through the etymological confusion with the name of the snake. According to the text, Adam called his wife Hawwah, which means "life," because she was "the mother of all living" (Genesis 3:20). Many commentators consider that verse a late addition because it does not tally with the context that the man after punishment calls his wife, full of hope, mother of all living. Other scholars such as Stade and Dillmann doubt that Adam could have called her thus before she had borne children. That verse 3:20 interrupts the context. No name is expected here, and that verse seems not to belong to the primal tale. Some scholars see in Eve a snake goddess to which some Semitic peoples trace their origin. (Mark Lidzbarski identifies the biblical Hawwah with the Phoenician goddess Hwt.[4]) H. Gressmann points out that the snake in the biblical story turns only to Eve.[5] He concludes that "Eve is still in the present story halfway a snake, the snake halfway a demon."

Let us return to the likely assumption that different myths were welded together in the story of the Fall, myths that had originally nothing to do with each other. It is very probable that there was also a myth of an ancient mother-goddess to whom was attributed all evil that befell mankind. There was further a myth in which a god, or rather a goddess, appeared as a snake. There was further the tale of a primeval sin through which mankind lost its original blessings. We cannot know which of those myths is older and which younger, especially since very ancient folklore can return in disguised and distorted shape and find entrance into a relatively recent level of sagas. We have no means of solving those problems of stratification and elaboration. No one knows when and how the different strands were woven

---

[4] *Ephemeris für semitische Epigraphik I* (Tubingen, 1902) p. 30.
[5] *Archiv für Religionswissenschaft,* X, p. 35.

together. We shall be content when we succeed in showing that there are various threads and in following the one we are interested in, namely the Fall story, through the multiform tissue.

The comparison with other myths, for instance those of the Babylonians and of the Greeks (Pandora) leaves no doubt that there was an ancient motif of sagas indicating that all evil came from women or from one woman into the world. Eve is thus only one of many mythological female figures—and in this context it is not important whether she is a goddess, a demon, or a human woman—who is made responsible for the downfall of men in primitive folklore and in ancient myths.

This motif, which presents perhaps the reversal of an earlier worship for women, is so conspicuous that it cannot be of a secondary nature. It certainly reveals a general negative or resentful tendency against women. This attitude emerges whenever Eve's part in the Fall story is mentioned to this day. Here is an amusing instance of such a tendentious reference to the Genesis story in our time: Megan Lloyd George, the daughter of Prime Minister David Lloyd George (who was the speaker for the Liberal party), a small, dark lady of twenty-seven, challenged the farmer, Col. Lawrence Williams, at a convention on the Island of Anglesey. She said that the world's first farmer had security of tenure only conditionally. When he violated the conditions, he was turned out of the Garden of Eden. Colonel Williams angrily replied: "And it was owing to a woman he was turned out, and let me tell you she was a young woman too."

It cannot be accidental that in the majority of those ancient myths the main motive, often the only one, for the

Fall of man is sexual desire or, as it was called later on, concupiscence. It is certainly significant that the tragic sense of life is concentrated on the sensual experience.

It is, on the other hand, very unlikely that the Fall story in its primal form could have had such a sexual concept. It is almost unimaginable with regard to the Semitic original tradition in which the biblical story originated, since "the idea that sexual desire is something sinful and deserves punishment was entirely foreign to ancient Israel."[6] It can only be that to the original tradition a sexual meaning was much later attached. Such a rearrangement of the ancient Fall story must have taken place many centuries before St. Paul and St. Augustine gave to the first transgression of man a sexual interpretation. The early fathers of the church, in attributing this distinct sexual meaning to the original sin, elaborated something that had been there in traces ages before their time. They reshaped the original plot in such a way that the first sin was a sexual one and Eve became a leading figure in the primal human tragedy.

The transformation of the material was a recasting to such an extent that almost a new play emerged before an audience that never had known the primal text. The significance of the redesigning and re-evaluating became increasingly clearer when Eve became the leading lady of the drama. Tertullian says that Eve's smile made angels cry. It is very unlikely that woman had such great power in the story that first emerged from the transformation of the ancient Fall tradition. Old Anatole France stated that Christianity has done much for l'amour in making it a sin. Nicolais Ségur heard the old master say: "One knew that there was a hell, but its geography was unknown until that

---

[6] *The Standard Bible Encyclopaedia, II* (Chicago, 1915), p. 1002.

violent African church father discovered its door at a
certain place between the legs of women."[7] Tertullian really
felt that the flames of hell-fire blazed there and, as Anatole
France remarks, men were eager to unlock this door to
enter perdition.

Yet woman could not have been merely an episodic
figure in the primal tale of the original sin. She appears too
often in the role of a malicious goddess or as prostitute in
the narratives of the ancient Orient, which the scholars
compare with the biblical story. Her lure was perhaps in a
very old version one or even the only motive for breaking
the law the deity had given. Freud guesses that the woman
who had been the "prize of the battle" and enticement for
that primal crime became in the hypocritical recastings of
the primal plot the seductress who induced the deed.[8]

And the Serpent? What was its part in the original plot
or had the reptile no role in it? The serpent or a fabled
dragon appears as the symbol of physical or moral evil
for men in numerous myths. These creatures are in many
mythologies, for instance in the Vedic and American sagas,
guardians of waters and trees. In the Greek myth the sleep-
less dragon Ladon guards the Hesperides. The reptile was
represented as winding from below around a tree which issues a well. It is very likely that the serpent represented
originally a god or demon whom the culture hero slew as
Hercules slew the dragon. The origin of serpent worship,
so widely spread in ancient civilizations and in primitive
societies, undoubtedly originated in a totemistic cult. Yet
there are traces of an ancient myth in which the serpent is
associated with the deep, variously called Leviathan, Behe-
moth, Raehab, whale, or dragon—and represented as con-

[7] *Anatole France anecdotique* (Paris, 1929).
[8] *Group Psychology and the Analysis of the Ego* (London, 1922).

quered by Jahveh (Psalm 74:14, Isaiah 27:1, 51:9) or bound by Him or set into the sea (Ezekiel 29:3-5, 32:2-8). The talking serpent in Genesis 3 is a late descendant of other mythological reptiles that were perhaps kindly disposed to man and wanted to help him to acquire knowledge and wisdom. Whatever the later recension made of the original tradition, the serpent appeared there as a sacred animal. We do not doubt that there was an ancient myth in which the reptile and its relations with men who traced their origin to the snake appeared in the center of the plot. It is even possible that there was a tradition of a conflict between the snake god or dragon goddess and a culture hero whom Adam replaced later on, as in the Sumerian myth of the "great serpent with seven heads," Tiamat, whom Merodach conquered and slew. Such a myth would have to be considered as an early totemistic variant of the biblical story, but this hypothetical tradition does not cast any new light on the origin of the Genesis tale.

We wished to penetrate to the core of the Fall story and hoped to accomplish that by clean cuts that separated the later versions from the original. We hoped that this task would not be difficult. No such luck. We encountered remnants of different myths in the tale interwoven so intimately that it seems almost impossible to reconstruct a primal tradition. The tale of the original sin is, thus looked at, as involved as the maze of the Minotaur in the Greek myth. Yet there is a thread even through this labyrinth. Is there a comparable thread in the Fall story, a thread we could bind fast at the entrance of the labyrinth, enabling us to penetrate the center of this rambling composite tale? In spite of all fusions and confusions, of various distortions and alterations, determined by many factors, the biblical text itself must help us to reveal the secret, must provide

that thread through the labyrinth. The tradition asserts that
the sacred text was dictated by Jahveh Himself to Moses on
Mount Sinai. Modern exegesis has, it is true, proved that
the text is the result of many editorial changes, but traces
of the original divine author probably remained intact. We
feel like Faust, moved to return to the sacred text. One
must also give God the benefit of the doubt.

CHAPTER IX

CRIMINAL INVESTIGATION

WHILE WE studied commentaries on the biblical account, followed the analogies of its content with the myths of other ancient civilizations and primitive societies, examined the exegetic and interpretive books and papers, our impatience to solve that mystery increased. But impatience does not secure clues; it rather retards our search for them. We have to control that unpleasant feeling of unrest, to overcome that diffusion of thoughts that go off at different tangents while we study that material. The work is, let us admit it, progressing very slowly and the abundance of overtones makes it difficult to discern the main motives of the symphony. The musical comparison reminds us of an observation Gustav Mahler once made to his friend Natalie Bauer-Lechner.[1] The young composer had found that his audience became restive sometimes at the slow movement of a symphony he conducted. Instead of accelerating the time, he made the orchestra slow down and asserted that the attention of the listeners increased. Let us try to apply the same tactics in dealing with our impatience while we proceed with our investigation that will, we hope, reveal clues to the solution of that mysterious crime.

[1] *Erinnerungen an Gustav Mahler* (Vienna, 1923).

We were bold to separate the story of creation from the myth of the Fall. We removed the figure of Eve and of the serpent because we think that they belong to other myths and became part of the story of the first crime only in a late version. The other myths are perhaps of a tradition much older than the Fall story, but our impression is that they became welded to it under the influence of religious tendencies during a late phase of the evolution of the Hebrew sagas. In those Semitic myths the predecessor of the Eve figure was perhaps the great Mother-Goddess, to be found in the prologue of so many theogonies. The snake was originally a god or a demon, conceived as the totemistic ancestor of the Hebrew tribes. The saga section resulting after those two bold cuts sees only two characters on the stage, Jahveh and Adam. In this moment it is immaterial whether we think of Adam as the first man or as some early representative of the species Homo sapiens. The dramatis personae are two: the Lord and the first transgressor of His law. The Garden of Eden and the Tree of Life are to be considered the stage setting.

But is the biblical tale not a unity? By what right do we perform such a vivisection, which cuts into living material? I consider the operation necessary and as legitimate as vivisection for scientific investigation. We have to establish a basis for the reconstruction of the original tradition, which we are undertaking. We do not deny that the Genesis story gives an impression of cohesion and logical sequence, but we assert that this appearance is the result of the work of late editors who tried to meld different sagas with the tradition of a Fall of Man. That impression is the effect made by secondary elaboration, by the synthesizing work of several centuries combining various sagas into a whole in such a way that the final product seemed to be consistent and coherent. The appearance of consequence and logic is deceptive and artificially established. Its true character is recognizable in small inconsistencies, inconspicuous contradictions, repetitions, and displacements, which reveal that later editors endeavored to reach sequence and consequence in the account. The processes in the formation of an ancient myth resemble in this direction the work of the psychic factors transforming an independent part of a dream into a co-ordinated unit and making it appear as if its elements had a logical connection. With regard to these effects of secondary elaboration myths have to be conceived as dream productions of the masses.

The modern reader of the Genesis tale of the Fall of Man is impressed by the coherence and unity of the composition and many commentators upon the Bible praised this tale as a pattern of simplicity, logic, and uniformity of presentation. To all appearances here is a report progressing from the creation of man to the birth of Eve, to the sojourn of the couple in the Garden of Eden, to the forbidding of the fruit, to the seduction of Eve by the Serpent and Adam's fall. In reality it is a compound of several substances, which formed a combination by the welding work of many centuries.

The similarities of secondary connections in the formation of the myth of a people and of an individual dream will become clearer by an example chosen at random. Here is the fragment of the dream of a young woman: *I am in the process of divorce from my mother. There remains only the property settlement*. Some information about the situation of the patient will be needed in order to understand the situation presented in the dream. Muriel is in her early

thirties and has serious marital difficulties. She sometimes
considers divorce from her husband. The dream seems to
displace this possibility to the relationship with her mother.
As a matter of psychological fact, she has had certain emotional experiences with mother in her married life. She has
not seen nor spoken to her mother, who has lived only a
few blocks from her, for many years, and she is still full
of hostility against the old lady. During the last weeks of
her psychoanalysis she had often spoken of that conflict,
discussing all the wrongs her mother had done to her.
Among many other complaints she stated that her mother
had not given her the rightful share of the estate her father
had left. The property settlement in the dream has thus a
basis of reality in the patient's claim on her mother. She
also had financial demands on her husband, to whom she
has given a considerable amount as a loan that he had never
repaid. A property settlement would have to be reached
also with him, if she should divorce him.

The dream makes the impression of unity and consistency. The only element of the dream that could appear
problematical is the legal process of divorce from her
mother. But this grotesque idea is partly explained by the
fact that I had compared her relationship with her mother
to that with her husband in the analytic session of yesterday.
With the exception of this tiny crack, the building of the
dream seems solid and logical. There were no associations
that could help in its interpretation except the patient's
insistence that her conflict with her mother has to be decided once and for all.

The patient was proceeding in her analytic session from
the report of the dream that could not be analyzed to
memories of her adolescence, particularly of her first dates
with boys in high school years. In her account she remem-

bered that mother considered it not proper that the young girl came home at a late hour from a date, or that Muriel remained for a long time in conversation with a boy in his car before the door of her house. Mother found fault with the flirtatiousness of the young girl. Quoting the expressions of her mother's criticism and disapproval, Muriel had three times repeated the words "not proper." It then became clear to me what the hidden meaning of the dream must have been. "There remains the property settlement" is an allusion to the thought: "I want to settle that old question of what is proper and what not. There remains that long argument between mother and me." The appearance of homogeneity and consistency of the manifest dream content is thus revealed as deceptive, designed as make-believe to pretend there is logic and reason in the sequence of divorce and property. The secret compartment or the latent dream content contains thoughts and emotions very removed from the area of lawsuits and financial claims. The surface logic in the individual dream is to be compared with the appearance of unity and continuity in the myth of the Fall. The work of secondary elaboration operating in the dream production is a process similar to that which changed the original tradition of the myth through some centuries until it emerged in its present, seemingly rational form.

The comparison between investigation of ancient myths and dream interpretation goes beyond the area here sketched. We do not forget that the reconstruction of the earliest tradition of the Fall story is only preliminary work, comparable to finding the original text of a dream. The preparatory work should enable us to undertake the essential task: to discover the concealed meaning of that old myth of the first crime. To return for a moment to our comparison: It is necessary to ascertain the pertinent facts in a criminal in-

vestigation in order to examine the available material in
search of clues. At this point it could well be argued that
anthropological and psychoanalytic research has already
found this hidden meaning of the myth. If that were so,
our labor would be superfluous. It would be comparable
to archaeological work in a field that has already been
excavated and scientifically exploited for many decades.

But this comparison, appropriate for this kind of research, reminds us that the argument is not valid. There
were many well-known instances of new archaeological
discoveries that were made in areas conscientiously examined. Excavations in Egypt and Palestine still unearth valuable material for the study of mankind's early history. There
were sometimes important findings made on the very spot
where earlier archaeologists at another layer had brought
potteries, tools, and weapons to light. Renewed digging revealed that, for example, an early Roman colony had been
built on the place where an ancient Greek city had been
destroyed many centuries before.

We reviewed in our survey of the exegetic anthropological
and psychoanalytic interpretations the various concepts
scholars of those disciplines attributed to the myth of the
Fall. We shall not enter into a discussion of the merits and
demerits of those interpretations, but only point out that
even important contributions to the understanding of the
tale did not solve the problem of the third chapter of Genesis. We take as an instance the psychoanalytic interpretation of the Fall myth as it is contained in the books of
Ricklin, Abraham, Rank, and even in Freud's letter to C.
Jung, quoted in a preceding chapter. The concept of the
original sin as forbidden sexual intercourse was known to
the early Fathers of the Church. Psychoanalysts added to
this general concept features of considerable import: the

sexual symbols they had learned to understand in dream interpretation were found again in the language of the myths. The analogy between infantile sexual theories and those of primitive people, the comparison of the biblical presentation with that of dreams led to surprising insights about some puzzling features of the narrative. The secret meaning of the myth in the analytic concept is that it presents in symbolic expression the incest of Adam with his mother and the punishment for it by the father-representative figure of Jahveh. This concept seemed to be confirmed by parallels in the myths of other ancient peoples, mostly neighbors of the Hebrew tribes.

We assumed that the Genesis account welds a creation myth to a report of a first crime and that the figure of Eve or of a mother-goddess as well as the serpent belong to another strand of tradition, later on intertwined with the Fall story. By the division of the myth into two parts and by the elimination of the woman the interpretation of the Fall as sexual transgression evolves as a secondary elaboration.

There was, it seems, an old tradition of sexual union of a mother-goddess with a son-god—it became an essential part of several ancient oriental religions later on—but this is not the original content of the Fall story. The emphasis put on the sexual character of the crime rather conceals than reveals its true nature. But even admitting that the sexual interpretation is a secondary one, it cannot be accidental that it was put into the foreground. (Psychoanalytic thinking insists that every element of mythical production is determined and asks why this particular form of replacement occurred and what is its connection with the concealed real crime.)

The necessity for clarification of the problem is obvious: the doctrine of the original sin became an issue of greatest consequence in the last two thousand years. The point need not be elaborated if the sexual nature of that primal crime does not become the source of the guilt feeling of mankind. Did we not go out to find the origin and character of that universal guilt feeling? It is of paramount importance to decide that question so that no ambiguity is left. The great interest of the problem will justify us if we refer to certain neurotic phenomena that have the most intimate connection with its aspects of original guilt feelings. Freud described[2] a case of obsessional neurosis in which a patient remembers the event that was the origin of some obsessional anxiety: when the man experienced for the first time the pleasurable sensations of sexual intercourse, the idea sprang into his mind: "This is glorious! One might murder one's father for this." What in this case of an obsessional idea would be the origin of the ensuing guilt feeling? The thought bridge would make it possible that superficially the sense of guilt would refer to sexual indulgence, but there is no doubt that the real source of guilt feeling is the idea of the father's death. We can fill the gaps and reconstruct the original thought: if father would interfere with the sexual urge, I could murder him. If later on the conscious guilt feeling concerned the fact of sexual intercourse and made sensual desire the source of guilt, we would have an excellent individual analogy with the process by which the original sin was conceived as sexual transgression in the doctrine of Christianity and Judaism.

The sexual interpretation of the Fall myth is not the result of an arbitrary uncritical inference. The Eve story is not a side show. The sexual note reveals one of the main motives of the primal crime, but the emphasis on it rather conceals its original character. Racine once remarked that

[2] "Notes upon a Case of Obsessional Neurosis," *Collected Papers,* III.

love cannot play a secondary role on the stage. ("L'amour au théatre ne peut pas être en second place.") But it has to be content with this restricted role in the *roman policier,* in the crime story.

All the preceding considerations have no purpose other than to clear the deck for the operation we want to undertake, to pave the way to the discovery of the oldest tradition in which the Fall myth originated. We exclude, of course, from this reconstruction the continuation of the Jahvistic story because we are now interested only in the nature of the primal crime. The expulsion from the Garden of Eden, the sentences of Man, Woman, and Serpent, and their futures are not pertinent within this framework. The report on Paradise lost is of a newer tradition, particularly of a Golden Age of Man, and is obviously added to and welded with the tale of a primeval crime. The narrative of the Garden of Eden and of the implied undisturbed happiness of the first couple can be discarded for the objective we have in mind. The Paradise story certainly belongs to another strand of sagas, to that of the Golden Age, also to be found in Egyptian, Babylonian, and Greek mythology. This later tradition follows Adam and Eve into the wide world after their eviction from Paradise. Even the first human couple could have said that they have seen better days.

To resume the anatomical comparison, our endeavor was to remove all muscles because we want to see the skeleton of the myth. What have we now after our bold transverse section? What remains as the core of the tradition of the Fall? It is almost impossible to answer this question. What can be done is to attempt to separate a certain solid substance from the many solutions to which it was subjected. We do not deceive ourselves: the precipitate we thus obtain is by no means the original tradition, but still thousands of years remote from it. Yet it is the closest we can approach and traces of the primal story in some changed form will be preserved in the late text as we now reconstruct it.

What is the frame of an old Semitic tradition? A narrative in which the Lord forbids man to eat of the fruit of the tree in the midst of the garden. "Ye shall not eat of it, neither shall ye touch it, lest ye die." To this old tradition belongs also the feature that "in the day ye eat thereof, then your eyes shall be opened, and ye shall be as gods, knowing good and evil." Can we include this piece although it is a part of the sentence the serpent said to the woman? But did we not dislodge both figures from the primal tradition of the Fall and shift them to another circle of myths? There are reasons why we can assume that this sentence in some form or other belongs to the oldest tradition. The statement that this is the effect of eating of the tree is repeated within the story. Not only the serpent points this out; the woman herself also "saw that the tree was good for food, and that it was pleasant to the eyes, and a tree to be desired to make one wise." It is furthermore reported that the Lord God said: "Behold, the man is become as one of us, to know good and evil: and now, lest he put forth his hand, and take also of the tree of life, and eat, and live forever." This is said, it is true, after Adam has already eaten of the tree. But most biblical scholars are of the opinion that this passage does not belong to the place where it stands at present. It lags behind the story and refers to a potential eating of a forbidden tree—after Adam had eaten of a forbidden tree. It sounds as though there were a slight variation on a theme that we presented before, a "doublette." We can surmise how this late variation came about. The ancient Babylonian myth of the tree of life had become

known to the Hebrews and was introduced into their tradition. That passage presents thus an attempt to harmonize
that feature taken from the other myth with the main motif
of the original Fall tradition. But if that passage, perhaps
referring to a single tree, was displaced, where was it before? Which was its appropriate location in this text? It
must have appeared in the earlier tradition as part of the
story preceding Adam's fall. The Lord expresses His worry
that man could put forth his hand and eat of the forbidden
tree and "become as one of us." Most exegetes agree that
this late expression reveals itself as remnant of a polythe-
istic belief in the middle of the Jahvistic text. "As one of
us" would amount to: as one of us gods or as one of us
superhuman beings.

If we now add this passage to the two others mentioned
before, the motif, eating of the forbidden tree, appears three
times in the Jahvistic text. Such repetition seems to indicate
that it belonged to the original tradition. We can guess why
it was there and what justifies the prominent place it must
have had within the early saga. It tells us why the Lord was
so much concerned, why He did not want man to eat of
that tree! It reveals not only the nature of the Lord's fear,
but also the main incentive for Adam's eating the forbidden
food. That passage and by implication the two previous ones
say: man should not "become as one of us." In other
words, Adam (or whatever other name we wish to call that
representative of early mankind) wanted to eat of the tree
in order to become as God, or to become a god. Jahveh
looks at His creature and thinks: Here but by the grace of
God goes God.

The blueprint of the early saga of the Fall is thus the
following: Adam ate of a certain tree because he was convinced that meal would make him like God or transform

him into a god. This is the nature of the original sin and
this is its motive in the old tradition. This is the core of
the early tale of a primal crime of mankind. We still do
not understand why the eating of this food should be punished by death, but this is not yet the time for an attempt
at interpretation. We wanted first to ascertain the facts. Here
they are: the original crime was a nutritional mistake. It
was not motivated by appetite, but by the wish to become
God by eating a special kind of food.

What kind of food? The text leaves no doubt that it was
fruit of the tree in the middle of the garden. The question
of what kind of fruit it was has been asked so many times
that finally some rabbis decided that it was forbidden to
speculate on its identity. The argument they brought forward was that the fruit is deliberately not named in the
Scripture so that man should not hate it for having brought
death into the world. As Josef Gaer points out,[3] the lore has
variously named the fruit as fig, apple, wheat, nut, lemon,
date, and orange.[4] The most popular concept is, of course,
the apple, which apears in early pictures and poems as well
as in scholarly comments. In most cases the sexual symbolism
of the apple is mentioned. In the Walpurgis night scene
Faust dances with a young witch and speaks:

> Once came a lovely dream to me
> I saw there an apple tree
> Two lovely apples on it shone
> They charmed me so I climbed thereon.

The young beauty answers:

[3] Joseph Gaer, *The Lore of the Old Testament* (Boston, 1952), p. 18.
[4] "If we may credit Clavigero, the banana was the forbidden fruit
that tempted our poor mother Eve." (*Stor. del Mexico,* I, p. 49. Quoted
from the *History of the Conquest of Mexico* [New York, Modern Li-
brary edition], p. 79.)

> The little apples men entice
> Since they were in Paradise
> I feel myself with pleasure glow
> That such within my garden grow.

The legend tells us that the "Adam's Apple" was formed when the forbidden fruit got stuck on its way down. In any case, whatever the nature of the forbidden fruit, it seems that the ancestor of all mankind bit off more than he could chew.

CHAPTER X

THE LEADING CLUE

AMONG THE historians of ancient civilizations who attempted to find the meaning of the biblical Fall myth, Salomon Reinach[1] was perhaps one of the first who traced it back to the phenomenon of primitive taboo. The French scholar states that after so many centuries of exegesis and so many heroic efforts that were in vain ("après tant de siècles d'exegese impuissante, tant d'efforts héroïques d'expliquer ce qu'est inexplicable"), one has to admit that the Jahvistic report has been changed and it is composed from elements that contradict each other.

In tracing the sources of those older myths in an attempt to unscramble the text, Reinach comes to the conclusion that the Jahvistic text contains remnants of old legends, especially of the taboo of food whose breach has caused the death of the first man. He adds that the core of the Fall myth is older than the concept of a personal, anthropomorphic god. In the original tale there was only man in the presence of a tree and its tabooed fruit. We postpone the discussion of Reinach's theory for a moment because we would like to point out one of the ambiguities or uncertain-

[1] Salomon Reinach, *Cultes, Mythes et Religions* (Paris, 1908), III, p. 351.

ties of the biblical text that he overlooked. In some passages, Adam is forbidden to eat the fruit of the tree, in others he is told not "to eat of the tree." This might appear a minor point, but such variants can gain significance if they are analyzed within the context. It is possible that the different texts are due to various editors, but it is also imaginable that they reveal divergent traditions or residues of older versions.

Returning now to Reinach's theory of a "tabou alimentaire" as the core of the Fall story, we like to add first an apparently trifling factor that confirms his thesis. In Genesis 3:3 God says: "Ye shall not eat of it, neither shall ye touch it, lest ye die." That is certainly the law of taboo: it is not only forbidden to eat certain food, but even to touch it means mortal danger. It is interesting that a Jewish legend says that the serpent took advantage of this variation by forcing Eve to touch the fruit. The serpent argued that since death had not followed the touch, it would not follow the eating (Ber.R.Ra.). A commentary is sadly mistaken when it calls this "a futile inference."[2] The arguing of the serpent is of irrefutable logic in the sense of the taboo law.

Here is an obvious incoherence in the biblical account: God predicts that Adam would die immediately after eating of the forbidden tree, but according to the Jahvistic text Adam lives another one hundred thirty years; nine hundred thirty years afterward according to the Elohistic text. We would expect that he and Eve after having eaten the forbidden food would drop dead, but nothing of this kind happens. They left the Garden of Eden hale and healthy and begot children afterward. With the exception of that unpleasantness between Cain and Abel, you could see them

[2] John Skinner in *The International Critical Commentary* (New York, 1925), p. 74.

as one happy family. The penalty the Lord inflicts on Adam
and Eve does not tally with the punishment He had predicted. It is as if He had ignored or forgotten His own
words. One can, as Reinach does, try to explain this and
other contradictions as resulting from awkward attempts of
various editors to amalgamate different and unreconcilable
sources into one unit.

It is conspicuous that immediate death does not follow
as threatened; this negative factor can well be used as argument against Reinach's assumption. None of the mental
contortions of some commentators can make us overlook
the fact that Adam and Eve lived more than a hundred
years after their crime. It is curious that the immediate
punishment we expect does not appear. One is reminded
of the famous comment of Sherlock Holmes:

"I would call your attention to the curious incident of
the dog in the night-time."

"The dog did nothing in the night-time."

"That was the curious incident."

It cannot be denied that there is some connection between the biblical prohibition against eating of the tree
and the taboo prohibitions of savage and half-civilized
people. The person who has eaten tabooed food dies almost
immediately. J. G. Frazer quotes[3] the instance of a New
Zealand chief of high rank and great sanctity who had left
the remains of his dinner by the wayside. A slave, who did
not know whose unfinished dinner it was, ate it. Informed
by a horror-stricken spectator that it was the chief's, he was
seized by convulsions and cramps in the stomach and died
about sundown the same day. A Maori woman who had
eaten some fruits from a tabooed place explained that the
spirit of the chief whom she had profaned would kill her;

[3] J. G. Frazer, *The Golden Bough* (abr. ed., New York, 1926), p. 204.

she was dead the next day. This and other cases quoted by anthropologists and missionaries can well be compared with the Lord's threat that Adam would die the same day, if he ate of the forbidden tree.

While these and other features—I remind the reader of the prohibition against touching the tree of knowledge—speak for the thesis that the Fall story is founded upon a tradition about the taboo of food, Reinach's theory cannot be maintained because the roots of the tale reach deeper into the dark subsoil of prehistory. In other words, there can be no doubt that an older tradition was used later on to explain the taboo of food or the sanctity of certain trees. The essence of the tale, its hidden core, precedes the social custom of taboo. The concealed meaning of the saga does not presuppose the taboo of food, but concerns events that led to the introduction of the prohibitions of taboo.

To my view the Fall myth is not explained by referring to the taboo of the savages, but rather the other way around. We would understand the meaning of food taboos better if we could penetrate the significance of the Fall saga. I would dare to assert that we have here a tale that, analytically interpreted, explains how and why the taboo of food was introduced into primitive society. Adam ate something and that brought death to him and into the world. We think that what the biblical tale reports, whether we undersand it or not, is not an average and everyday occurrence, but an action of great pith and momentum, a death-worthy deed. We return here to our problem: if we conceive of Adam as a nameless representative of very early mankind, the question concerning this first crime is not Who done it, but What did he do? What was the crime he committed?

The answer to this question can be given only when we

understand the part of that fateful tree within the tradition. We know that the view that there are two trees "in the
middle of the garden" was determined by a textual mistake.
There was only one tree there, or at least only one tree was
forbidden to Adam. This misunderstanding is partly due to
the fact that this tree is sometimes called The Tree of Life
and at other times The Tree of Knowledge of Good and Evil.

Scholars have argued that the tree in the biblical narrative is the original concept of the symbol of immortality
and have pointed out that there are many parallels in the
mythology of the ancient Orient, for instance in Babylon.[4]
But this argument that gods and men can obtain immortality by eating from the sacred tree cannot possibly be used
in favor of a primal tradition. The people of the ancient
world, just as the primitive tribes of our own time, did not
possess the modern concept that gods are immortal. Gods
were supposed to die, to be resurrected, and to die again.
It is very unlikely that the quest for immortality belongs to
a very primitive stage of evolution of mankind; it is a result
of more mature thought and has to be attributed to a late
and progressed phase of civilization.

What about the other attribute of the tree, that of
knowledge of good and evil? What do these two words
mean? In a discussion the British writer G. K. Chesterton
once spoke of the ambiguity of the word "good." He said,
"For example, if a man were to shoot his grandmother at
a range of five hundred yards I should call him a good shot,
but not necessarily a good man." The original theological
view that the words signify the good and evil in a moral
sense has been discarded long ago by exegetes and has been
maintained only by fanatic fundamentalists. It gave way

---

[4] Further instances in Thomas Barns, "Trees and Plants," *Encyclopedia
of Religion and Ethics,* XII, p. 448 f.

to another view that referred to the passage stating that Adam and Eve recognized after eating the fruit that they were naked. The knowledge that they missed "is that of sex." In the sense of this concept the first couple became then aware that they were male and female and felt ashamed. This sexual significance of the terms "good" and "evil" is still believed by some theologians, but most modern exegetes follow another concept. They point out that the knowledge here meant scarcely refers to what is good and bad in a moral sense, but to something that is a divine prerogative. The knowledge that man acquires by eating of that tree would be dangerous to Jahveh. Since Wellhausen, most biblical scholars assume that the knowledge thus acquired would make Adam in the sense of Genesis Lord of Nature. The narrative presents Jahveh as hostile to man's intellectual development. Tennant considers[5] such an idea "in keeping with the rudimentary theology to which in the earlier form at least the narrative belongs." The reason for the prohibition of the Tree of Knowledge is in this concept of Jahveh's fear that man could become a rival of His. An attentive study of the biblical text confirms this view. Does not the Lord Himself express His concern: "Behold, the man is become as one of us, to know good and evil . . ."?

Even if we accept that interpretation as essentially correct there remain several problematic points. Let me formulate them in the form of questions: Of what nature is this knowledge that could make man equal to God? What is meant by good and evil in the account? And why is that knowledge or power acquired by eating of the tree?

The first two questions are easier to answer than the

---

[5] *Sources of the Doctrine of the Fall and Original Sin* (Cambridge, 1903), p. 14.

third. When we consider the phase of cultural development to which the original tradition belonged, we do not hesitate to assume that the word "knowledge" is an intellectualized replacement for another expression, namely power over nature or, to make it more specific, magical power. The quality here alluded to is similar to what the Australian aborigine means by the word "mana," namely the magical power he ascribes to certain persons such as kings or sorcerers. Yet the words "good" and "bad" must have a meaning in this context too; they specify this power. It is the power to do good or evil, black or white magic. We can thus translate: Jahveh is afraid that by eating of that tree Adam could obtain the magical power that is a prerogative of the deity and thus become God Himself. Why by eating? Well, that is in the primitive mind the main way of acquiring some envied quality. To incorporate something means to possess it. But that implies that the tree itself possesses that power and here we have to ask: What is the magical character of the tree? In other words, we have to find out what is the place of that tree in the primitive mind.

"Whence art thou?" inquires Penelope of the disguised Ulysses, "for you are no sprig of oak or rock as old tales tell." Zeus fashioned the race of man from the ash of a tree. The ancient Romans considered the oak the first mother of man. We still call the part of the body below the armpits the trunk. Virgil tells a dramatic legend: In order to nourish a sacrificial fire, Aeneas plucks boughs from a myrtle. Suddenly blood runs down from the place of the breach and a plaintive voice is heard: "Stop, you hurt me, you tear me to pieces." The view here expressed can be traced in every form of religion and is to be found in the folklore of all people. The life of trees is identical with human life. The sacred tree is in the earliest stages not a symbol, but is instinct with divine life. It is not the sanctuary or the home of the god or ghost, but the god himself. The burning bush, living and aglow with the divine voice, is the living god.

Tree worship is to be found in all ancient Semitic tribes. W. Robertson Smith says[6] it is in its pure and simple form attested for Arabia "in the case of the sacred date palm at Neyran. It was adored at an annual feast when it was all hung with fine clothes and woman's ornaments." The sacred Erica in the temple of Isis at Byblos was a stump wrapped in a linen cloth and represented the dead Osiris. According to Mrs. Philpot,[7] a fruit tree was dressed as Dionysus. Survival of tree cult in Greek ritual is the concept of the Oak-Zeus, that was traced through all the earliest sanctuaries of the Mediterranean area, especially in Dodona and Crete. The tree cult of the aboriginal Africans is associated with worship of their ancestors. With the Wanika in Eastern Africa destruction of a coconut tree was regarded as equivalent to matricide. The Tomori place little ladders against the trunks to enable the spirits to descend in safety. The inhabitants of Sumatra would assure the tree they were about to cut down that it was the Dutch authorities who forced them to do it and if they disobeyed they would be hanged. One tree is hailed by the Hereros with the words, "Holy art thou, our ancestor." It accords with the character of Osiris as a tree spirit that his worshipers were forbidden to injure fruit trees. The Roman *flamen Dialis* was forbidden to eat or even name several fruits.

The identification of tree, god, and king is general. The

---

[6] *Lectures on the Religion of the Semites* (Edinburgh, 1889), p. 169.
[7] J. H. Philpot, *The Sacred Tree* (London, 1897). The material contained in the following paragraphs is taken from this book and from Thomas Barns' article, "Trees and Plants," in the *Encyclopedia of Religion and Ethics*, XII, p. 448 f.; John Stewart Collins, *The Triumph of Tree* (New York, 1954); J. G. Frazier, *The Golden Bough*, and other works on tree cult.

chain of evidence is unbroken from East to West: from the
Celts and Romans to the prophetess Deborah who "dwelt
under the palm tree . . . and the children of Israel came up
to her for judgment" (Judges 4:5). The sacred stump is a
survival of the worship of the sacred tree. The spear is perhaps a variation of the sacred stump that represented the
tree god and the sign of its power continues to live in the
scepter. The Etruscan kings were representative of Jupiter
and their crowns were of golden oak leaves; the oak was the
sacred tree of Zeus, originally identical with the god. The
great God Brahma is represented in Hindu theology as having emanated from a golden lotus as Balder takes his origin
from the oak. The Bo tree of the Buddha in Ceylon is endowed with wisdom. In India each Buddha has his own tree.
After having passed through forty-three incarnations, Gau-
tama himself eventually found wisdom under the sacred
tree of Brahma, the pipal tree.

The gods being trees or dwelling in trees were often replaced by spirits and demons. The devils of the Old Testament, the jinn of the Arabian stories, the centaurs and
cyclopes, fauns and dryads of Greek and Latin, wild men
and elves of German fairy tales, the wild women of the
Tyrol, and the green ladies of Neufchâtel, in their different
degrees of mischief and maliciousness, were haunting terrors of the old world. The Nereids of Macedonian folklore
are tree spirits. "Daphne" is the name both of the laurel
and of the spirit within it. Each variety of tree had its
nymph, as did many individual trees. Mrs. Philpot notes:[8]
"In later times an attempt was made in some cases . . . to
explain the connection by metamorphosis . . . but it is
extremely probable that this was an inversion of the primitive nexus. . . ." The oak was also sacred to Ceres, the wil-

[8] *The Sacred Tree,* op. cit., p. 59 f.

low associated with Hera at Samos and with Artemis in
Sparta. The laurel is sacred to Apollo, the olive is at
Athens connected with the cult of Athene. The pine is
associated with Pan, the cedar with the Acadian deity Ea,
the sycamore with the Egyptian goddess Hathor. The vine
and the ivy were closely connected with the rites of Dionysus. Zeus survives perhaps in Windsor Forest as Herne the
hunter who walks

> . . . round about an oak, with great ragg'd horns;
> And there he blasts the tree, and takes the cattle,
> And makes milch-kine yield blood, and shakes a chain
> In a most hideous and dreadful manner.
> *The Merry Wives of Windsor,* Act IV, Scene iv.

Most if not all races at some period regarded the tree as
the home or embodiment of a spiritual presence. "The god
inhabits his body."[9] Osiris has his origin in a tree as Adonis
in Syria and Attis in Phrygia. The cult of Osiris was associated with acacia. On an old sarcophagus is the inscription
"Osiris shoots up." The ancient Egyptian monuments depict
his body enclosed in a tree. In Boeotia the title of the god
was "Dionysus in the tree." Among the trees particularly
sacred to him was the pine tree. The Delphic oracle commanded the Corinthians to worship a particular pine tree
"equally with the god" so that they made two images of it.
The sacred cedar of the Chaldeans was not only the tree of
life, but the revealer of the oracles of earth and heaven. The
name of Ea, the God of Wisdom, was supposed to be written
on its core. The early cult of the sacred tree among the Jews
left its mark in the temple of Jerusalem. Robertson Smith
notes that, as the two pillars Jachin and Boaz, so also the
golden candlestick has associations with this ancient cult. The
candlestick was a budding and blossoming almond. The

[9] W. Robertson Smith, *Lectures on the Religion of the Semites,* p. 84.

tree of life reappears in the seven-branched candlestick that
marks the origin of the Menorah.[10] The voice, vocal at
Dodona and Delphi as well as in the burning bush and in
the vision of the seven candlesticks (Revelation 1:12-15),
is the voice of divine wisdom. The Tree of Life was the
source and the sustenance of life. The soja plant, the Iranian
haoma, is the sacred food of the gods in Asia and corresponds to the ambrosia of the Greeks. The Vedic amrita or
soma had in it the principle of life and was withheld from
ordinary men.

The god Ningishzida in Babylon is "master of the tree
of life." The Norse Yggdrasil is the central tree of the universe. The chief and most holy seat of the gods is by the
ash Yggdrasil; there the gods meet in council every day. It
is the greatest and best of all trees; "its branches spread
over all the world and reach above heaven."[11] Hercules in
the garden of the Hesperides "conquered the protecting
dragon and secured the golden sun fruits from the central
tree" (Hesiod, Theogony, 215 ff.). The garden of India
contained five wonderful trees, the chief one being the
paridjata, "the flower of which preserved its freshness
throughout the year, contained in itself every scent and
flavor, and gave happiness to whoever demanded it." It was,
moreover, a test of virtue, losing its splendor in the hands
of the sinful, and preserving it for him who followed duty.
Atlas originally carried the world as a tree among Chaldeans, Japanese, Egyptians, Persians, aborigines of Europe
and Japan, but also among aborigines of America and New
Zealand. The Heaven of the Mohammedans knows a tree
which is so large that a man mounted on the swiftest horse
could not ride round its branches in a hundred years. It

[10] *Jewish Encyclopedia*, III, p. 531 f.
[11] Philpot, *The Sacred Tree*, p. 129.

sent forth a pleasant aroma over all the land, while its boughs were laden with delicious food to be plucked at pleasure.

Widengren shows[12] what an important role the idea of the tree of life played in Mesopotamian myth and ritual, where Tammuz is constantly hailed as the cedar. The king functions as the custodian of the tree of life and is often called the "gardener." There is also the mythical idea of a paradisaic garden in ancient Mesopotamian religion. The gardener and waterer is the priest-king. He performs certain acts of libation with the view of reviving this tree, which is also the symbol of the dying god who is called to life. The king is later thought of as the possessor of the tree of life and his scepter is a twig from it. The rod of Moses was according to a Christian tradition a branch from the forbidden tree. The last Athenian kings appeared on solemn occasions as oak cutters armed with an ax, according to Cook "the ancient ritual costume of an oak-king." The king is supposed to be the tree or plant of life. In Ezekiel 31:2-9 the king is compared to the tree of life in whose shadow people dwell. In Hosea 14:8 Jahveh says: "I am like a green fir tree. From me is thy fruit found." It is impossible to avoid the conclusion that the origin of the comparison is that Jahveh was once thought of as a tree.

We collected representative instances of an abundant material that shows that the sacred tree was considered originally not as the dwelling place of the deity, but as the god himself. We followed the long development from this earliest animistic phase to a late period at which the sacred trees were conceived as homes of the gods and demons and to another one, closer to our own age, in which sculptures

[12] *The King and the Tree of Life in Ancient Near Eastern Religion* (Uppsala, 1951).

of God were shaped from tree stumps. Jahveh compares
Himself with a green fir tree. No doubt the god of the
Hebrews was once conceived as a sacred tree. We also
found in the material gathered by historians of civilization
and by archaeologists many instances of food taboos concerning those sacred trees, prohibitions against breaking
boughs from them, or even approaching them. We saw that
S. Reinach meant to recognize in the Fall story the remnants of such a food taboo.

How can we make use of that material in the interpretation of the Genesis narrative? It seems to me that that can
be done when we treat the tale as though it were an equation with two unknowns. The one unknown would be the
significance of the tree and the other the nature of Adam's
crime. We found the first quantity: the sacred tree is the
totemistic god. If we insert this recognized quantity into the
equation, we reach the following result of the primal tradition whose traces have been preserved in the Scripture:
Adam—or the man of the primeval time—ate his god.

The understanding of the significance of that clue of the
tree in the middle of the Garden of Eden as a totemistic
god does not solve the mystery, but it promises a solution.
From the point we have reached, how remote seem the
many interpretations we have left behind! We remember a
very old rabbinical tradition according to which the tree
from which Adam ate was the Torah and his deed was the
study of God's law.[13] We remember a recent analytic interpretation: according to this concept the first crime was
committed because Adam wanted to become immortal and
therefore ate the forbidden fruit. But immortality does not
grow on trees.

[13] August Wünsche, *Die Sage vom Lebensbaum und Lebenswasser*
(Leipzig, 1905), p. 17.

CHAPTER XI

THE FAÇADE AND THE INSIDE STORY

WHEN WE now reread the Genesis narrative of the Fall of Man and translate it into the language of tree totemism, we look at a new picture. The old one has been transformed by the now recognized significance of the forbidden tree. The core of the dark tale is an ancient tradition that in primeval times man ate his god. In other words, there was a lore saying that once, in forgotten times, a man killed and ate God-Father. That ancient tradition certainly did not have the character of a myth of an original sin, which it obtained only after many thousands of years. It was at first a story like many others: a "just so" story. Yet the echo of great events of forgotten times lived on in it and was orally transmitted from generation to generation.

What were the motives for that primeval deed? If we can trust the traces left in the Jahvistic tale, it was the urgent wish to become a god ("Behold, the man is become as one of us . . .") or rather to become God. The only way to reach this goal in the primitive mind is to incorporate the admired, loved, and hated object. The cannibalistic aborigines of Central Australia still believe that they can obtain the magical power they attribute, for instance, to a European missionary by the simple act of eating him.

That original tradition of the murder and devouring of a powerful chief to whom godlike qualities were attributed was subjected to many changes and distortions during many thousands of years. We have already mentioned some we could guess: it was fused with other traditions like that of the creation of the world. That amounted to an attempt at synthesis. But this was not the only purpose of that combination. Another and more important reason was to place that event as far back as possible or, otherwise put, to remove it as much as possible from the present, so that the distance between then and now appeared enormous. By such a regressive process the responsibility for the crime was shifted to the first human couple. In Greek philosophy we often meet the view that the first crime was committed not by man, but by his soul in a previous existence. The chain between the first criminal and the generation now living is thus broken or has become at least almost infinite.

The second incisive change: the original tradition of the killing and eating of a father who much later became God was displaced to the tree totem. This change appears to us today as tremendous. Not so to the primitive mind. We have heard that the native tribes of Australia and Africa do not hesitate a second to call a tree or a plant their ancestor. They consider them children of nature, not only equal but often superior to themselves. To modern man who considers himself the crown of creation the concept of God as a big tree is entirely alien. It was very natural to an animistic age in which the tradition of a primal crime against a powerful chieftain was transmitted in a tree-totemistic language. To recognize in a tree a god was familiar to the primitive tribes, "familiar" also in the sense that they considered themselves descendants of this tree god.

A later phase of cultural evolution did not understand this language any longer. In the Genesis narrative Jahveh takes a walk in the Garden of Eden and speaks with a human voice to Adam. Many thousands of years earlier Jahveh had regained a human or rather superhuman form. He had become anthropomorphic. At the time when the tradition was first written down, only remnants of the original tree cult had survived in Palestine: the asherah, a wooden pillar, represented the god in its old form. Traces of the tree cult are in the sanctuaries at Samaria (II Kings 13:6), at Bethel (II Kings 23:15), and even in the temple at Jerusalem (II Kings 23:6). There were still sacred trees, not recognized any longer as dwelling places of Jahveh, but attesting to an earlier cult of trees among the Jews; for instance, the two pillars Jachin and Boaz in the temple at Jerusalem. David consults the oracle of the mulberry tree before he attacks the Philistines (II Samuel 5:24). Tradition reported that Jahveh appeared to Moses in a burning bush and the rod of Aaron was the token of priesthood. The language of the prophets, for instance the riddle of Ezekiel of the highest branch of the cedar, or Jeremiah's vision of the blossoming of the almond tree, is still colored by the image of Jahveh as a tree god.

At the time when the tale of the Fall was written by the Jehovists only traces survived of that phase in which the tree was a god whom it was severely forbidden to touch. The old continues to live side by side with the new. On the fringes of the high and sublimated monotheistic cult of Jahveh features of the prehistoric totemistic concept of a tribal god still existed. The situation is comparable to that of a household in which an old grandfather lives while his grandchildren have children of their own.

The early tradition that was handed down from generation to generation recounts that aeons ago man had murdered and devoured his god. When the tradition was transmitted to writing, its original meaning was not recognized any longer. The idea of killing and eating their God was not even imaginable any longer to the worshipers of Jahveh. In oral tradition that atrocious deed of God-murder was mitigated to an act of disobedience and the devouring of God-Father was displaced to eating forbidden foods. Expressed in the language of tree totemism and distorted to an extent that made its significance unrecognizable, the tradition still preserves features of its original meaning, not understood any longer by later generations. In spite of forceful suppression increasing in intensity through the centuries of religious development from a barbaric and crude totemistic belief to the sublimated worship of Jahveh, traces of a saga of the devouring of a God succeeded in living on in the Hebrew tradition. The early drives that expressed themselves in that tradition must have been so intensive that they could not be wiped out or annihilated by the combined forces of religious intolerance and moral condemnation.

We do not dare to state that we have cut through to the core of the Fall myth, but we arrived at a reconstruction whose blueprint strikes us as highly probable. Here are the essential features of the tradition as it presents itself to the exploring mind:

1. Once man killed and devoured his God.
2. This deed was told in a later tradition in the language of tree totemism. God was presented in it as a sacred tree.
3. The main motive of this cannibalistic act of man was

the wish to become God Himself—to take His place.
This wish should be fulfilled by incorporation, by taking God into one's own body by eating Him.
4. The act marked an expression of utter rebellion against
God.
5. God was jealous of man and afraid man could usurp
His powers or magic.

These are the essential features of the old saga. All others
are the result of fusion with other traditions and of processes
of distortion and elaboration.

A few added remarks about this tradition will be necessary in order to characterize it and to determine its evolutional place. We have a tale here that is already very old,
even in the primitive shape at which our reconstruction has
arrived. It is the diluted descendant of a primal myth whose
content and form we cannot guess. That original myth belonged to an age to which the killing and eating of a god
was quite imaginable and did not appear as monstrous. It
is almost certain that this myth of a pre-Mosaic time did
not tell the story in a tree-totemistic language that amounts
to a translation of the crude saga of an early phase. The
biblical story of Adam's transgression in eating a forbidden
fruit forms the façade. The preceding interpretation offers,
to use the slang expression, the "low-down" of that primeval
story.

CHAPTER XII

PREHISTORIC REALITY IN THE MYTH

A MYTH is for us an invented story, a tale of imagined persons or events: the idea is akin to that of a fable or even a fairy tale. But an old tradition like the Fall myth was for the ancient Hebrew tribes not a story, but history; in other words, a narrative of their past, of real happenings. The old myths were literally believed by the generations to whom they were told. The tablets and scrolls on which they were written were read by their early readers with the same trust with which our children read their history books. They *were* the history books of antiquity. A listener or reader of those legends would doubt their truth as little as our children would doubt that the Declaration of Independence was pronounced in Philadelphia. The difference from historical reports is that myths were at the same time sacred, that they had almost the character articles of faith have for us.

We are searching in ancient myths for clues that point to the human situation in prehistory, to events in an age of which no record is preserved. In order to find prehistoric residues in the Fall legend, we have to consider the typical form of mythical presentation and to remove the wrappings in which the original tradition is enveloped.

Jahveh is not a historic or prehistoric figure, but a theological entity. One is almost tempted to say that God is not a figure of the primordial past of mankind, but rather a figure of speech. But this is not correct. We have to assume that there was once a very human figure behind that elevated image of the deity, that the idea of the God father developed from that of a most powerful and terrifying chief of the tribe, a despotic father of the family. There is no God, but there was a God—a hundred thousand years ago. God or His prototype once really walked on earth in the shape of the head of the first organization of the family or clan and His will was law for all its members.

And Adam? We have already heard that this is not a proper name, but that it denotes simply a primitive man. We learned that the chronology of the Genesis legend is determined by the fact that two stories, that of the creation of the world and of man and that of the primal crime, became fused and confused. The first human being was as capable of "falling" or disobeying his father as a baby a few weeks old. We have also to assume that behind the figure of Adam is simply the representative of primitive or prehistoric man. In other words, the original tradition recounted a terrible act of rebellion that was later conceived as the Fall of Man and many thousands of years later as original sin.

Our reconstruction gives us information about the character of the atrocious deed of that representative, prehistoric man. He ate his father; he killed and devoured the head of the primitive family. This is the central part of the prehistory that is concealed in the Fall story. Nothing of this kind is reported in any biblical or other source. More than this: if such were the real core of the tradition, no biblical story would have been possible. Translated into theological language, the tradition would report that primordial man killed and ate God. But that would be the end not only of Jahveh, but also of the Bible. Theology would become superfluous. What is there to say about a god who is dead? He was done away with and is done with. A dead Jahveh is impotent. He is powerless and will not be worshiped. The concept of a God whose figure gives His worshipers not food for thought, but for their bodies, is utterly incompatible with the character of the sublimated religion of the Hebrew tribes and of the writers of a late tradition, known to us as Holy Scripture. The barbaric idea of killing and eating God is intolerable to the progressed civilization of the Hebrews at the time of David, at which time the biblical stories were written.

The situation we face is the following: either our reconstruction of the core of the Fall story is a mistake or we have in the Genesis narrative two different gods. The one is Jahveh, the Almighty Lord of the world and its lawgiver, originally an anthropomorphic deity. The other god is the successor of the crude figure of a despotic father whom the rebellious son kills and devours. We have thus two versions or two traditions of the Fall story, corresponding to the different characters of the two god figures. In the first, the primal crime of mankind was an act of disobedience, a transgression comparable to that of a child who was forbidden to eat an apple and who swallows the forbidden fruit nevertheless. The second version was that of the atrocious act of deicide, of the cannibalistic murder of a god. We cannot doubt which version is the older and more primitive one.

But does the Genesis story not make the impression of an undivided unity? Is it not a tale of homogeneity, consistency, and continuity? There is no trace of two versions, no evidence of different gods, no manifestation of a split within the narrative. Its surface is smooth; no crack within it can be discovered. One part logically follows the other and the plot has sequence and consequence. We reconstructed a primal tradition of the murder and devouring of god-father and saw this original tale beneath the Genesis legend as clearly as a scholar sees in a medieval parchment an erased Roman poem underlying a chapter of the Old Testament. This very comparison leads us to another assumption. The old tradition had been erased, pressed, and pushed down under the influence of powerful tendencies that could not tolerate the idea of God's murder and that had elevated Jahveh to the eternal and almighty Lord of the world. That deed of primitive man was replaced in the tradition by the breach of a taboo, the forbidden eating of a fruit reserved for Jahveh. This new version superseded the old, barbaric saga.

The picture of the stratification becomes clear. The newer tradition was not only elaborated from the old one. It also took its material from the original tale in a manner similar to that of tailors in remaking an old suit. By chemical and mechanical methods such as cleaning, dyeing, ironing, and so on the suit seems to become almost new. The appearance of consistency and harmony is obtained by a process of transformation and secondary elaboration by which contradictions are removed, gaps filled, and an imitation of sequence and consequence is reached. A synthetic or pseudo coherence of the Genesis text is the result of this effort. The reconstructed tradition, reduced to the human level and cleared of mythical weeds, is a tale of the killing and eating of a prehistoric father by his sons. The old legend of Genesis is the transformed and distorted primal tradition of a prehistoric parricide.

If we tentatively accept that the tradition reflects a prehistoric truth, the deed in ages beyond all memory must be determined by the particular part and position of the father and his relationship with the sons in the earliest primitive society. That position must have been very different from that of the head of the family today even when we imagine an extremely authoritarian and severe father. That primal paterfamilias was certainly an utterly brutal, beastly father of unrestricted power over every member of his kin. Life with father was then different. You cannot say that his words were law for all because he had not many words, if he had any; perhaps he had rather gruff grunts and shouts. As our analytic experiences prove, the image of God, almighty and dreadful, is shaped from the figure of such a father in the conception of the child, and the dire and terrible God of primitive tribes was certainly formed in the likeness of such a father in early family life. The primal parricide we reconstructed from residues of the Genesis narrative was the original crime of mankind and continued to live in the tradition of people as deicide, as murder and eating of the god of the tribe. Its memory survived in the transformed and censured legends of many other peoples and in the myths of other ancient civilizations.

The result of our search for clues, concealed in the biblical tale of the Fall, led us to conclusions similar to those at which Freud arrived. He developed in 1912 a hypothesis about the state of the early human family and about the events that must have taken place within it, events whose repercussions led many thousands of years later to the beginnings of primitive religion and social organization. Following remarks by Charles Darwin and suggestions of Atkinson as well as making use of analytical material, Freud attempted a reconstruction of those prehistoric events in his book *Totem and Taboo*. The main features are the following: in primeval times men lived in small, unorganized hordes, under the domination of a strong and despotic father. The expelled sons, living together in small hordes themselves, were all consumed by the passionate wish to overcome the father, to take his place, and to possess the women. They killed the tyrant and ate his body by which primitive method they, according to primeval belief, took part of his superior force and power. Freud assumes that this great crime in which the sons got rid of the tyrant was not a single act, but one that was committed in all the hordes and repeated through the centuries. The succession of parricides had tremendous direct effects and repercussions, which determined the whole development of mankind. Those events beyond all memory are the most important that happened to mankind and their significance cannot be compared to any of the things that happened to men in the following millennia. Their impact surpasses and eclipses that of the events history records. The reactions to that atrocious deed led to the first social ties, to the basic moral inhibitions, and to the oldest forms of primitive religion, to totemism.

How Freud, Roheim, I, and others added to and modified this hypothesis about the events in the primeval hordes cannot be repeated. Putting aside for the moment what prehistory, anthropology, and comparative studies of religion tell us about the long development from an animistic state to totemism, we wish only to point out that the memory of the primeval father of the horde lives still in the image of the totem animal and in the figure of god-father after he regained human shape in an evolution that took many thousands of years.

What is the relationship of the analytic interpretation of the Fall story I have attempted in the preceding chapters

to Freud's hypothesis? It has been mentioned that there is
no published interpretation of the Genesis story by Freud.
His remarks, contained in a private letter to Jung, strongly
state that the primal crime related in the Scripture is to be
analytically interpreted as Adam's incest with his mother.
This interpretation contradicts, of course, the character of
the primal crime reconstructed in *Totem and Taboo*. There
is no doubt that Freud discarded his older concept after
he discovered the origin of totemism in comparing the
analytic material obtained in the observation of childhood
neurosis with anthropological data. There is, however, no
further attempt by Freud to reinterpret the biblical tale in
the light of his new insights. My interpretation took its
point of departure from the biblical text, used the result of
exegetic studies and of comparative mythology, and arrived
at a hypothesis about the original tradition of the Fall of
Man. Independent of Freud's theory, but applying his
method of analytic investigation, the exploration of the Fall
myth came to the conclusion that the core of that prehistoric
tradition is a tale of killing and eating the god who was
Jahveh's totemistic predecessor with the early Hebrew
tribes. A comparison of this reconstruction with Freud's
theory shows that the two concepts are close to each other.
Some important divergencies that make a modification of
Freud's hypothesis necessary will be discussed later on. As
far as I know, no other attempt at interpretation of the
biblical Fall story has arrived at conclusions similar to the
one here presented.

The results of the analytic exploration of the Genesis
myth of the Fall attempted here seem to concur with the
inferences Freud drew from his material. The "scientific
myth," as he once called his reconstruction, and the conclusions we have reached are likely to converge at a certain

position. This point commands a blurred view of the remotest past of man's evolution. We recognize in dim light human or rather subhuman figures, each of them "passion's slave" even more than we and inclined to outbreaks of violence.

There is a far cry from the tradition we discovered in the biblical Fall story to the events in the primeval hordes. Yet remains of a primordial God father figure, concealed behind the tree totem, are entombed in that tale of the first crime as bits of extinct prehistoric plants and animals are preserved in a piece of translucent amber.

CHAPTER XIII

THE MAN WITHOUT A PAST

NOT ALL in that myth of the Fall is mythical. There is a piece of historical reality hidden in it. When and where did those tragic events that overshadowed the whole future of mankind take place? This is a moot question. Wherever we try to penetrate the deep darkness, we find our way blocked. This is the realm of prehistoric jungle that cannot be entered or pierced. The comparison brings to mind that there is really the possibility that those primordial events, warded off and forgotten, took place somewhere in the forests or in the caves of Africa.[1] We have to assume with Freud[2] that all primeval men underwent the fate described in *Totem and Taboo*. This would imply that those great conflicts were experienced at a phase when mankind was still at its original home, which means before its differentiation into races.

As Freud himself admitted, his story is told in a very condensed way. It is certain that the drama in the primeval horde was not a singular event, but took centuries and was repeated innumerable times. "For how many centuries?"

[1] The paleontologist John Talbot Robinson assumes that the cradle of mankind was in South Africa. (Herbert Wendt, *In Search of Adam* [Boston, 1956], p. 502.)

[2] *Moses and Monotheism*, p. 127.

one would like to ask. No one can answer. It is extremely difficult to give an estimation of the time certain developments took in those prehistoric ages. One is tempted to find analogies with the source of events in recorded ancient or modern history, but such comparisons can be very deceptive because prehistoric changes took much longer and were certainly much more of the character of trial and error. There is, for instance, a modern analogy to those events of the primordial parricide, an analogy to be used only as a touchstone. It seems we will soon see the end of monarchy or of the ancient institution of kingdom. Recently the Egyptian regent, Farouk, deposed as were so many others, predicted that before long only the king of England and the king in card games will be left. How long will it take until all kings on earth are done away with? Our comparison concerns, in the first line, removal of kings by organized violence because this case comes closest to the parricide in the primeval hordes. There were king-murderers; there were Ravaillac, Damiens, and others, but as Albert Camus justly points out,[3] they attacked the person of the king, not the principle. "They wanted another king and that was all. It never occurred to them that the throne could remain empty forever." We choose thus with the author of *L'homme révolté* the date 1789 as the starting point of the modern age of modern regicide because, with the execution of Louis XIV, the murder was committed by the people for the people.

The revolt of the primeval sons against the father of the horde and the violence committed against him can well be compared with the rebellion of the people against the king they assassinated. Since January 21, 1793, we have seen the murder of the czar, of the Serbian king, and of other

[3] *The Rebel* (New York, 1956), p. 12.

monarchs, and there will certainly be others because there are still kings governing people on this planet. Can you therefore say that the whole process of the violent discarding of kingdom by the people took about two or three hundred years? Not at all. The historical development we can observe is only a small part of an evolution that took place during many thousands of years. Our time presents only a certain form of the regicide; there were others and at least as well-organized ones. J. G. Frazer has collected impressive material from comparative religion and anthropology to prove that there was even in prehistoric Egypt a custom of putting the divine kings to death at the first symptom of infirmity or old age. Such a ritual of execution of kings and chieftains is still alive in many primitive and half-civilized people in Africa and Asia. Is the killing of crowned heads in our time more than an episode within a succession of similar happenings, comparable to a new, slightly revised edition of a book published ages ago?

Are there any circumstances to date those fatal events in the primeval hordes? We understand, of course, that it cannot be a question of dating them as though they belonged to the realm of recorded history. A few thousand years more or less cannot make any difference. Freud emphasized that no attempt was made to guess even approximately the phase in which the catastrophe of that remote past occurred or even to attribute it to a certain geological age. Homo sapiens is more than half a million years old and there is no record of history until about six thousand years ago. More than 99 per cent of the story of mankind is prehistory.

Who were the men who rebelled against the fathers of the hordes? Were they men at all? Did they belong to the species of man, or were they still a kind of ape-man? Can we think of them as though they belonged to some known types of fossil men such as the Pithecanthropus, Neanderthal, Cro-Magnon men? The Neanderthal type, for instance, belongs to the beginning of the second glaciation of the Ice Age (about four hundred fifty thousand years ago), but there are findings of a Neanderthaloid in Europe in the earlier part of the last great glaciation (one hundred thousand to fifty thousand years ago). To imagine those aeons for only one type of prehistoric man, a type preceding modern man, means to form an idea of how difficult, if not impossible, it is to make any statements concerning the date of those primeval events.

Are there any clues for an informed guess—for instance, from the character of those changes within the primitive hordes? Freud mentions two clues, but he himself considers them problematical or attributes to them only the value of probabilities. He thinks it likely "that mankind was not very far advanced in the art of speech"[4] and he assumes that some cultural advance, perhaps some new weapon, had given the brothers a sense of superior strength so that they dared to attack their father, of whom they were in mortal dread.

A detailed comparison with the development of the individual is not indicated, because of our lack of knowledge about the evolution of prehistoric man. The nature of the topic makes reserve necessary and restricts the explorer to the statement that that critical time belongs to the infancy of mankind, comparable to the age before the fourth or fifth year of a child. Since no point of contact with geological data can be established, any added attempt at dating would be mere surmise.

Not much more precision can be reached when we try to determine how far back we can trace the oral tradition

---

[4] *Moses and Monotheism, op. cit.,* p. 127.

we reconstructed from traces in the biblical story. We cannot refer to any significant previous research on this special problem. There are, of course, many books and papers dealing with the question of traditional sources of the Genesis narrative, but almost all of them choose their points of departure at a time to be considered too late. Some of them, for instance, deal with an amazing degree of sagacity and penetration with the changes to which an older alleged tradition was subjected by the different editors of the Holy Scripture.

Many ingenious and even some correct hypotheses were thus obtained by solving certain problems of text criticism and exegesis. The point at which the research finally arrived is the fixation of the tradition in writing. The changes of the oral tradition itself through some thousands of years are rarely considered. The knowledge of very remote experiences seems to have been forgotten; late generations have received tales already obscure and incomplete, which had gone through many changes.

What has happened to those early experiences? They left permanent traces in the human or subhuman individuals who passed through them, but they themselves are warded off; this means that they have fallen into the deep well of oblivion. They were not lost, but they became submerged. The analogy with processes in the individual emotional life is helpful in elucidating the development that follows. We know that early experiences of childhood, especially those to which we attribute the character of the traumatic, seem to be entirely forgotten. In some form or other, mostly distorted, they are remembered at the time of puberty after a long phase of latency. It seems that something similar happens to the events of the early phase of human prehistory. If we assume that those great conflicts in the life of the human family occurred in the infancy of mankind, we would, in analogy, expect a similar long latency period—perhaps a hundred thousand years or more—and then a slow rise of the forgotten at the dawn of civilization. This reproduction of the past in memories, this late return of the forgotten can well be compared with the ascent of buckets from the bottom of a very deep well.

We can only dimly perceive that all kinds of alterations and deletions had been performed before that material became accessible to oral transmission. We become at this point aware of how mistaken we had been in our belief that we can penetrate in our reconstruction to the core of the original tradition. The primeval tale that had been conveyed from generation to generation, the original story told in caves and miserable mud huts, perhaps knew nothing of a god, nothing of totems and taboos. The outline of a tale we mistook for the primal myth was a late and already transformed version of the original, primitive memory of the great deed of liberation and murder. And how great is the interval between that early oral tradition and the first version of the Fall story that was never discovered!

The beginning of the art of writing may go back to 3300 B.C. It took certainly more than a thousand years until the primitive Hebrew tribes learned it from their Egyptian teachers. The Jehovist to whom we owe the first tale of the Fall of Man certainly edited and drastically changed the tradition known to him; the Elohist and his successors continued this censuring, correcting, and distorting work. From this survey we can imagine what distance existed between the primeval myth and its written version in Genesis. It is remarkable that the core of historical truth concealed in the Fall story is preserved as though it were protected against all influences that transformed, distorted, and elaborated the oral tradition. The kernel of the prehistoric reality had withstood the power of eroding forces, gradually wearing away the content of the original tradition. What a monument to the conservation and loyalty of memory!

The core of oral tradition tells of the killing and devouring of the totemistic god by early man. The biblical version has blended the account of the first crime with an old tale of the creation of the world and has made the first transgressor the first man on earth. The most incisive change in the primeval tradition is, besides this transference, the substitution of the primordial father of the primitive family by the figure of God. How did it come about that the deity was introduced into the original myth? How was the barbarous and raucous tune of a savage phase transposed into the majestic melody of Jahveh?

In order to understand the origin and the nature of that substitution, we have to follow the hypothesis about the events within the early human family after the death of the primal father. The development is, in great outlines, the following: after the atrocious deed a long phase of quarrels among the brothers took place. Each of them was eager to usurp the vacated place of the murdered father. Their fights were futile and led, after many trials and errors, to a kind of "social contract," as Freud calls it. That means they resulted in a primitive form of social organization in which each renounced full instinctual gratification and acknowledged the right of the others and his own obligations. None of them could take the desired place of the father, none could possess the females of the horde. The social institutions, by and by developed, marked the beginning of unwritten morality and law. By a kind of, as one is tempted to say, "gentlemen's agreement," incest became forbidden and exogamy was necessitated. All members of the "brother-horde" were frustrated and compelled to renounce the fulfillment of their most urgent wishes. Their situation must have somewhere resembled that of the people of the old Austro-Hungarian monarchy whose democracy had, as someone remarked, the principle that each was equally wronged.

Freud assumed that in the phase following that beginning of primitive organization was the time of matriarchate, of which many traces are preserved in myths and customs. The power of the dead father was now to a great extent given to the older women of the horde. It was a situation similar to that in a family in which the father has died and the mother takes over his authority, including authority over the adolescent sons. It is very likely that ten thousand years later, when religion evolved, the memory of those domineering mother figures helped to shape the great goddesses of early civilizations. Those idols, primeval and very earthy predecessors of the Holy Virgin, had later on as consorts son-gods who were their lovers, Osiris, Attis, and Adonis. But with the introduction of those son-gods we are already at the dawn of history. It is more than probable that their reign preceded that of a tribal father-god, who was re-created from the material of memory traces that returned from the repressed. The figure of Jahveh is perhaps the latest re-creation of such a powerful father-god who, in the beginning, continued to show many of the characteristics of that tyrannical, unpredictable, and vengeful master of the primitive horde.

The evolution of the religious ideas would thus be the following: mother-goddesses, later on accompanied by young sons with whom they are sexually associated and whose early, violent death they mourn. The worship of

those figures of young gods gains in importance while the
cult of the mother-mistresses recedes. A powerful and
brutal father-god who had occasionally emerged as revenger
of the incest becomes more and more the boss of the divine
household. By and by he is transformed from a hostile and
malevolent demon into a figure who is no longer walking
on earth, but looks down at men just as Jahveh, who says:
"The Heaven Is My Throne and the Earth My Footstool."
With the resurrection and sublimation of the father of the
primeval horde in the shape of a supreme and almighty god,
henotheism and later monotheism were actually attained.

A great part of this whole evolution of religious ideas
belongs to the dawn of history at which the gods had already
regained human shape. In the middle of the long preceding
night that covers the evolution of Homo sapiens, the beginning of religion is marked by totemism, the worship of
an animal from which the members of the tribe traced their
descent. This original god was the representative of the
primal father in his beastly shape. Religion in this early
form replaced an even more primitive concept of the world,
that of animism. In this view the whole of nature, including
inanimate objects, has a will and a soul. Rocks, trees,
and clouds are really demons and ghosts; the world is peo-
pled by all kinds of malignant or benevolent beings to be
seen and heard around us. In later phases of totemism trees
and stones also became gods, until they finally were conceived of as dwelling places of deities.

In this very condensed survey we reached the point from
which we return to our original topic, namely to the interpretation of the biblical Fall story. We said that the significance of the forbidden tree in the middle of the Garden of
Eden has not been understood until now because it was not
recognized as a remnant of the tree-totemistic god of a

time preceding the Jahveh concept by many centuries. Only in this way can we understand the fact that eating from the tree is the crime of all crimes in the biblical narratives. A memory of that primal murder within the horde, distorted and disguised, has found its way into the lore of an age that has no direct knowledge of events beyond any human recollection.

The biblical tale, written around 1000 B.C., was founded on an oral tradition of long duration. Even if we could trace the original tradition that survived in a myth, we cannot imagine how the memory of those events within the horde could have succeeded in keeping alive. Even for the contemporaries of the beginning of writing, let us say for Sumerians and Egyptians of 4000 before Christ, the great catastrophe in the human family belonged to a remote prehistory of which no record existed.

A comparison, used before, may now become useful. We conceived of the neolithic age in which civilization began as analogous to prepuberty years in individual life. Carrying this comparison further—and we remain aware that it is only a comparison—we learned that events of childhood begin to be remembered at puberty. Only then memories of childhood, often distorted and disguised, emerge and become objects of conscious recollection. We can compare early oral traditions that formed the material for myths of a later age to the recollections of the individual at puberty. But where do those recollections come from? Where had they been in the long interval? Let us say a boy of eleven years remembers something that took place before his fourth year. Where was the memory entombed before? The child at that age was still unable to put his experience into words that would emotionally master it. The intensive feelings awakened by the experience could not be appropriately expressed and the conflicts resulting from the clash of the contradictory emotions remained unsolved. Tendencies that were frowned at by the parents and later on by the child himself were, in the subsequent phase, repressed and continued to live in the psychic underground.

In a similar manner those dramatic events in the childhood of mankind and in the early human family remained unremembered because only what can be verbalized or at least thought in words can be recollected. Freud must have had this in mind when he ventured the guess that man at the time of the catastrophe within the horde had not progressed very far in speech. Certain analytic observations and conclusions, made in his practice, concerning early traumatic childhood events must have led him to this comparative assumption. For many thousands of years man remained mute with regard to those events within the primal hordes. Only dimly remembered, they entered the preconscious mind of mankind in the early Stone Age. They emerged in the form we call oral tradition and were first written down several thousand years later, so to speak in the early puberty years of man's evolution.

The myths, told in the Bible, could thus be compared to a primitive autobiography that a high school boy, thirteen years of age, writes as homework. The character of those myths corresponds to that of daydreams of a boy, not yet arrived at full maturity. Yet in that autobiographical attempt there are, distorted and disguised, certain historical memories from childhood that resemble those remnants of prehistoric reality to be found in ancient myths. The mythical hero can be likened to the person of the juvenile writer who remembers—sometimes in terms characteristic of dreams of glory—his past.

Returning to the myth of the Fall of Man, we guess that

the figure of Adam is not only a representative of prehistoric man, but takes the place of all the brothers combined who killed and ate the feared father of the primal horde. In the myth he alone committed that terrible crime or dared to undertake that deed of liberation. Many thousands of years later he will be made the mythical hero who commits the outrage against the deity and is punished for it by the father-god, as was Prometheus by enraged Zeus. In the myth the deed is his alone and he is later made responsible for the curse that befell all future generations and for "the heartache and the thousand natural shocks that flesh is heir to."

The prehistoric events whose memory is concealed and preserved in the Fall myth overshadow in their importance all historic happenings just as traumatic experiences of the individual's early childhood overshadow those of adult life. Mankind has never been quite the same since.

CHAPTER XIV

YOU ARE WHOM YOU EAT

GEORGE CUVIER, professor at the Jardin des Plantes, developed a new theory that was enthusiastically received by some Paris professors, but passionately contested by others. From his observations and comparisons of animals he came to the perception that all the parts and organs of an animal stood in a mutual relationship to one another. He deduced that an animal which developed a distinct organ will show a particular other set of organs developed. Animals equipped with hooves and horns will have teeth of a kind that makes them vegetarians. Other animals, for instance with claws and anklebones, have invariably a system of teeth that points to their being carnivorous. Cuvier believed that this connection, which he formulated as the "Law of Correlation," is so stringent that it would be theoretically possible to reconstruct the entire body of an animal from a single bone that was known.

The great naturalist, who formulated his famous "Law of Correlation" almost one hundred sixty years ago, showed on more than one occasion the courage of his conviction. There is the amusing incident of the plot of some students of his at a time when the professor was already at the zenith of his fame. One of the gang put on the mask of the Devil, with horns and cloven hooves instead of shoes. While the other students observed the scene through the window, the boy, dressed up as Devil, broke into Cuvier's house at night. He shouted into the ears of the sleeping professor, "Wake up! I am the Devil!" Cuvier awoke, lit a candle, and looked very interestedly at the monstrous appearance. The intruder shouted again at the top of his voice: "I am the Devil! I have come to eat you up!" Cuvier shook his head and said. "Eat me up? I am skeptical about that. You've got horns and hooves. According to the Law of Correlation you can eat only plants." Turning on his other side, he went to sleep again.

The Devil in goat shape is not likely to be a man-eater. No one knows anything about the physical endowment of Satan's divine counterpart, but the history of religion shows that gods like human sacrifices. And men, created in God's image, in His likeness, were cannibals since the Ice Age. Their ancestors too were, to quote the words of an American humorist, such "gastronomers of the old school." We now know that they were already using fire to cook human flesh. In a discussion of the question whether certain very early specimens, found in South Africa, are apes or men, the famous anthropologist Hans Weinert at the University at Kiel remarked a few years ago:[1] "To slaughter, roast, and devour members of one's own species is a thing no ape ever does. It is the action of a human being."

The cannibalistic aspect of the great event in the primal horde has its place in Freud's theory, which is one of the great achievements of research, comparable only to the

[1] Quoted from Herbert Wendt, *In Search of Adam* (Boston, 1956), p. 493.

magnificent discoveries of medicine and biochemistry of our time. Freud says of the brothers:[2] "Cannibal savages as they were, it goes without saying that they devoured their victim as well as killing him." He takes this cannibalistic act for granted as the consequence of the first. From the viewpoint of those cannibal savages themselves—if you can speak of a viewpoint at as low a level of evolution—the priority of aims belongs obviously to the eating: the killing was, so to speak, the necessary act preparatory to devouring the victim. I am of the opinion that the cannibalistic part of the primal deed, casually treated in Freud's reconstruction, is of paramount importance and is the central seat of most of the social and religious developments originated in the emotional reactions created by that crime. Superficially considered, the divergence in Freud's theory and mine would be comparable to a difference in pronunciation, for instance emphasizing the second syllable in the name Beethoven instead of the first. We know that the accent should be on the first syllable, but we would, of course, recognize the name of the great composer, even though incorrectly pronounced. Yet the difference in the theory amounts to more than a shifting of emphasis.

The change I am suggesting makes a modification of Freud's great hypothesis a logical and psychological necessity. It leaves the core of his reconstruction, but brings certain features to the fore that are more appropriate to the character of the early Old Stone Age and of that great drama whose late repercussions led to the beginning of civilization. It seems to me that the "shift of emphasis" leads to a new design and reassessment in the interpretation and reconstruction of many tribal customs and myths. We start, then, from the premise that everywhere the

[2] *Totem and Taboo* (New York, 1950), p. 142.

earliest stratification will be found to be concerned with cannibalism rather than with murder and violent death. The act of killing is, of course, implied in that other feature, but it is a necessary condition like the defeat of an enemy garrison before the occupation of a city.

It needs a certain mental reorientation to recognize the cannibalistic aspect of the crime as the more important part, but more than that it needs an emotional effort to focus on this side. Cannibals devouring a body with relish present a picture of "nature red in tooth and claw." Father-murder is an atrocious crime. The eating of the killed father is for persons of our civilization so unimaginable that the act is outside the range of our imagination. We can still imagine, although even that is difficult, that a young son in rage kills his father, and we sometimes read of such cases in our newspapers, but eating of the killed father is not believable and is unheard of in every sense of the word. Killing of fathers is outdated, but eating them is decidedly obsolete. Yet the killing as well as the eating of parents is well proved by the testimony of missionaries and anthropologists who lived with cannibal tribes of today. It is, however, remarkable that even with those savage people dead relatives are often killed and eaten by a neighboring tribe, which is asked to dispose of the old ones.

It speaks for the psychologically greater significance of the devouring when we hear that certain totemistic tribes are willing to kill totem animals at certain occasions, but would not eat them and leave them to other tribes who are allowed to enjoy the food. In this case the killing is allowed, but not the eating which secures—so to speak—an inner evidence of the greater importance of the food taboo and indirectly of the devouring in the primitive horde, from which much later the totemistic forbiddings originated. The

ganging up of the brothers to kill the father is a grim and
gruesome picture. Their ambushing him to devour him is
an idea so horrible that imagination recoils from it. ("The
eyes of all wait upon thee; and thou givest them their meat
in due season.")

No religion or social organization is known whose laws
forbid cannibalism while almost all religions and societies
condemn and abominate murder. Even the savages seem to
obey the commandment, "Thou shalt not kill," but there
is no commandment, "Thou shalt not eat human flesh."
The millennial repression of cannibalistic tendencies became so internalized that outside prohibition is no longer
necessary, while homicidal trends are in every society alive
and effective enough to make their legal prohibition indispensable. The conclusion from this situation could not be
that the cannibalistic trends are originally weaker than the
murderous impulses, but that they were repressed so drastically and so early that they remain banned into deep
layers of the unconscious. The original repression of the
cannibalistic drives must have been so severe and forceful
that its effects became lasting. Since cannibalism was universal among our prehistoric ancestors, that repression has
to operate many millennia to become so internalized that
the very existence of those tendencies remains unknown to
us. A faint echo of those drastic measures is to be felt in
punishments and menaces for transgressions of the taboos
of totemistic animals and plants to which the cannibalistic
forbiddings were displaced.

About one hundred years ago a French writer, Théophile
Gautier, complained that man did not even succeed in in-
venting an eighth deadly sin. Yet at the time at which the
list of deadly sins was fixed, man had left cannibalism
behind him so long ago that it was not mentioned. The

people of the ancient Orient who had reached a high level of cultural development at the time of the Fall myth did not remember that they had to be weaned from cannibalism. Only single memory traces, like the myth of Osiris, testify to the overcoming of cannibalism, which was one of the greatest achievements of mankind in its slow evolution from its bestial past to a more progressed stage of civilization.

The comparison of universal repression and of intense drives such as the cannibalistic appetites and of mass education with individual training is illuminating in more than one direction. It is difficult to convince an adult person, man or woman, that there was a time in his infancy when he not only ate his feces and smeared himself with them, but also liked to do that. In the best case a purely intellectual conviction can be reached while no emotional echo of such inclination can be awakened. Yet such a phase existed in everybody's infancy. No social or educational measure of defense or prohibition is longer needed against a revival of those coprophilous tendencies, because their successful repression is the result of the education that took place at an early age in which the ego of the individual child was still weak, plastic, and easily influenced. A strong reaction formation of disgust and revulsion has taken the place of the primal infantile impulses. The analogy with the vicissitudes of cannibalism in the early evolution of civilization is too obvious to be pointed out.

In emphasizing the importance of the parricide and in neglecting the emotional weight of the cannibalistic act, one has unconsciously followed the direction of our progressed civilization. But one has renounced the understanding of primitive beliefs and superstitions entertained by the criminal brothers, savages of the Paleolithic Age, and their later descendants in whose elementary feelings and thoughts eating, especially of human flesh, was much more important than murder. What appears to us as an impossible motive, namely to kill a person in order to eat him, was then one of the main motivating powers. Our modern concept and interpretation of primitive customs and myths often goes astray and is misleading because we do not consider the impact of these cannibalistic tendencies.

Let me, returning to a subject mentioned before, insert a literary remark at this point: The sleuth of a mystery story dealing with a crime dated at a paleolithic or even early neolithic age (for instance, predynastic Egypt), is in danger of being sadly mistaken if he takes into account only the motives for murder as they appear in modern times (greed, revenge, hate, and so on) and neglects the various impulses operating in primitive cannibalism—even excluding hunger. It is an amusing thought that a modern writer of mystery stories planning a prehistoric murder plot would fail in his task, if he were to neglect this motive—which he need not consider in a story of our time.

Among the inherent tendencies of early cannibalism the belief that one can acquire the qualities of the victim by incorporation is perhaps the leading motive. In the primitive mind the hostile and affectionate components of cannibalistic trends are not yet sharply differentiated; they coalesce in the desire of incorporation and possession of the object. It is remarkable that the few remnants of cannibalistic trends to be found in our emotional life have only affectionate character. A lover can well say to his sweetheart that he would like to eat her up and thus express his tender desire of incorporation. The other aggressive and hostile component of cannibalistic strivings has become lost to our conscious thoughts and continues to live a disavowed existence in the area of repressed impulses. It appears only rarely in colloquial phrases, for instance, "I cannot stomach him."

The decisive role of the primal ambivalence toward the father is already apparent at the cannibalistic stage. The factor of affection and admiration, of longings for him after his death has its roots in this aspect of the deed. It is with the killed father as with the cake: you cannot eat him and have him. There is, however, a third possibility, alien to our thoughts, but familiar to those of prehistoric savages, namely: you can eat the father and become he. The cannibalistic version of the well-known saying is: you are whom you eat. However fantastic or bizarre such a thought possibility may sound to us, it was very close to the primitive mind and continues to live in the imaginations of our little children. It is not astonishing that it is still alive in the idea of the Eucharist, in which the worshiper becomes united with Christ by incorporating Him. This renewal of a savage and infantile belief in the possibility of acquiring the superior object by eating it is tied to the condition: "Except ye be converted, and become as little children, ye shall not enter into the kingdom of heaven."

The re-evaluation of the cannibalistic part of the parricide is necessary for the apportionment of the psychological consequences of the deed. While murder does not figure in the ritual of the great monotheistic religions, cannibalistic rites are daily performed in the Mass of our churches. Not the slowly vanishing customs of Central Australian tribes, but the living liturgy of Christianity bears witness to the strength and ineffaceability of cannibalistic trends in our civilization. The eating of Christ's body and the drinking of His blood are the most important parts of the Eucharist.[3]

[3] J. I. Lloyd, *God-Eating, A Study in Christianity and Cannibalism* (Cambridge, 1921).

Religion, the loftiest and most sublime creation of the human mind, has at its center the most savage and blood-thirsty ceremonial in a cannibalistic rite.

Freud's reconstruction of the great event in the primal horde "which, since it occurred, has not allowed mankind a moment's rest," as he once remarked, will certainly be modified and qualified by future research—and its full impact will only be recognized in the future—but its partial alteration is introduced by the emphasis of the cannibalistic character of the primordial crime. This factor serves as a key to open many doors and make us understand connections that have puzzled us.

There are a few instances of such illumination: first, the reconstruction of the Fall myth dealt with in the preceding chapters. The clue to the unravelling of the myth lies in the assumption that God was eaten. In the manifest content of the myth neither the murder nor the devouring appears, but, as our interpretation proved, the cannibalistic act succeeded in entering the narrative, so to speak, by a hidden side entrance, namely in the displacement to the substitute tree totem. Thus displaced and distorted, the original alimentary character of the primal transgression was sufficiently camouflaged so that the concealed meaning of the tradition could not be consciously recognized any longer. This displacement tallied with the local description of the place in which that drama was performed. Nothing is more natural than a tree in the Garden of Eden. The original tradition conveyed and concealed thus the content of the myth in choosing an excellent hiding place in the obvious. At the progressed stage of religious evolution reached when the myth was transmitted, the enormity of the idea of devouring Jahveh was not any longer imaginable. Yet it found a way of expression in that trick of secondary elaboration.

The puberty rites of the savages are the most important religious and social event of the native tribes of Australia, Africa, and America. They are, to quote J. G. Frazer, the "central mystery of primitive society."[4] This prominent anthropologist, who has an impressive collection of material on puberty rites from all parts of the world, characterizes the general nature of the festival as death and resurrection. Careful inquiry into the important features of the puberty rites will confirm that Frazer has indeed grasped the quintessence of that ritual in his characterization. All observers, missionaries, and anthropologists agree that the main idea of the rites is that the young people are killed by a monster or demon and are then resurrected. Afterward they often behave as though they were little children who have to learn to walk and speak and so on. All this takes place after the young men are circumcised, which is the central part of the ritual. Yet this same description leaves no doubt that the two-act drama of death and resurrection is the result of a secondary elaboration, so to speak, a rewrite of the original play.

Let us cite only a few instances: in the Jabim tribe of New Guinea the principal rite consists in circumcision, which is performed in the forest. The lads are supposed to be eaten up by a monster called Balum, who will release them from his belly on condition of receiving a sufficient number of roast pigs. The scene is a hut about a hundred feet in length, representing the belly of the monster who is to swallow up the candidates. A pair of great eyes is

---

[4] *The Golden Bough,* II (London, 1913), p. 278. Compare "Puberty Rites of the Savages," in my book, *The Ritual* (New York, 1940).

painted over its entrance, and above the eyes projecting roots of a palm represent the monster's hair and so on. This is the stage set. When the procession of the lads arrives at that monster, pigs are sacrificed to him in order to induce him to spare the lives of the novices. They remain after circumcision in strict seclusion for three to four months living in the long hut, the monster's belly. After this period of digestion they come forth safe and sound.

In the rites of the Dukaua and the Tani the lads are supposed to be swallowed by a monster who is induced by the sacrifice of many pigs to vomit them up again. In spewing them out of his maw he bites or scratches them and the wound is circumcision. These and similar examples of which an abundance has been quoted by Frazer and others speak in favor of the primal meaning of the puberty ritual that the boys are supposed to be eaten and then be unswallowed. But the educational purpose of those rituals is to intimidate the young men and to frighten them away from the temptation to attack the generation of fathers.

The presentation of death and resurrection has become a secondary one and replaces the original, quite realistically performed spectacle of being eaten and vomited up. The central place of the cannibalistic devouring of the father of the horde is also indirectly proved by this terrifying display of being eaten in the puberty rituals in which the fathers of the tribes deflect the boys from the original objects of their appetite. Only with the late repression and recession of cannibalistic impulses was the primal character of the puberty rites ameliorated and the savage and crude ceremonies of being eaten replaced by others in which the candidates are supposed to die and to be reborn.

The belief in the transfer of power, in the physical assimilation of the qualities of other persons by incorporation is still alive in the later developments of the totemistic system and in their religious manifestations. Here is the second advantage of the displacement of emphasis on the act of devouring in Freud's hypothesis. It paves the way to a better understanding of the great importance of eating, not only in the totemistic systems, but also in the later and more developed forms of religion. (The table companionship of early social organizations, even of our family, has its roots in the renewal of that primitive belief in the kinship and community of persons eating together.) The Last Supper of Christ is a totem meal in which the victim takes part although He is the victim to be eaten. The superior role of the ceremonies connected with food (the totem meal of the ancient religion, the sacrifice of animals, the avoidance of the flesh of certain animals, the fastings as well as the rituals of slaughter) is understandable only if we attribute the greater importance to the devouring of the father in the great event in the primordial family.

The emphasis on the cannibalistic character of that crime facilitates also the understanding of later developments of food taboos and dietary laws such as those of the Jews, Hindus, of the ancient Babylonians and Egyptians. It is very likely that the early Hebrew tribes lived chiefly on vegetable food and fruit and that animal food was partaken of by the common people only on festive occasions in connection with sacrifices. Shylock says to Bassanio: "I will buy with you, sell with you, talk with you, walk with you, and so following; but I will not eat with you, drink with you, nor pray with you." (Merchant of Venice, I. 3.) It is to be assumed that the first form of isolation or segregation is older than the others. Within the totemistic phase the person who avoided eating the eagle was religiously and nationally or, as one might rather say, tribally well differentiated from the one who was permitted to eat that animal. A man (or a woman) was marked with regard to his kinship by the kind of food taboo he observed. In this sense one could conceive of the strict observance of the dietary laws of Jews as an alimentary expression of their loyalty to their God. The astonishing tenacity of those food taboos even in Jews who no longer have religious ties with their faith, especially the revulsion against ritually unclean ("treife") meat, for instance pork, would thus correspond to an unconscious fear of eating an ancient totem animal. The expression of such avoidance is equivalent to the creed, "Sch'ma, Yisrael, Adonoi Elohenu, Adonoi Echod." ("Hear, Israel, the Lord is our God, the Lord is the only One.")

It seems to me that the inner evidence of the greater importance of the cannibalistic part of the primordial crime is very strong. We can follow it from the time of the Orphic theogony to the Christian and Jewish visions of the last things. Kronos devours his children in Greek myths, Zeus swallows Metis or Phanes, and the Titans devour Dionysus. According to R. Jechanan (Talmud, Bab. 74a) the Lord will give a banquet where the righteous and the pious will all eat the flesh of the Leviathan, that totemistic sea monster whose strength and invulnerability are praised by Jahveh in His dialogue with Job. It is highly significant that, according to tradition, that primal deed will be repeated in the displacement to a totemistic substitute at the time when the Messiah will come. In Christian eschatology God promises (Revelation 2:7): "To him that overcometh will I give to eat of the tree of life, which is in the midst of the paradise of God." At the resurrection the circle is completed with the repetition of the original sin.

CHAPTER XV

THE ANSWERS OF SCIENCE
AND RELIGION

A CRIMINAL investigation has as its first task to ascertain when and where the crime was committed. Our research, dealing with the first crime, was compared with such an investigation. Yet we are unable to say when and where it all took place. The Bible gives, it is true, precise answers to those questions. It locates the crime in the Garden of Eden and dates it shortly after the creation of man. But we have to be content with guesses and conjectures.

The other day one of our generals was invited to the Soviet Union to be a guest at maneuvers of their air force. Returned, he was asked about the information he had brought home with him, but he refused to be acknowledged as expert about the Soviet armaments, saying: "There are no experts about Soviet Russia. There are only different degrees of ignorance." Similarly, there are no experts about the events that took place in Paleolithic times. There are only different degrees of ignorance on the part of the scholars in various fields. They are all separated from that area by more than an iron curtain—by the impenetrable curtain of the Old Stone Age.

Can we apply with regard to those events the colloquial phrase: Your guess is as good as mine? It seems to me that we are too ready to say that about things that are very difficult to explore. What, for instance, do we know about the situation on the planet Mars? Very little. Yet the astronomers who have instruments and methods not at our disposal know or can at least conjecture much more than we laymen. Our guess is certainly not as good as theirs. They have reached certain conclusions and hypotheses, founded on observations of many decades and on results of scientific research that are often even beyond our grasp. Theirs is an informed guess while ours is utterly fanciful. To use a modern simile: theirs is a guided missile into space —ours is an unguided one.

Good or better guesses—but can there be no facts that cannot be doubted, no certainties? There are, but they are not ascertained by science, only by religion. They are not found by research, but by revelation. The verities that the church proclaims are not verifiable. They are not even verisimilar.

Yet science has certain significant premises in common with religion. The dogma of original sin proclaims that man became a sinner by the Fall and the church describes the nature of that sin. We assume that certain events in his early evolution are responsible not for the guilt of man, but for his sense of guilt. We try to discover the character of those events. The difference is obvious: on the one hand is dogma as authoritative belief, on the other is an assumption or hypothesis as a basis for reasoning. That contrast of belief and reason will be the decisive factor in the realm of problems that, by their nature, cannot be solved unequivocally. The sentence of Theodor Fontane, "We cannot get along without hypotheses," is applicable to problems such as the primeval origin of the sense of guilt in human civilization. If science cannot dispense with hypothesis, religion cannot exist without certainties. Assumptions, conjectures, and tentative opinions are within the realm of reason. We are not ready to leave this territory and to enter the area of alleged certainties. Reason is a weak instrument to find the causes of things of this kind, it is true, but it is the only one at our disposal. We like the comparison of Diderot, used two hundred years ago, "All I have to guide me at night in a dense forest is a flickering little light. A theologian comes and blows it out for me." The answer religion gives is not acceptable to us because it is not founded on inferences from facts, ascertained by research, but is based on the reference to the Holy Scripture.

But what answers has science to give to the question of where the collective guilt feeling of man originated? There was a funny saying in old Germany: "If I had to tell the truth, I would have to lie." By the same token we, challenged at this point, would be tempted to lie and say that science has made various attempts at a solution of the problem of collective guilt feelings. But courtesy aside, the crude truth is that science has scarcely raised the question and almost never tried to answer it. Here is one of the cases in which religion or theology has tried to solve a problem that science has either not seen or not considered worthy of its attention. It is only fair to concede this priority. But the answer theology gave was unsatisfactory— there is the rub.

There are, however, a few scientific attempts to discuss the problem and to make a contribution to its solution. Freud's theory in *Totem and Taboo* is until now the most daring and original essay on the subject. The point of departure of Freud's inquiry was a comparison of a number of mysterious social and religious beliefs of primitive people and some puzzling phenomena in the emotional life of children. Using and analytically interpreting data from anthropology, archaeology, and comparative history, Freud arrived at a reconstruction of the events in the paleolithic family, of the explosion that created the first feeling of guilt long before the dawn of historic time.

Freud's hypothesis will be qualified, modified, and corrected by future research. There is the possibility that new findings from paleolithic times will open undreamed-of avenues to insights and conclusions about the prehistoric situations from which the first sense of guilt in human evolution sprang. Methods of research whose character we cannot foresee may lead to new discoveries. Finally, analytic research itself will be able to choose another point of departure; but we do not think that those modifications will affect the essential results of Freud's excavations. The priority of religion in posing the problem of universal guilt feelings was acknowledged. It is not astonishing that religion preceded research in this area, since magical and religious assumptions were everywhere the forerunners of scientific exploration. The fact of which science should be ashamed is that the problem was not even seen and certainly not dealt with until a few decades ago. When we finally try to characterize the results of the religious and scientific attempts to solve the problem of the genesis of guilt feeling, a comparative assessment would suggest itself. The Christian and the analytic attempts have the premise of a prehistoric happening as the cause of a collective, common sense of guilt. They resemble rays sent into the dark unknown from different points. The religious answer, intended to reach a certain spot, overshoots the mark. Freud's attempt comes near the target. We cannot say how far distant it still is. The scarcity of data and the very limited amount of circumstantial evidence do not allow reaching conclusive facts. Clues are few and do not establish truths. Science has in cases such as this to be content with uncertainties, with doubtful and indefinite answers. It concedes without envy that only theology can offer certainties about the beginnings of morals. In the area of reconstructing that unknown past, a Latin proverb consoles us; it claims that it is enough to have tried one's best in great issues.

My own contribution is an attempt at a solution to the problem independently of Freud's reconstruction, but applying his analytic method of exploration and interpretation. We wished to penetrate the jungle from another side or to probe into the secret in our own way. To change the simile: Freud's analysis had penetrated the darkness, digging a shaft at a certain place and excavating a most valuable piece of antiquity. We chose another place to enter the underworld: the area of ancient myths.

The mythological material, especially the myth of the Fall of Man, has provided us, by an analytic investigation, with a number of pieces of circumstantial evidence. It was the same material that theology used, but which it considers to be divinely revealed truth. As such it cannot be subjected to critical or analytical exploration. In our concept, the Genesis narrative was not a revealed truth, but a story whose analysis and interpretation could reveal some prehistoric truth. Our reconstruction of the unknown past, of early mankind, starting from mythological clues, was not of gigantic or Cyclopean shapes as was Freud's and did not reach farther than the interpretation of the Fall myth. In certain points we differed from Freud, particularly with regard to the kind of sense of guilt which, in our view, concerns rather the cannibalistic than the murderous aspect of that primeval deed. Departing from a different angle, our attempt reached results that seem to confirm Freud's reconstruction.

The many uncertainties and ambiguities inherent in that reconstruction were not concealed. We still do not know where the atrocious crime was committed in paleolithic times: perhaps in the grasslands of Africa where many suggestive remains of early human civilization have been found. It seems that the Sahara desert, East Africa, and Arabia formed the life center of prehistoric human development. But we are perhaps mistaken and the great events within the primal hordes took place in the caves of South Africa and spread north. When? It was in the infancy of mankind, at the time when men were becoming human. Was it in the glacial or interglacial period? If we might judge by analogy, it must have been many hundreds of thousands of years ago. Man has lived on this planet for more than a million years now. The Pleistocene age in whose beginning he evolved into Homo sapiens is now considered to have lasted around seven hundred thousand years. Ape-men and Homo sapiens competed with each other. At the end of the Pleistocene age, Homo sapiens won over the Rhodesian, Solo, and Neanderthal beings, races that have vanished from the earth. The first cultural advances belong to the late Pleistocene. If it is permissible to conclude from analogy, we would date that great, fateful event of earliest prehistory of our race to a phase in which speech was not far developed, but which already had various weapons and a primitive form of social life. Psychologically speaking, the time would correspond to the age between three and five years in the life of the individual, the age in which decisive changes are taking place. We cannot say more without becoming fanciful.

The other day, I listened to another doubt concerning Freud's hypothesis. Is it possible, a student asked, that Freud's sketch of these primal events is correct, that the father and leader of the horde was killed and eaten, not by his own sons, ganging up against him, but by young men of a hostile band who coveted his women, were envious of him, and eager to incorporate his power? Freud's reconstruction would thus remain intact in its main features and the first crime would really be the killing and eating of the father of the primal horde, elevated to a god by later generations. Many atrocious and repulsive aspects of the reconstructed story would appear mitigated, if he were killed not by his own sons, but by men of another tribe. Even among the last Australian cannibalistic tribes, or for instance among the Papuans of New Guinea, the killing and eating of old people is done by warriors of another, neighboring tribe. I just read the report by the French missionary André Dupéyrat,[1] who spent twenty-one years among those barbaric tribes that still live in the Stone Age. One of his native friends showed the priest the skulls and bones of his parents. When they became old and feeble, the dutiful son asked people of a neighboring village to take care of them. Those friends brained the old couple with clubs, cut up the bodies, cooked them in a stone oven and ate them with great relish. Other missionaries and anthropologists report that many cannibalistic tribes usually trust the killing and eating of old fathers to members of another clan.

Such a transaction is, it is true, a revision, because older reports show that the task was originally done by one's own folk, so to speak, "en famille." We must not forget that the Papuans and other cannibalistic peoples also have a long past and in it a "cultural" evolution that changed their old

[1] *Savage Papus, A Missionary among Cannibals* (New York, 1954).

customs. But this and other arguments are really unimportant since the traces left in primitive myths speak clearly enough, and observations in children and neurotics—analogies of those processes in individual life—confirm the conclusion that the course of events was as Freud sketches them. The circumstantial evidence, provided by remnants in myths, religion, and social organization as well as by emotional analogies in children, points irrefutably to the concept that the atrocious deed was done by one's own folk. Traces of this character can be discovered in so late a myth as the murder of Christ. One of His own disciples in whom we recognize disguised remnants of the brother bond delivers the Lord to His judges. Also, He is betrayed by His own folk. A French proverb says: "On n'est trahi que par les siens."

Arrived at an elevated point, we look back at the road we took before we set out to continue our march. We have left the myth of the Fall and its interpretation far behind us. It was not our goal, only a station on the road. Our quest was not to discover the secret meaning of an old Semitic myth, but to find the origins of guilt feelings in human evolution, in primeval times long before the dawn of civilization. We assume that in individual development there is an analogy, that there must have been events in prehistory upon which our earliest ancestors reacted with an emotion for which they had no name—they had few names anyhow—but which was akin to that which we today call guilt feelings, something between anxiety, depression, awe, and regret.

We cannot say farewell to that myth and turn to other problems before we at least attempt to resolve another doubt about the tradition of the Fall. We cannot state with any conceivable certainty that we succeeded in arriving at that primal tradition of which traces are seen in the biblical tale. We can only assert that we perhaps grasped a very old tradition—or better still, fragments of an old tradition—preceding the biblical story by many thousands of centuries, and which was until now undiscovered. This piece of a forgotten and suppressed tale must once have existed as a living myth among the Semitic tribes, perhaps a thousand years before it was suppressed by the religious authorities, long before obscure and distorted remnants of it found their way surreptitiously into a tale written at a time when the Israelitic tribes had already acknowledged a new anthropomorphic god called Jahveh.

If we assume that Freud's reconstruction of the traumatic events in the prehistoric family is in all essential points correct, several questions concerning the Genesis story of the Fall of Man remain unanswered. They concern the period before such a myth emerged, that is, before a tradition such as we assumed became a live myth in the oral transmission from generation to generation. If there were no memories of those fateful, prehistoric events, how was it possible for it to emerge in an oral tradition, to be remembered in one form or another?

CHAPTER XVI

THE BREAKTHROUGH OF MEMORIES

EVEN WHEN we accept that those oral traditions can be traced back to many thousands of years before the Jahvistic report, the generations that transmitted them were many hundreds of centuries, perhaps even hundreds of thousands of years, remote from those prehistoric events. How could a tradition of events beyond all memory emerge? The answer to this question was given by Freud in his book, *Moses and Monotheism,* comparing this situation with the processes that had been studied in the psychology of the neurosis. The analogy with these phenomena of the individual psychology starts from the fact that the neurosis always goes back to the very early impressions of childhood, mostly to traumatic events before the fifth year. The most important period seems to be between two and four years, the age when the child begins to develop his speech. Those experiences are entirely forgotten and are inaccessible to memory. We call the period latency, lasting up to puberty, in which almost no memory of those early experiences emerges. During the long latency phase, all seems to be forgotten, submerged in an abyss of oblivion. In early puberty, obscure and incomplete, often distorted memories of early traumatic experiences and conflicts of a sexual-aggressive nature begin to occur in the individual.

If we compare the early conflicts within the prehistoric human family with individual and sexual-aggressive experiences of early childhood, we have to assume that they left permanent traces in prehistory, memory traces that were mostly warded off and forgotten, and came to life and to memory only after a long period of latency at a later phase of man's history. How did the memory of that primeval crime survive? This question, like so many others concerning the psychology of prehistory, was answered by Freud in a general manner. He refers to the phylogenetic inheritance keeping memory traces of past experiences of the race. "Le passé en nous," as the French would say, is not restricted to personal memories, but reaches also into the collective childhood of humanity. The assumption is that the masses as well as the individual retain impressions of the past in unconscious memory traces that are inaccessible to conscious recollection. This repressed material, containing fragments of phylogenetic memories, transgresses the threshold of consciousness under certain psychological conditions.

I would dare to assert that the analogy Freud drew would have been even clearer if he had tentatively compared the phases of prehistory with which he deals to particular ages of the individual in childhood, with phases to which the traumatic events and their emotional aftereffects can be traced by psychoanalysis. We understand very well which consideration prevented his following such a comparison. While many clinical observations of children are now fully available and complement the reconstructions made in the analysis of adults, no such data about prehistoric developments are at our disposal. Freud rejects even the possibility of attributing the traumatic events in prehistory to any geological age. Aware of those justified doubts and well-founded considerations, we are attracted to the idea of such a parallelism. It seems to be so illuminating and clarifying that it should be followed—whereupon its speculative character has to be strongly emphasized. It would, of course, be as impossible as silly to strive here for accuracy. All elements of the comparison have the nature of great uncertainty, at best of approximation.

Modern science thinks that man in the form of Eoanthropus lived on this planet longer than a million years and was a contemporary of the Pleistocene period. During the Paleolithic or Old Stone Age, he evolved from an ape-like creature into a worker of tools and weapons. He thus lived at the same time as the Cro-Magnon Man, Neanderthal Man, and the Heidelberg Man, as well as other genera distinct from Homo sapiens. Comparing the individual childhood with the infancy of mankind, we would guess that the events Freud considered traumatic within the prehistoric family took place before the ice age, which marks perhaps the most important and decisive demarcation line in the evolution from an ape-like predecessor of man to Homo sapiens. The glacial period represents the end of the prelude of human evolution. The trauma in human prehistory took place in a paleolithic phase, comparable to the age of three or four years in the individual's life. The only piece of data available for our guess is Freud's suggestion that mankind was not very far advanced in the art of speech, which would well tally with the early paleolithic age. The assault on the father of the horde by the brothers, his murder, and his incorporation would thus be roughly dated a few hundred years before the first glacial phase.

We have another argument for this conjecture: we assume with Freud that those traumatic conflicts must have been experienced by all mankind, living closely together; that means before there was a possibility of dispersion and distribution in different continents. When the last ice retreated, opportunities for migration appeared and early Neolithic man invaded new countries. We compare the phase before the invasion of the glaciers to the individual childhood period before the fifth year and the end of this age to the onset of the prehistoric latency period that lasted many hundreds of thousands of years. During this long phase, no memory of the traumatic events separated by the glacial age and the following period of protracted readjustments can be discovered.

Does that mean that those fateful events were entirely forgotten, that there was a complete amnesia regarding them? To all appearances yes, but some memory must have been kept alive underneath the void surface. Otherwise, no traces of that trauma could have been preserved in myths and, as we shall see, in other productions of the imagination that are crystallized around a bit of historic reality. But where are those memories?

Before we give up the attempt to find them, we want at least to try to follow that comparison of the evolution of all mankind with individual childhood a bit further and to pick up the analogy at a point in later years. When would a boy at school have to write a composition, say with the theme "My Earliest Memory" or "What I Remember from Childhood"? Let us assume the appropriate age for such a school paper would be twelve years. We take the liberty of comparing such a written record with the Jahvistic account of Genesis. That means that mankind as a whole was at the age of early puberty when it began to write its his-story, a strange mixture of mythological fantasies, folk lore, obscure traditions, and little bits of historical truth. The Jahvistic report, written about a thousand years before Christ, is founded on traditions living in Canaan for several thousand years. Those traditions glorify the early days of the Hebrews, who were poor and uneducated Bedouin tribes. Here the analogy leads us further, because it is in early puberty that boys begin to remember in some form or other their childhood experiences, when first memories of early years emerge, isolated and distorted, to the mental surface.

Emerge from where? Where have they been? We do not know; we can only guess that they were submerged and slowly ascended like buckets from a deep well. But that is another way of saying that they were latent. At this point we become painfully aware of how misleading the comparison of the collective with the individual evolution is. The child learns to write at six, perhaps sometimes at five years and a boy in the years of puberty will, we said, write a school essay about his early childhood experiences. The interval is about six years. Science assumes that rudimentary writing as pictographic representation dates back as far as thirty thousand years before Christ, very likely even a few thousand years earlier. But the first clumsy attempts at writing by a child, compared with the early picture writings, are separated by only a few years from the first "history" writing of the boy. The crude pictographic writing of Egyptian predynastic times precedes the first historians— even when we think of Herodotus as the "father of history" —about thirty thousand years, a relatively short interval. We cannot avoid the conclusion that the character of our comparison has to be very elastic. Those six years of indi-vidual development from grammar school to high school

writing can be considered analogous to the interval between paleolithic pictowriting and early history presentation
only in a very rough estimate. A thousand years plus or
minus cannot play a role when we think of the scarcity of
data about prehistoric development at our disposal.

But back to our comparison: traumatic experiences of
early childhood are not remembered during the long
latency period of the individual. They are "forgotten" and
memories of them arrive at the surface only piecemeal
during puberty. But being forgotten does not mean being
ineffective or inactive; it is not identical with being lost.
The little child who has experienced something traumatic
does not talk about it because he cannot express what he
thought and felt in words. His faculty of speech is not
advanced enough to tell what has happened to him or what
he has done. His way of expressing himself, his manner of
reacting is nevertheless vivid and dramatic enough. As a
matter of fact, it is more so than the act of speaking.
The child's reactions show clearly enough what experiences
have done to him by his manner of acting afterwards—
you can say by what he does with them. Let us imagine a
little boy three years old who has a traumatic experience;
for instance, he was examined by a doctor or had even a
minor operation. The little boy tries to master that traumatic
experience not by talking about it, but by playing it. That
means he repeats the experience of examination in his play
innumerable times. He "acts" the doctor, imitates his movements and actions, accompanying his mimicry by noises,
half words, or songs.

This way of emotional conquering of traumatic experiences in repeating or, better still, re-enacting them, continues even when the child has somewhat advanced in his
speech faculty. It seems that the possibility of re-enacting

the traumatic scene is not only older and more primitive than the spoken report, but more natural and appropriate to the child. In acting out with cries, gestures, pantomimes, the intensive emotions that the child had felt are not only expressed, but the experience is also emotionally mastered, its original overpowering effect reduced. Such behavior, the acting out of an experience of traumatic character, is not restricted to painful or unpleasant events. A kind of repetition compulsion develops, which Freud characterized as reaction to impressions whose intensity threatens to overpower the still weak ego. This kind of remembering is preverbal, not yet connected with word presentations, but with activities by which "forgotten" memories are relived and renewed. Compulsive acting out of traumatic experiences will later on be replaced by telling or recounting them. This becomes possible when they have been diminished in their reactive effects and when the child has learned to describe them and to express his emotions and thoughts in words. Words, poor substitutions for acting out and pantomiming, become in early puberty the vehicle upon which memories of childhood are transported across the threshold of conscious thinking. The boy has then learned to tell a tale, to recount what he once experienced or did as a child. He becomes potentially the historian of an early part of his past.

Do we dare pursue that analogy into the realm of prehistory? We risk it. We grant that the primordial murder and devouring of the horde father by the band of brothers must have taken place at a phase when the faculty of speech was not much advanced, in the infancy of the genus homo. Every memory trace of the atrocious deed seems to have been effaced. It is as though those traumatic events of mankind's childhood have fallen into the abyss of oblivion.

During the long latency time in the evolution of man during many thousands of years memories of those events were buried, but not dead. Vague impressions of the dark deed had not vanished, but had found a means of expression that was closer to the primitive nature of infant humanity than rudimentary speech. We imagine that those tremendous events had to be re-enacted because their power could not be mastered in any other way. An experience that had stirred young mankind in its depths could not have lost its emotional power in aeons. We cannot guess in what way those horrible happenings were re-enacted, but through the re-enactment it became possible to re-experience the passions preceding and following them.

We have here to admonish ourselves not to carry the comparison with children too far. The cannibalistic killers of the brother tribe were savages, however childlike in their thinking; their deed was no child's play. Their reactions must have had an explosive character. The emotions that led them to the crime and those that were awakened by it could not be expressed in words because there were not enough words within their reach. But they were also not speakable because their intensity was overwhelming. Those original repetitions certainly run the gamut of emotions: rage and triumph, frenzy and fear. The result of the crime looked different to them before it was committed and after it.

We know with certainty of at least two kinds of compulsive repetitions of a later age. That means we can reconstruct their content and form from survivals to be found at the dawn of history. Their character of repetition of that ghastly crime is clear although they are displaced on substitutes for the original victim. The beginnings of the repetitive actions have to be dated many thousands of years after the catastrophe in the primal human family. They both belong to the area of primitive institutions and have been evolved as social reactions of late descendants of the brothers who had committed that crime. The first is a tribal custom that was repeated periodically within the groups which, much later, had replaced the smaller hordes of primal times. The wider units that marked the first social organization had chieftains, late substitutes of the family father. The chieftain was absolute head of the tribe and usurped in later phases the place and authority of a king. Those primitive chiefs of tribes and their successors, for instance the godlike pharaohs of prehistoric Egypt, were periodically killed and eaten. These regicides developed later on into ritualistic acts performed whenever the chieftain or king became too old or too weak to enforce his authority.

Another repetition, acted out on a substitute object, was the totem meal of the tribe. As Freud has shown, totemism was the first form of religion in which a sacred animal took the place of the primal father, who was much later deified. The totem animal that the clan considered its ancestor and that it was forbidden to kill and eat was from time to time slaughtered and devoured by all members of the tribe. In this common totem meal, whose character was first recognized by Robertson Smith, not only the old crime was re-enacted, but also the incorporation by which the whole clan took possession of the envied power of the primal father and became united with him. By the by, the primitive totem meal also developed into a ritual whose traces can be found as late as in the Passover Festival of the Hebrews and in the Eucharist of Christianity. These two representative instances, historically and psychoanalytically explored, cast an excellent light on the origin of ritual in general. Ritual is in the form or system of ceremonies that evolved from tribal acts, performed under the influence of repetition compulsions. Those acts were originally reactions to the forgotten primal crime, measures of defense by which its repetition was warded off. Later on rituals included as well the provisions and conditions under which the repetition of the primal crime (on a displaced substitute) was allowed and finally evolved into sacred actions that repeated the forbidden deed. The tribal rites were originally activities or gestures, pantomimes, and dances without words or with only rudimentary verbal expressions. Only very late were the ceremonies accompanied by words and whole sentences.

Maybe the preceding digression is pardonable because it led us to a new concept of the origin and psychological character of ritual, but it is perhaps also justifiable because it continues the line of our inquiry into the nature of emotional repercussions from the fateful events in the primal family. We learned that memories of them were not entirely lost. They did not continue to live by word of mouth, but by means of actions, of compulsive repetitions displaced on a substitute for the primal father. The periodic killing of tribal chieftains and the totem meals are such repeated substitute acts, which were to develop into rituals of primitive societies. We still attribute the beginnings of these repetition compulsions to the Paleolithic or Old Stone Age, meaning the infancy of mankind; but the development of the repetitious acts can be pursued until late into the age of Neolithic man.

The lost memories whose traces we discovered in those rituals of the communities found new means of expression with increased speech faculty. With growing ability of articulation, experiences could be verbalized, memories could be caught and held in crude sentences—a process whose analogy can well be observed in the development of our children. Old experiences could be told and reported, formed into primitive narratives. That which once had to be played out could now be recounted. Here is the origin of what we call oral tradition and with it the beginning of myths, of stories in which the superstitious and animistic beliefs of the primitive mind try to formulate memories of the past. Here is thus the first crude form of history. It is appropriate to compare this breakthrough of memories—perhaps at the close of the Old Stone Age—with the emergence of childhood memories at the puberty of the individual. When boys and girls began to remember experiences of their early years, there is also observable an odd mixture of fantasy and truth in their stories. From the early transmission of tales about the past to the beginnings of writing, originally in pictorial representation, is a long way, an interval of many thousands of years. The fixation, and with it the early codification of myths, is to be found written in Egyptian hieroglyphs.

Our interest is less directed to this development whose continuation leads to the threshold of the writing of the Holy Scripture than to the relation of those repetition acts, later tribal rites, to the oral form of myths. Myths tell that which was once acted out in rituals. They present the verbal expression of the performances of the ritual, which is a plastic repetition, so to speak, a stage observance of the tribal history. The new instrument of the written word gave to the oral tradition of myths a durability that made it possible for us to examine them and to enter into research such as this. We started from the question: What possibilities are there of reconstructing that remote prehistory of mankind in which that family catastrophe took place, with the handicap of having lost all memory traces of the event?

We found obscure traces of memories in rituals, early reactions to the prehistoric happening. They finally took the shape of ancient oral traditions and then of myths, written down. We have completed a circle and return again to the Jahvistic myth in whose analytic exploration we discovered hidden traces of the primal murder and devouring of the father in whose image a hundred thousand years later Jahveh was formed.

The obscure character of the process justifies a second approach to the question from another angle: how did unconscious memories of the primal crime succeed in reaching the threshold of consciousness? Freud answers that a number of influences, some of which are unknown, may be responsible for such penetration. There are cases in which a spontaneous course is possible. An awakening of memory traces through a recent, real repetition of the event "is certainly of decisive importance." Freud[1] mentions as such repetitions that became causative agents the murder of Moses and the supposed execution of Christ. Freud alludes here to his hypothesis of a compulsion of repetition that operates when experiences of an overwhelming intensity threaten to flood a weak or not yet firmly constituted ego.

George Santayana summed up in one pregnant sentence the essence of Freud's theory of those compulsive tendencies. He said: "What man cannot remember, he is destined to repeat. . . ." Destined by what? Obviously, in the first place by the intensity of the impulses that press for satisfaction in those repetitive actions. Most powerful drives had found an explosive outlet in that crime. The brutes who had committed it were certainly not haunted by memory of that scene. Yet memories of it must have been

[1] *Moses and Monotheism* (New York, 1949), p. 160.

preserved in unconscious traces in many subsequent generations until they emerged in a dim and vague form at the
threshold of consciousness. In that long phase, unconscious
memory traces were kept alive and transmitted in phylogenetic inheritance. They were also reactivated by two
kinds of experiences, in which those precipitates from the
past of human civilization were revealed. From time to time,
revolutionary movements resulting in the murder of chieftains repeated the primordial crime and violent fights for
supremacy shook the foundation of the societies in the
making. Not only kings and tribal autocrats were killed,
but also the first lawgivers, priestly authorities, and prophets
fell victim to the unleashed aggressive drives of the crowd.

The second kind of repetitions had another form, which
emerged from the midst of already organized societies that
had acknowledged and submitted to a primitive order of
moral and religious laws. In these repetitions the repressed
impulses return out of the very center of the repressing
forces. As a matter of fact, they fit into that primitive frame
of early social and religious rule and regulation and were
made part of the tribal life. Not recognized as such repetitions, they nevertheless formed breakthroughs in which
these repressed impulses periodically found a displaced
and distorted substitute gratification. I mean the totem
meals, the clan ceremoniously killing and eating the animal
totem who was considered their ancestor, and ordinarily
tabooed. There is a direct line leading from the tribal totem
meal to the eater of the sacrifice to the gods.

We have still to answer the question of how the unconscious memory traces succeeded in penetrating the conscious mind; how they finally arrived at a tradition—
however distorted and altered—and how and when the
amnesia of mankind was broken. The sincere answer is, of

course, we do not know. We can only venture to express a guess, founded on the remnants of ancient myth and legends, on the one hand, and on analogies from child psychology and clinical observations of neurotic patients on the other. To begin with the second: We realize in analytic practice that many significant impressions and experiences of early childhood were repressed and are inaccessible to efforts to remember them. Some of them re-emerge later on in the form of screen memories behind which the real ones are concealed and whose significance and meaning are not recognized. Those memories from, say, the second to the fourth year were only recaptured at puberty. If we may reach a conclusion from this analogy, we would say that the ancient myths are such distorted or screen memories from the collective childhood of man and the time of their appearance in oral tradition can be compared to individual early puberty.[2] How does primitive man arrive at such oral tradition? It is obvious that this is not possible as long as his dictionary is not sufficient to tell a tale or verbalize a fantasy. Nothing can become conscious that cannot be grasped in word presentations. Again thinking of analogies from childhood psychology: strong impressions and experiences of great power are mastered by the small child not in talking about them, but in playing them. Playing them means renewing them, means emotionally conquering and

[2] One knows how misleading, even odious such analogies can be, yet cannot always resist the temptation to indulge in speculations of this kind. Science believes (Herbert Wendt, *In Search of Adam,* Boston, 1956) that "the human animal" assumed an upright posture about fifteen million years ago. That would roughly correspond to the individual age in which the infant makes the first step. The pictographic representation of the paleolithic man, from which developed later writing, traced as far back as 30,000 B.C., can be compared with the earliest attempts of a child to draw lines. Early mythical traditions, to be dated perhaps nine thousand years before our time, would thus correspond to the individual age of twelve years and present man has, comparatively speaking, reached the mature age of thirteen years—the age of juvenile delinquency.

absorbing them. In this sense the child applies, so to speak, elementary self-psychotherapy, play therapy. He is repeating and re-enacting things that threaten to overwhelm his psychical apparatus in order to diminish their reactive capacity. In a similar way, primitive man will try to "act out" in gestures, bodily movements, pantomimes, and dances the things that most impressed and affected him.

Words are at first very few and far between in those activities and will accompany them only much later, similar to the character of early children's play that contains more inarticulate shouts and murmurs than sentences. Slowly, and with words accompanying the doings, actions will be replaced and a song or tale, still very vividly told and with "telling" gestures frequently interrupted by pantomimes, will play a greater role. Running, dancing, and gesticulating as on a stage have an important part in those early narratives. What was first played or acted out is now told, yet the oral traditions have still a dramatic or even rather melodramatic character. The early myths were tragic plays, half acted, half recited. All passions and emotions of the "remembered" experiences were vividly expressed as though the past had become present and what had been was actually done or suffered. The first oral tradition of the past of the tribe was not simply a tale, but a dramatic presentation.

Such was the character of the original myths, conveyed from one generation to the next. The narrative form we know is the result of a later development. Telling a tale is a diluted, weakened, and thinned expression of acting or repeating the events in performance. Such reactivating has a freeing and cathartic, a "telling" effect. Even the narrative, which repeats the experience in words, has to a minor degree such a liberating, easing, and relieving effect. It is very likely that the undeniable therapeutic influence of confession is mainly due to the unconscious verbal gratification of those impulses that were satisfied in forbidden actions. In the memories connected with confession they are not only regretted but also repeated, not only repeated but also enjoyed.

In surveying the development from unconscious memory traces to the transformation into mythical tradition, we reached the point of junction with a problem from which we departed. We stated that experiences that had been preserved only in unconscious memory traces were repeated because intensive drives claimed periodical satisfaction. We observe in our analytic practice that a patient does not remember definite features of his childhood behavior, for instance that he was at a certain phase of his growth a naughty, rebellious, and quarrelsome boy, but he behaves naughtily, rebelliously, and quarrelsomely during the analytic sessions and toward the analyst. In this acting out, not only the elementary urge to express and gratify those old repressed impulses is operating.

The compulsion to repeat becomes complicated by a new, later emotional agent, namely by the influence of an unconscious need of punishment. The patient acts not only under the pressure of his instinctual drives, but also under the counterpressure of the moral powers that condemn their aim and unconsciously demand punishment. It is as though his objectionable and defiant behavior were not only an expression, but also the demonstration of those forbidden tendencies, returning from the repressed. In my book, *Geständniszwang und Strafbedürfnis,* I endeavored to show with the help of many clinical instances from analytic practice that the function of that behavior is unconscious confession. The old compulsion for repetition, caused by the inability to conquer intensive experiences, is modified

by the work of this new tendency emerging from unconscious guilt feeling. This new power has acquired an intensity equal to that of the primitive drives and is in its
dynamics and effects similar to them. It has its representation in an unconscious need to be punished. Its aim can
easily be guessed. The patient shows in the demonstration
of his behavior how wicked or malicious he was and that
he wants to be punished. But his behavior also proves that
he desires to obtain pardon and to regain love after and
through the punishment. The confession that is acted out
has its religious counterpart in the masochistic wish to
suffer and to acquire salvation by it. Punishment itself can
thus become the unconscious goal of instinctual drives and
suffering can be evaluated as proof of being loved. It is
this emotional soil from which the view sprang that "whom
the Lord loveth he chasteneth" (Hebrews 12:6).

CHAPTER XVII

THE EMERGENCE OF GUILT-FEELING

SOMEONE has said that without death we would have no philosophy. We could add that, without the violent death of the despotic father of the primal hordes, we would perhaps have no religion or morals. Both evolved, it is true, a thousand years later, in the phase when the social structure was that of the primitive clans of brothers, but both religion and morals were reaction formations to the great explosion that shook the foundations of the earliest human groups.

But we have progressed too rapidly and must return to our point of departure, the scene after the murder of the primal father. There he was, knocked down by clubs. It was all over but the shouting. There followed a wild outburst of victory and triumph. What were the immediate consequences of the dark misdeed, the reactions experienced by the murderous sons? "Did they sleep well after life's particularly fitful fever last night?" We guess, quite well—if they had no troubles of digestion after that gruesome meal together. We do not believe those killers were remorseful. They were savages and not very far removed from the ape-men, their kin and enemies. It would be obviously mistaken to attribute to them our human feelings; they were just at the process of becoming human. They certainly differed very much from criminals of today who would have committed such an atrocious deed.

We have no right to compare them with even the crudest and most barbaric lawbreakers of our time. No guilt feelings were felt by the murderous sons. Something akin to such a reaction, one could say, a kind of primal psychosomatic herald of it, was perhaps experienced on the day after the gruesome meal of the brothers.

We have no direct knowledge; all is reconstruction and guesswork, though informed guess. The mind of our most distant ancestors is as alien to us as that of another species. Yet on some strange and long detours some fragmentary bits of insight enable us to discover traces of the primeval crime and to conjecture what its nature must have been. "Murder will out," also in the evolution of our race. Before we inquire into the miraculous tongues that speak it, we would like to know what happened in the following time, what were the consequences and repercussions of that dark and terrible crime. Here also we can only guess and we had best follow the guidance of Freud, who sketched a picture of the subsequent development.

After the end of the patriarchal horde came a long phase of a fatherless society, an interregnum. It was filled with wild fights among the sons, who fought with each other, and each of whom tried to occupy the place and to exert the power of the father tyrant. Violent struggles among the brothers often led to fratricide, to a repetition of the primal deed, displaced to the competing brothers. As a matter of fact, the first murders of which the Semitic tradition tells, the primal crimes, are not the killing of a father, but of a brother. The legends of Osiris and Set, of Cain and

Abel present prominent cases of such murderous strife within the primitive society. In these and other myths—some of which are familiar to us since the days when we were told biblical stories—echoes from that phase of brother jealousy and brother hate reach us children of a progressed time in which murders of brothers became rare and are replaced by mass destruction within the brotherhood of mankind. When and how, after many centuries of wild competition and fights, the first form of social organization emerged is not known to us.

After innumerable violent episodes, trials, and errors in arriving at some tolerable form of living together, man finally founded a primitive kin company. There were perhaps at first attempts among the victorious brothers to share the females who had been the father's possessions. There were perhaps incestuous associations with mothers and sisters that could not be maintained on account of the envy and jealousy of the other members of the band. Whoever usurped the place of the murdered father within the clan and with the women he had left behind soon became the victim of strong hateful passions in his competitors. At the end, bands of males with equal rights emerged and after a long period families or clans with a father at the head evolved again, so to speak, as modified restorations of that primal form. The new fathers or chieftains were not any longer unrestricted in their power. Still despotic, they had to subject themselves to the supervision of the society. Their power was that of a tyrant, but of one whose life is not charmed, but rather endangered. The oldest primitive societies were dictatorships without much to dictate. (The late Karl Kraus once characterized the old Austro-Hungarian monarchy as "absolutism mitigated by sloppiness," "gemildert durch Schlamperei"!) The inflation of the person of the chieftain or king in the form of taboo belongs to a later phase.

Before this renewed or restored patriarchal form evolved, the interregnum was interrupted by matriarchy, by the rule of mother figures. They took over control in a way similar to that of widows with children after the authority of the father had passed into their hands after his demise. Bachofen[1] and many scholars following in his track have sketched that long phase of social order that was much later replaced with a new patriarchal order. This transformation came about by a combination of slow changes and revolutionary upheavals within the society. The dominating mothers had to yield their rule to their grown-up sons, a transition of which memories survived in legends and myths such as that of the Amazons. Again men were heads of the tribes; chieftains became, by and by, kings when many clans formed greater social units.

A very abbreviated history of the evolution of religion marks totemism as the oldest and most primitive form of religion. A most powerful, feared, and admired animal was the first god clansmen worshiped, from whom they traced their descent, and with whom they thought to be as intimately associated as children with their father. Our early ancestors, to whom our condescending attitude toward animals was alien, saw in that beast an impersonation of their tribal ancestor. Remorse about that old crime, reactive admiration and love for the primal father, and the striving to undo that deed worked together in the establishment of the most important command, forbidding the killing and eating of the totemistic animal. The subsequent development, passing through many transformations, characterized

[1] Bachofen, *Das Mutterrecht* (Stuttgart, 1861).

by mixed figures such as the centaurs, satyrs, and sphinxes resulted finally in the restoration of human anthropomorphic gods.

It is likely that the first deities in human form were great mother-goddesses. Those female figures were certainly conceived originally as very earthy, and as endowed with abundant bodily curves. Aphrodite Calypigos is still a voluptuous woman with a hypertrophic behind and the "Venus of Willendorf," excavated in Austria, proves that this was for paleolithic man an indispensable attribute of goddesses. A late echo of such idols was still found when female figures were symbolizing countries. Heinrich Heine, returning from his Parisian exile to Germany, runs into the goddess of the city of Hamburg. He first thinks her an average woman, but the superhuman backside showed a divine being:

> I first believed
> Her to be a woman average,
> But the superhuman posterior
> Revealed a higher personage.

Those goddesses were first conceived as embodiments and incarnations of sexual desires: Venus, Astarte, Isis, and Ishtar were all great mother-idols of sexual fulfillment. Only much later did they acquire also the character of charity, of desexualized love, and of sympathy and became patronesses of the unhappy. But cruelty and destructiveness were also not alien to their character; they were often imagined as goddesses of death and destruction. Their resemblance to the Holy Mary of Christianity was restricted to their divine nature and their position of mothers of son-gods.

Otherwise they were rather the antithesis of the virginity and chastity attributed to the mother of the Saviour. The most popular goddess of the Babylonians, Ishtar, had Tammuz as her lover, as Isis had Osiris, Astarte had Adonis, and Cybele had Attis. All those young lovers shared a terrible end; they were killed, castrated, or torn to pieces by wild animals. Each death was lamented by their mistresses and mothers. In their deep mourning for their sweethearts, those divine women resemble the pietà figures of medieval art. All young son-gods are resurrected, finally elevated to the kingdom of Heaven or Olympus, and their re-emergence is celebrated with the greatest joy.

In the evolution of religious ideas the appearance of great and supreme father-god figures who pave the way to the monotheistic deities, such as Aton of the Egyptians and Jahveh of the Hebrews, marks a very late and progressed phase. The incomparable majesty and superiority, the omnipotence and ubiquity, but also the ferocity and venge-fulness of those figures idealize the memory of fathers of the primitive hordes. Prehistory repeats itself in the emer-gence of the more recent figures of a divine son, who is sacrificed and tortured, is resurrected and ascends to heaven. He is destined to take his place at the side of the God-father, to replace him at the end.

We said before that the cannibalistic sons felt no guilt after their murderous deed. "The access and passage to remorse," to use Lady Macbeth's words, were not yet open to those subhuman creatures. It is possible that the first reactions to their gruesome act were of the nature of digestive disturbances. Perhaps the flesh of that body, hastily and voraciously gulped down, did not agree with them and caused fits of indigestion. The dead father within them seemed to bite back. This is the first and elementary ap-pearance on earth of what was known, a hundred thousand years later, as remorse. The meaning of the expression "remorse" can be traced etymologically: re = back + mordere = to bite. The eaten object bites back, so to speak. The delusions of paranoiac patients and their stomach symptoms, in which the regression to the oral phase manifests itself, seem to confirm the origin of the metaphor.

The analysis of a case of obsessional neurosis, treated almost thirty years ago, provided an excellent opportunity to guess the origin of the metaphorical expression, "remorse."[2] During the analysis, the father of the patient, who was a British physician, died. Besides the doubts that usually arise after such an event, for instance the question of whether or not everything necessary was done for the father during his illness and whether or not the patient had always shown enough affection for him, anxious dreams and unpleasant ideas tortured the man. There was, for example, the half-conscious fear that a ghost or a skeleton would come into the bedroom of the patient during his sleep. An especially absurd fantasy, connected with intensive anxiety, announced itself first in a rather vague manner: the patient reported that he was sometimes bothered by the image of a horse as he sat reading and smoking in the room of his father. The complete text of that compulsive idea, as could be reconstructed in the analysis of the dreams, was: the horse of the father's funeral carriage will come into the room and bite the patient. The character of the obsessive idea, which disappeared after its analysis, casts a light on the original meaning of the metaphor of remorse. The analytic reduction of the obsessive thought confirms the assumption that the primal fear of being eaten emerges in remorse, a fear which will be transformed later on into ambiguous, social anxiety. At the core of remorse was the

[2] The case was first presented in lectures in Vienna in 1924, and is described in *Geständniszwang und Strafledürfnis* (1925), p. 122.

archaic fear of being devoured by the father or the father totem.

The opportunity provided by the analysis of this case could be used to illustrate the difference between this infantile anxiety and its later part as the concealed core of guilt feeling. In the mysterious dreams of the patient after the death of the father, an uncanny, somber figure appeared again and again. He had puzzling and strange features and seemed to look at the patient threateningly. I was attempting to identify this person with the dead father, but many characteristic trends did not tally with this assumption. The figure had also something—but what?—to do with the horse that had emerged in those bizarre obsessional thoughts of the patient. To the astonishment of both analyst and patient, and after many conjectures and misinterpretations, we had to acknowledge that the mysterious figure was Napoleon. The patient had at no time experienced any special interest in the great Corsican and it was puzzling why he should enter into his dreams. The solution of that little problem came from a memory of early childhood. The patient had spent an important part of it (until nearly the third year) on an island near Saint Helena. The natives there had preserved in their tradition the memory of the sojourn of Napoleon. The patient once remembered that his old, colored nurse had often threatened him: "Boni will catch (or eat!) you if you aren't a good child." He had first confused Boni with a small horse. A later inquiry must have conveyed to him the knowledge that the dreaded Boni was identical with the great antagonist of the British.

There is a far cry from the obsessional and superstitious fear of my patient to the elementary and crude emotions of those brutes, the subhuman members of the gang who killed and devoured their father. Yet emotions similar to those that emerged in the neurotic patient might have announced themselves in a dull, unclear way in the prehistoric murderers. There was perhaps that transitory psychosomatic symptom of a digestive complaint. It was followed and replaced many generations later by another form of fear, in which the dread of retaliation consciously appeared without any connection with its origin. It is very likely that whenever we now feel remorse, that deep, painful regret for having done wrong, the fear of cannibalistic retaliation is unconsciously experienced. (It "gnaws" at us.) Remnants of that feared punishment, whose nature became utterly alien to our conscious thoughts, still survive in many myths and in the fairy tales of our children, such as Hänsel and Gretel, the Gingerbread Man, and so on. It is that fear that is at the hidden core of the dread of imminent calamity in the thoughts of our obsessional patients.

The preceding paragraphs claim to be acknowledged as legitimate modification, complement to, and continuation of Freud's theories as presented in his *Totem and Taboo*. They continue the sketch of the events within the primitive horde and fill the gap left there, concerning the reactions of the murderous sons. At the same time they bridge the gulf between the emotional situation and that of many millennia later in which the first signs of guilt feelings emerge. We characterized those first reactions as psychosomatic representatives of elementary remorse. They were replaced by superstitious fears of cannibalistic retaliation. The hypothesis here presented has perhaps provided the missing psychological link and tied the first digestive remorse reactions with later forms of guilt feelings, undoubtedly of an aggressive and masochistic nature also ("pangs of conscience").

A phase of the emotional life of our most distant an-

cestors, until now undiscovered, becomes understandable
in the unfolding of this process of neurotic and psychotic
patients in whom similar emotional processes can be
conjectured. Tracing back of remorse and guilt feelings has
a bearing on the analytic theory of the origin and character
of the collective sense of guilt. It makes necessary a modification of Freud's hypothesis, contained in *Civilization and
Its Discontents*. Freud asserts that guilt feeling is a reaction
to the unconscious emergence of aggressive drives and is
really the anxiety resulting from the temptation of aggressive actions. Analysis of the origin and nature of the sense
of guilt, its reduction to archaic cannibalism, modifies this
characterization. It has to be changed into an evolution-
ary explanation of the sense of guilt as reaction to fear
of the temptation of cannibalistic trends, originally as
retaliatory fear of being eaten. This seems to be a purely
theoretical consideration, but it has far-reaching consequences with regard to our understanding not only of
neurotic pathology, but also of the psychology of early
childhood. Continuing Freud's research, we arrived at a
point far beyond that reached by psychoanalysis today. As
a by-product of the exploration of prehistoric events, a new
insight into the developing process of unconscious guilt
feelings dawned on us.

Without planning it, yes, without even being aware of
it, following only the course of prehistoric development
and compelled by the immanent necessities of the psychological material, we have returned to the general subject
material of this book, to the origin of the collective sense
of guilt. We have picked up the thread with which we
started this work. Again we turn our attention to the question of how finally, after years of obscurity, a conscious
sense of guilt emerged in ancient civilization. We will, it is

true, not encounter it in this defined shape, but as a feeling of sinfulness, because it first reached consciousness in the area of religion. In the situation after the murder, several emotional factors favored a slowly emerging negative reaction among the brothers. The deed could not fully satisfy the drives that had propelled it: each brother wanted to have the place, the power, and the women that belonged to the father. None could usurp them because each had to share them with the others. In a certain sense, the crime was committed in vain. This want of success, certainly not recognized but vaguely experienced, was responsible for a kind of depression that heralded the birth of guilt feelings.

Another powerful element, increasing in intensity, was longing for the father. The brothers had not only hated him; they had also admired and loved him. Now when he was not around any more and his brutalities and savage cruelties were not any longer painfully experienced, he was missed. Unconscious memory traces awakened in them a kind of elementary longing for him and his presence. The part that this love plays in the genesis of guilt feelings was often overlooked, but the importance of that desire or yearning grew with time. It intensified the strange anxiety that occurred when a new situation awakened the temptation to repeat the old crime. The ghost of the murdered father haunted the guilty mind.

CHAPTER XVIII

THE TENSION BEFORE CHRIST

ONLY MEMORY traces of that evil deed had remained in the late descendants of the generations following the brother horde. The totemistic systems had been replaced by religions in which many gods, a hierarchy of gods, reflected the greater units such as the tribes and nations that had evolved from the primitive clan. Those gods slowly regained human shape and appeared first as despots, but later also as the benefactors and protectors of man who submitted to their will. The higher forms of society had brought rules and regulations of conduct that were partly determined by the necessities of self-preservation, partly by the compulsive defenses built to prevent a repetition of that misdeed. By and by, there developed laws decreed in the name of the powerful gods. They should check murderous and violently aggressive drives against members of one's own people, chieftains, kings, and priests. As reward for "good behavior" and as recompense for the control of antisocial drives, God was supposed to love and take care of the tribesmen who worshiped him and obeyed his commandments. With their compliance and yielding, renunciation of the most urgent and impatient strivings of the masses was connected.

The first inhibitions and prohibitions originated in practical interests of the primitive society, especially as reactions to the explosions of violent impulses. They had taken the form of taboos, setting apart certain objects and persons as sacred or considered untouchable. Those persons and things were such that they aroused the temptation to transgress the primitive laws erected against murder and incest. The emergence of temptations at their nearness or presence awakened a dark but intensive anxiety, the first form of what we now know as guilt feelings. Their original nature can be characterized as temptation anxiety, anxiety at the certainty that yielding to the temptation will bring not only punishment but also condemnation, loss of the protection one enjoys as a member of the community, expulsion, and with it the state of the outlaw; that means perdition. This gloomy outlook is precisely the collective analogy to the anxiety a small child experiences when he wants to do something naughty and is afraid of losing the love of his parents and being deserted by them.

With the repeated emergence of temptations, this social anxiety becomes more emphasized and oppressive. In the place of the chieftains and of the members of the tribe from whom punishment and expulsion are dreaded, gods will, later on, function as guardians of the unwritten tribal laws. All dangers and miseries are now feared as coming from them. Safety and protection are only in submission to them, in unconditional surrender to the prohibitions and renunciations they demand. With the raising of moral standards and with the enforcement of the laws of larger unities, the temptations became more urgent and unconscious guilt feelings increased the more conscientiously they were avoided. We remind the reader of what was said in the beginning about the origin and character of unconscious

guilt feelings. They are born as anxiety at the emergence
of temptations, remain at their core a social anxiety, and
increase in intensity the more frequently temptations occur.
Re-emergence of temptation reinforces the vigilance of
conscience, makes a sharper and more rigorous maintaining
of precautions and avoidance necessary. It produces, also,
more measures of defense against the dangers of yielding,
raises the moral demands of the inner watchman on the
ego which, in turn, arouses the reaction of new and more
urgent temptations.

A vicious circle appears in the sense, too, that the forbidden and repressed desires obtain the character of most
dangerous vices, which they did not originally possess. Thus
it comes about that the person who has high moral demands
on himself and lives a life of renunciation of his most urgent desires has a more intense guilt feeling because the
denial of satisfaction causes an increase of temptations,
which produce new anxiety. Saint Anthony, living in the
desert, is not only more tempted by most voluptuous visions
and lascivious images, but feels guiltier, too, than the
habitual visitor to burlesque shows. Repression surrounds
the desired objects with an allure they do not have otherwise, and attributes to them power and peril beyond
reality.

We understand that the victory over temptation, the
conquest or mastery of desires, aroused pride and sometimes
even conceit and self-righteousness. This pride is founded
on the awareness that one is entitled to reward for good
behavior, comparatively speaking, to the praise and love
of one's parents to whom one was obedient against the
heavy odds of tempting and forbidden gratification. The
loyalty of the Jews is thus rewarded by Jahveh in the

promise that they are His chosen people, His favored children. It cannot be denied that the Jews maintained a special kind of pride or conceit on account of this belief in their being chosen by the Lord. In correspondence with the ubiquity of the development in which increasingly severe moral codes demanded and exerted obedience to religious laws, every nation at one time or another has asserted itself to be the favorite of its god—otherwise put, to be the "chosen people." The character of this claim reminds one of the remark of Anatole France that while the relative strength and scale of the navies of different nations is known and acknowledged, every country justifiedly claims to have the first army of the world.

Here is the psychological and lawful succession: inhibitions of drives—temptation—guilt feeling—increased temptation—increased guilt feeling. This sequence has more than sociological significance in the evolution of civilization. It is plausible that the vicious circle dominated the development of ancient and modern culture, or was at least a decisive factor in the process of evolution of human civilization. In other words, it is part and parcel of the pathology of our society. If this be correct, we will have hit upon another discovery in the realm of collective psychology. Fumbling and groping about in the dark for the solution of the problems of unconscious guilt feeling of the masses, we stumbled over the difficulty of finding a connection between obedience to the severe laws and the sense of guilt that grew sharper and more acute.

Looking back like a person who glances at the obstacle that made him trip, we found that we had not seen or not acknowledged the important factor of expanding unconscious temptation. To our own surprise, we came by that

slip upon a still undiscovered psychological law operating
with the inevitability of the laws of physics, and governing
the course of human civilization. The far-reaching consequences of the discovery of this law cannot be foreseen.
From time to time revolutionary changes within religion
itself bring about a lessening of the guilt feeling conditioned
by accumulated temptations. The pressure from that social
anxiety, the feeling of sinfulness has then become so great
and self-pervasive that it has become unbearable. There
remains only one possibility of mastering the omnipresent
temptation: yield to it. It was in this sense that Luther
proclaimed, "Sin bravely!" (Pecca fortiter!)

The succession of aggravating observances of religious
and moral laws and increased guilt feeling (in the theological term the sense of sinfulness) must have been a general
phenomenon in the different civilizations of the ancient
Orient. We restrict ourselves to the discussion of the civilization that became most important for our Western World,
namely that of the Judaeo-Christian section. In support of
this preference, I can bring forward the likelihood that the
new point of view, resulting from the introduction of that
psychological law, will most probably correct the false assumptions and replace prejudices and biased opinions about
that era. It will perhaps change our views about the course
our civilization has taken and is going to take in the near
future.

As the ages rolled by, the unconscious guilt feeling,
dimly and shallowly perceived, had reached such an intensity and acuteness that a breakthrough into consciousness
became an organic consequence. It seems that to a great
extent a general depression determined by that guilt feeling
had taken possession of the Mediterranean peoples around

800 B.C. In the case of the Hebrews, the national disinte-
gration was helpful in this development. The agony and
anguish of the nation did not have the consequence that the
Jews turned against Jahveh who had prepared their doom.
They turned against themselves. A child who is punished
by his parents and who does not understand why assumes in
his feelings, nevertheless, that he must have been naughty.
He does not conclude that his parents were wrong. He does
not doubt the wisdom and justice of the elders—he must be
guilty. Thus the Jews felt that they must have sinned since
Jahveh had surrendered them to their enemies and had
delivered them to oppression, poverty, and misery. But the
national misfortunes were only one of the causes of the
increasing depression in Judaism. Faith had developed, in
the course of centuries, more and more into a religion of
instinctual renunciation. Such renunciation has not been
present in religion from the beginning, but now plays a
prominent part in it. The prophets insisted that God demands, above all, the virtuous life from His people—in
Freud's words, "abstention from the gratifications that,
according to our present-day moral standards, are to be
condemned as vicious."

The prophets were not the initiators of the sense of guilt
that is a phenomenon of the masses, but they kept it alive,
nourished it and, again and again, made the sinfulness of
the Jews responsible for the bad times of the nation and
for the doom they foresaw. Behind the superficial motivation that the Jews did not observe the laws of Jahveh
appears the deeper source of the guilt, the unconscious
knowledge of the primordial murder. We have already
said—and we agree here with Freud—that the Jews accepted the severe judgment of their sinfulness. Their guilt

feeling manifested itself in a need for punishment that was only partly satisfied by the national misfortunes. Freud pointed out that this insatiable feeling of guilt made them render their religion ever more strict, more exacting, but also more petty: "In a new transport of moral asceticism the Jews imposed on themselves constantly increasing instinctual renunciation." While Freud emphasized that they thereby reached "at least in doctrine and precept, ethical height that had remained inaccessible to the other peoples of antiquity . . ." the second great achievement of their religion besides its pure monotheism; and it is the reverse side of this development that we want to make the object of psychological exploration.

We turn, in a sense, the stone the Jewish prophets erected as an eternal memorial for Jahveh's glory to glance at what is beneath it. Behind the sin of idolatry and of worship of pagan cults the sin of aggression and attack against Jahveh is concealed. Not desertion, not apostasy was the real crime of which the prophets accused the Jews, but revolt against their God and the moral commandments He had given. It is a misconception to assume that the corruption, moral laxity, and dissoluteness of the nation were much greater at the time of the prophets than before. The rituals and ceremonials of Judaism were more conscientiously followed. That means that the Jewish people, in the time of national disaster, turned anxiously to service and sacrifice. Did the prophets not again and again proclaim that such conscientiousness in observance is not enough? What they felt and unconsciously feared was something else: that the anxious observance of the laws was constructed only as an external bulwark. It was built against the increasing temptation to throw off the intolerable prohibitions. It blocked gratifica-

tion of drives more and more on account of the condemnation from within. The sinfulness or the sense of guilt of
the nation sprang from the repressed temptations that pervaded the everyday life of the Jews.

The guilt feelings that Jeremiah, Ezekiel, and the other
prophets kept reiterating were meant to protect the Jewish
people against the danger of a breakthrough. They served
as a defense more powerful than sacrifice and the other
rites against the urgency of unsatisfied and insatiable drives.
The comparison with the dynamics of obsessional neurosis
is here most illuminating. These emotional disturbances set
in with symptoms of defense or rejection of the intense, forbidden impulse, mostly of a sexual nature. (In the case of
religion, the drives that are warded off are for the greatest
part cruel, aggressive and hostile.) Measures of defense,
for instance, puzzling and irrational actions that have to be
repeated, certain individual ceremonials, have to be observed. They protect the patient from the anxiety he feels
when he is tempted to yield to those forbidden trends. The
more urgent the temptation becomes, the more severely the
compulsive actions have to be performed. They become
more extended and expanded to the point that, at the end,
they preoccupy almost the whole day of the obsessional
patient. The danger of their slightest transgression awakens
an intense anxiety, corresponding to the feeling of sinfulness
in the religious field. Suspending the observance of the
compulsive ceremonials, of the performance of these pro-
tective actions, threatens the patient with all kinds of
dangers, illness, misery, and death. It is unconsciously
equivalent to a full breakdown of all moral restrictions that
he acknowledges for himself. Trapped between the urge
of vital desires that he forbids himself to gratify and the

tyranny of his obsessional, enforced, and aggravated duties, the patient is a helpless victim of the conflict that produced his serious affliction.

This is exactly the situation of the Jews in the period of the prophets and of the centuries before Christ. The prophets fought the increasing temptation, deepened the sense of sinfulness of their people, and threatened them with the danger of perdition if they yielded to temptation. But they also encouraged them, gave them hope, and promised the eternal support of the Lord if they resisted the temptation. At the same time, they devaluated the external performance of ceremonies that correspond to the compulsive ceremonial of the obsessional neurotic and emphasized the value of virtuous living, raising the ethical standards of the nation. In other words, they tried to break down the religious compulsiveness, but blocked the road to instinctual gratification.

It cannot be denied that the prophets prepared for the emergence of a religious upheaval such as that of Christianity by putting the sinfulness of the Jews into the center of their message. Christianity in its Paulinic form, that is, in the essential doctrine that conquered the world, continued to abolish the ceremonial laws, re-enforced the prohibitions of instinctual gratification, and elevated the ethical demands beyond human tolerance. The prophets who had proclaimed perhaps the noblest and most spiritual values of the world had also prepared the revolt against Jahveh in whose sacred name they spoke. In the message of Deutero-Isaiah the figure of the suffering servant appeared whose part Jesus Christ took over and perhaps unconsciously wished to act.

In the speeches of the prophets, a new idea emerges or rather an old idea had obtained a new content and significance: the thought of salvation.[1] At the same time the expression "Messiah" was filled with a new meaning. The Redeemer or Saviour was originally conceived as a king who overthrows the enemies of the Jewish people and rebuilds the temple, destroys sin on earth, and reconciles God with mankind.

If we want to discover the deep psychological significance of the idea of salvation, we have to put aside all later theological and eschatological meanings. Salvation, redemption from what? Obviously, deliverance from sin and from punishment for sinning. Since "the wages of sin is death," that would mean deliverance from death, thus immortality. This is one side of the idea: it means that the anxiety connected with temptation or, as we can now substitute, guilt feeling should be removed. This can be reached by sinlessness, by purification from sin, by release from the dangers that threaten the transgressor.

The other side is: temptation can also be removed by fully indulging those forbidden desires, by revolt against the severity of God's prohibitions. Both sides are contained in the thought, properly speaking, in the utopian idea of salvation; the one conscious and conspicuous, the other repressed and hidden. They meet in the most urgent wish of redemption from the tension under which the ego suffers

[1] According to the article, "Salvation," by Morris Joseph, in the *Encyclopedia of Ethics and Religion,* XI, p. 138, Judaism has no equivalent for the word used theologically. The one aspect of the idea, redemption from sin, is covered by the term "nekiyouth"; there is no phrase for the other, deliverance from its consequences. Salvation in the Old Testament has various meanings and stands for deliverance from enemies, victory, redemption from captivity, and so on. In Isaiah 45:17, 49:8, 60:18 it connotes fulfillment of Israel's mission and the conquest of the Gentiles. The essential premise of redemption is the worship of the one true God. One of His instruments is Israel: "I will also give thee for a light to the Gentiles, that thou mayest be my salvation unto the end of the earth" (Isaiah 49:6).

between the two extremes of instinctual renunciation and satisfaction. The aim is the same: to extricate oneself from temptation, to get rid of the intolerable double pressure from the side of the drives and from the side of guilt feeling. Liberation from this emotional impasse can be reached in one of the two directions. Heinrich Heine has pointed them out in the lines:

> When sinful desire I could suppress,
> I was blissful beyond measure.
> But when I did not succeed,
> I also had considerable pleasure.

It was scarcely acknowledged in the pertinent literature that salvation has unconsciously also an instinct-liberating aim. The misery of guilt feeling in the fight and conquest of temptations had become as oppressing as the anxiety following gratification of forbidden desires. People were more frustrated, wretched, exhausted when they had resisted the evil than when they had yielded to it. The struggle was beyond human strength.

Only a god, only that God who had condemned weak mortals to the fatal suspense, could release them from the impasse. Only a god who was subjected to the same temptations, but who remained sinless, could be the Redeemer. Only a superior being who shared all the frailties of human nature, but was at the same time divine, could carry all the sins of mankind and remain free of guilt.

We know the outcome of the experiment that the Almighty made in sending His son who met those requirements. That result was not very encouraging. It has not fulfilled the hope that a guilt-ridden mankind had cherished. Also the hope for the atonement of guilt is an illusion. Man continued to feel guilty even when he did not sin, when he conquered the temptations.[2] The anxious suspense, springing from the free-floating feeling of guilt, had been lifted for a very short time, but it grew again. It has since reached an almost intolerable degree in our civilization. The faint sound of a sigh has become a cry of tormented mankind, heard over the world: Redemption for the redeemed!

---

[2] For the history of mankind in whose memory the original crime lives on in repressed forms Freud considers it not really a decisive matter whether one has "killed one's father or abstained from the deed: one must feel guilty in either case." (*Civilization and Its Discontents,* p. 128.)

PART THREE

THE PUNISHMENT

Breach for breach, eye for eye, tooth for tooth;
as he hath caused a blemish in a man, so shall
it be done to him again.

Leviticus 24:20.

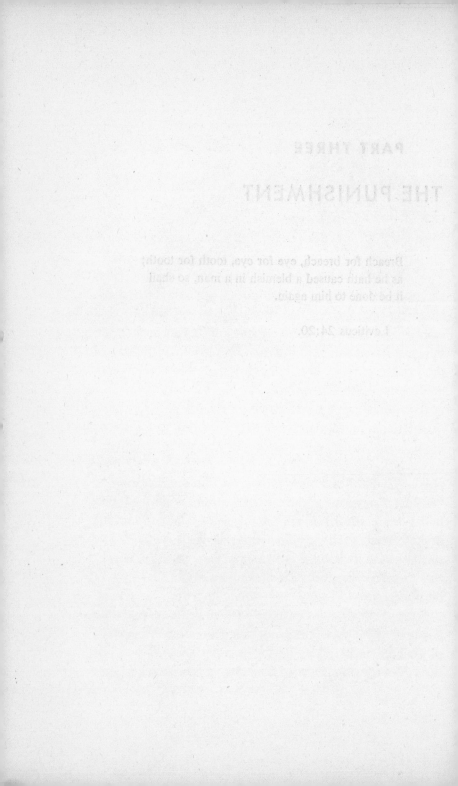

CHAPTER XIX

TOWARD REPEAT PERFORMANCE

THE GREAT slogan in present American psychoanalytic literature is emotional maturity. With the charming optimism of our young nation we imagine that emotional maturity can be reached by anyone who tries. It is just a technological question of know-how. As one of the easiest ways of obtaining that desirable aim psychoanalysis is recommended.

In contrast with such refreshing naïveté the wise men of all times agree that emotional maturity can only be approached in old age and at the cost of suffering and renunciation. Confucius, one of the great figures of religious philosophy, said of himself almost two thousand years ago: "At fifty I understood the law of heaven; at sixty nothing that I heard disturbed me; at seventy I could follow the desires of my heart without transgressing the right." Only so late was this wise man near to obtaining "peace of mind," an almost-balance between the impulses and demands of the superego.

So much or so little for the individual problem, but what about emotional maturity of man in general? We conceived of civilized mankind as having reached about the age of early puberty with all its crises and conflicts. Our species is obviously not very progressed on its march to emotional maturity. We often see a kind of make-believe prematurity, it is true, but that is a funny pretense similar to that of a little boy who puts on the hat of his father and carries his cane. Thinking of historical phases in comparative terms, how long ago was it since Christ died on Calvary? Considering the ages of evolution of human civilization from the early Stone Age, it was only yesterday. We are in the middle of the same painful dilemmas, trapped in the same impasse from which He vainly searched for an escape. There is still the same emotional misery for which no religion can offer more than short-lived and deceptive palliatives. There is still the same basic conflict between the innate aggressiveness of man and the cultural impossibility of satisfying its urge, between gratification of drives and guilt feelings since their repression and renunciation are necessary in the interest of civilization. The German poet, Friedrich von Schiller, a noble idealist if ever there was one, said:

> No other choice is left to man; he has to find
> His way between sensual pleasure and peace of mind.

But has he a choice? That's the question here. The psychologist will confirm that not even the chance of a choice is given to man as long as he is young and vigorous. The other day a wise writer thoughtfully remarked that it is not true that when we grow old we leave our vices behind us. They rather leave us. It seems that man is condemned to oscillate between a restricted and uneasy gratification of his drives and a regretful and guilt-loaded renunciation.

Perhaps we have not considered sufficiently that all religions have tried to cope with this problem and all in vain. Think of a culture that is very alien to ours, the

Chinese civilization. After a long, early phase of ancestor worship of the people of Shang (fourteenth to twelfth century B.C.) came a critical phase (after 700 B.C.) in which skepticism attacked the old superstitions and no strong authority was generally acknowledged. Two great schools of thought finally emerged, that of Confucius and that of Lao-tzu. Both searched for a way to satisfy natural instincts and at the same time to avoid social conflicts. Lao-tzu's disciple, Chuang-tzu, interpreted the doctrine of the old master in such a way that asceticism as well as wild orgies could be found in the originally simple school of Taoism. About the time of Christ, Buddhism coming from India invaded China and its doctrine of asceticism, sometimes reaching even to the extent of self-mutilation, conquered the Chinese people. In spite of all modifications of the doctrine in the following centuries the state of Nirvana, the extinction of craving or passion, remained the core of Buddhism. But this doctrine, which appears so alien to our western civilization, also presents a desperate attempt to escape that old conflict between the urge of the drives and the suppressing powers that owe their strength to the memory of distant ancestors. But that is essentially the same conflict that Jesus Christ tried to solve on the cross, the same impasse into which the religions of the Greek and Roman Empires, the Persian and Jewish doctrines inevitably led. There was no easy escape from the pressure of the drives and none from the pangs of conscience. It was impossible fully to renounce instinctual gratification and almost intolerable to go through life crushed by guilt feelings.

The feeling of guilt increased in prophetic and post-prophetic times until it reached one of its peaks and crises with Christianity, strictly speaking, with the concept of

Jesus Christ in the mind of Saul of Tarsus. As Freud points out, the consciousness of guilt in that epoch was no longer restricted to the Jews: "it had seized all Mediterranean people as a vague discomfort, a premonition of misfortune, the reason for which no one knew."[1] Freud surmised that modern history, speaking of the aging of antique culture, apprehends only some of the adjuvant causes for that mood of dejection prevailing among the Mediterranean people. He finds the deeper sources of that depression in guilt feeling, owing to the repressed aggressiveness of the masses.

Yet there must have been special motives for such increased guilt feeling in the emotional situation of that epoch. The atmosphere in Rome, in Greece, in Judaea, everywhere that civilization had reached a high point, was wrought with discomfort and a kind of moral malaise. The feeling of impending calamity on one side and an ardent hope for salvation on the other were pervasive. A sense of urgency filled the emotional air, as if doomsday were near or redemption were around the corner. This mood announces itself in the sayings of the Hebrew prophets and is clearly expressed in the Gospels and in the epistles of Paul.

But it is also to be perceived in the documents of Greek and Roman civilizations, in the speeches and writings of Greek philosophers and Roman observers of life. The maxims of Marcus Aurelius, the teachings of the Epicureans, the arguments of Lucretius bear witness of such a defeatist attitude. Thus are the principles of the Stoics who strove for ataraxia, which is somewhat akin to the Buddhist goal of a state of peace undisturbed by human passions. All these, and many other manifestations of the urgent desire to find a way into the open, show that the human situation

[1] *Moses and Monotheism*, p. 213.

in the centuries before Christ had reached a critical point. The general explanation that the ancient civilizations were on the decline does not satisfy us. We would like to know what were the special reasons for the mood of dejection and defeatism pervading the civilized world. Doubtless some of them we shall never know.

Some others we can only guess, but there are a few that can be defined with some accuracy. To the second group belong certainly some economic and sociological changes, for instance the accumulation of riches in the hands of a small class of society, the increasing misery of the masses, the luxury in the highest layers of society in contrast with the indescribable poverty on the lowest stratum. There was, furthermore, the increasing rebelliousness of the slaves and of the oppressed masses. It is not accidental that Christianity started with poor Galilean fishermen and day workers and spread especially among the poor. Nietzsche intuitively recognized that condition when he called the spirit of the new religion a "Sklavenaufstand in der Moral."

Religion and morals had erected mighty roadblocks to instincts that most urgently demanded gratification. Aggression that had been forbidden in primitive society against members of the tribe became increasingly condemned in general and the demand for an affectionate or charitable attitude toward members of one's own clan was extended to such a degree that it finally reached the absurd command to love one's enemy. Moral laws to which the authority of priests gave most efficient force put higher and higher demands on the people in other directions also. A net of rules and regulations had, in the name of religion, entangled and complicated the lives of all. Sacrifices, ceremonials, and rituals that became more and more petty and exacting claimed energy, time, and material privation. The progress of civilization—if progress it was—was paid for by loss of joy of life in other directions as well.

Love in the romantic sense was unknown in prehistoric times. With the exception of Egyptian love poems and perhaps the Song of Solomon, antiquity had no notion corresponding to our experience of romance. To the Greek of the classic period, to the Hebrew even of postexilic time, to the Roman of the early empire, Goethe's statement that the "Eternal Feminine" draws us above would have been incomprehensible. At best, he would perhaps have acknowledged it as valid for the male genital since the fulfillment of sexual desire was highly appreciated.

Aggravation of prohibitions and extension of restrictions on sexual activities appeared at the end phase of the declining ancient civilization. It had two opposite effects: on one side, as in Palestine, a wave of asceticism, an inclination to sexual restraint and abstinence, in early Christianity even the demand for chastity; on the other hand, as in Rome, breakthroughs that did not acknowledge any frontiers and led to orgies in which all aberrations were not only allowed, but preferred. By the devaluation of sex, life became impoverished, but with the lifting of all prohibitions life itself lost much of its color and content. Christianity heralded by the mystery cults gave sex a new stimulation. Anatole France praises this effect of Christianity, which did much for l'amour in rendering it a sin.

If I might digress a few moments, I would take this occasion to differentiate three decisive changes in the evolution of sexuality, from which I exclude the earliest transformation determined by the loss—strictly speaking by the decrease—of the periodicity of sexual desires that man had in common with the animals. At first, gratification of the sexual appetite or release of sexual tension was the only goal of the drive. The object was not important. It was instinctual satisfaction without respect for the person. Freud once remarked that antiquity greatly appreciated sexual satisfaction itself without discrimination of objects, while modern times allow sexual gratification only when the objects are appreciated.[2] Slowly the qualities of the object, especially the physical endowments, were acknowledged and appreciated. With the entrance of ascetic doctrines, but especially with that of Christianity, the sexual interest received new stimulation by the alleged sinfulness of sensuality. The new obstacle had been erected to be conquered. A resistance had to be overcome and with that new enticement the sexual desire became intensified. The forbidden object enhanced the attraction and removed the casual and condescending attitude of declining ancient civilizations toward sexuality.

The third modification is characterized by the introduction of the romantic factor into sex. As a continuation of the chastity that the church recommended and in the wake of new values, favored by the Renaissance, especially by virtue of chivalry, sexuality received a new stimulus and the object seemed to have an augmented lure.

The subject of unfulfilled sexual urges is welcome to us when we return to the theme of general dissatisfaction and discontent among the Mediterranean peoples. Many men had submitted to religious concepts that were antagonistic to sexual gratification and favored abstinence. We heard earlier that repression of sexual urges indirectly increases guilt feeling because the temptation strengthens the unconscious hostility against the prohibiting persons or laws. We made the paradoxical observation in analytic practice that

[2] *Three Contributions to the Theory of Sex* (New York and Washington, 1910).

guilt feeling grows when, for instance, an adolescent boy
remains victorious in the fight against the temptation to
masturbate while in a previous period of indulgence his
sense of guilt, connected with sexual satisfaction, was
moderate. We now understand why this is so: the sense of
guilt is only secondarily connected with the sexual activity.
It really originated in the repressed aggressiveness awakened
by the increased temptation and lack of gratification. The
increase in guilt feelings during sexual abstinence is due
to the rising hostility and rage against the forbidding
authorities.

But the repression of sexual desires is only one of the
sources of human aggressiveness, although it is one of great
force. There are others that feed that subterranean stream
springing from the psychophysical heritage of man. The
unconscious guilt feeling that originates in the repression
of that aggressiveness produces that anxious feeling of impending calamity whose manifestations can be observed in
all centers of the declining ancient civilizations. It is a mood
in which punishment or retaliation for the repressed aggressive drives is expected and feared. In some form or
another—the day of the great judgment is one, the collapse
of national Israel is another—doom is foreseen. What Freud
suggests is correct: that failure or misfortune favors the
emergence of guilt feelings. But this describes only the
initial phase in which an unconscious need for punishment
is the representative of the sense of guilt. A partial gratification of that need has mostly the effect of reducing the tension of guilt feeling and of mitigating the severity of the
inner conflict. If, for instance, an aggression from outside
occurs, the effect is often that the inner fight is, at least for
the time being, interrupted and a kind of integration of the
personality takes place. The process reminds one of the

situation of a country that is divided by the violent struggles of two parties and is suddenly attacked by an enemy.
The internal strife within our own country was in this way
immediately stopped by the assault of the Japanese in the
last war, and national unity was reached overnight after
Pearl Harbor. A bit of funny dialogue between the come-
dian Edgar Bergen and his dummy Charlie McCarthy
illustrates what is meant here. Bergen complains: "I am
my own worst enemy," and Charlie says: "Not when I am
around."

Unconscious guilt feeling will, when its intensity is growing, press either in the direction of self-harming acts in
which the need for punishment is gratified or to a repetition
of the forbidden deed that caused the guilt feeling. The
aggressiveness will either be turned inside, be transformed
into masochistic self-torture, or push man to acts that are
displaced substitutes of the old crime. Pent-up aggressiveness that has no possibility of expression was perhaps the
deeper cause of the general dismay and unhappiness of the
age before Christianity. Discontent drives man on one hand
to intensification of religious acts, that should mitigate the
pressure of guilt feelings, and on the other hand to aggressive tendencies, thriving in the dark and fed by many instinctual frustrations, pressed to new violence, to a repetition
of the father-murder. The time was ripe. Rising unconscious
guilt feeling that had formed an entente cordiale or a
concealed alliance with the aggressive trends asked for a
new victim, for another representative of the father-god or
his son. The pressure from those unconscious guilt feelings
could not be endured any longer. The old murder had to be
avenged and to be atoned and at the same time to be
repeated. Penalty had to be paid and mankind had to
confess to the bloody crime and to be freed from over-

whelming guilt feeling. The Divine Son appeared and was sacrificed. His death was interpreted by Paul as ransom for the original sin and as redemption from the blood-guiltiness with which all men were burdened since Adam. But with this atonement the old deed was repeated and re-enacted. In the very action that should expiate the primeval crime of man, it was committed again.

CHAPTER XX

THE CHRIST MYTH AND
THE HISTORIC CHRIST

THERE ARE many and decisive reasons why we put the mythical figure of Christ into the foreground to which the historical events in Palestine under the regime of Tiberius serve only as relief. In contrast with other investigators we do not refer to the scarcity and dubious character of the information we have about the life of that rabbi from Nazareth because they have little significance for the kind of problem with which we are dealing. In the preceding part, we endeavored to penetrate the darkness of prehistory to discover the situations in which the sense of guilt originated. We were not very concerned with the precise data of those prehistoric situations. It was essential to show that at the bottom of that myth was some historical or rather prehistoric truth. It was not important whether the reconstructed reality existed a few ten thousands of years earlier or later, whether in South Africa or in Arabia.

The name of Adam, to be found in tradition as the first criminal of mankind, did not mean the same to us as to the religious people. We accepted that name for reasons of convenience although we know it is not a proper name and we seriously doubt that the prehistoric criminal had any name. It is very likely that in accordance with the sub-human state of the family he was not christened at all. He was as nameless as his deed was unheard-of. He is to us not a person, but a representative of paleolithic man. It is also likely that he did not act alone, that the atrocious deed was not his, but that he was one of the members of a gang who committed that murder. The brothers killed the victim and ate him together. Their crime was primitive but efficient teamwork. The mythical Adam is thus more important to us than a potentially real human being who might have committed parricide. In our reconstruction we were content with having made the core of truth in the mythical wrapping likely.

The situation we face when we now continue our exploration to the time of Christianity is different. We need not grope any more for our way in the dark vault of paleolithic times, but we move, if not in the daylight, at least in the semiobscurity of early history, whose events are recorded, even though the records are few and ambiguous. Furthermore, interested in the development of that sense of guilt, we would now like to find out how man, many thousands of years after its first emergence, dealt with that "certain feeling" whose nature slowly had dawned upon him. In this perspective the historical person is not the significant and relevant factor, but the personality, reflected in the minds of others, in its effects and aftereffects upon the contemporaries and, even more so, upon the following generations. In other words, the mythical Christ figure is more important to us here than a possible historic person who was called Jesus Christ.

The situation has its paradoxical and odd aspects: the more we learn about and understand the times and works of the historic Christ, the more He seems to be just one Jewish prophet or teacher among others. The more we think of Him as a mythical figure, the more He gains an almost unique place. The historical person viewed as representative of his nation and of men generally seems to shrink. The mythical Christ grows to a gigantic form and reaches to heaven.

Not even the destiny of Jesus is an especially conspicuous one in his time. Josephus Flavius reports[1] that that "joy of human kind," Titus, crucified so many Jewish captives and fugitives during the siege of Jerusalem that there was not sufficient room for the crosses, nor sufficient crosses for the condemned. (Titus had occasion to read Josephus' book and in it the tale of his triumphant accomplishment.) According to Josephus,[2] Alexander Jannaeus commanded eight hundred rebel Pharisees to be crucified. On one occasion alone, two thousand Jews were crucified. In the light of Josephus Flavius and other contemporary writers who report the crucifixion of a particular rabbi, it loses its special character. The scrolls of the Dead Sea, discovered in 1952, and the report about the Teacher of Righteousness who was perhaps also crucified, and what we know about the teachings of the Essenes as well as of other religious contemporary doctrines, threaten to reduce the uniqueness of the historic Jesus figure. G. B. Shaw has rightly remarked that in Heaven an angel is no rarity.

The man Christ, if there ever was a man of this character, was a defined and definite individual and as such different from others, while the mythical Christ was one of those son-gods such as Attis, Adonis, Osiris, and Dionysus and His destiny followed in all its essential features a mythologi-

[1] *Wars* V; IX: 1.
[2] *Antiquities* XIII; XIV: 2.

cal pattern shaped through many centuries, different only in the teachings and sayings that are recorded. It is very possible that there is some reality in the life story of Jesus Christ, while His message of redemption and salvation has the characteristics of a fairy tale.

In the analysis of the Fall story we discovered a core of historic truth. We will perhaps find also in the analysis of the Christ myth some secret connections that have eluded the attention of historians. Myths belong also to the realm of truth in a higher sense. They reflect a piece of life that is not contained in the realm of material or of "shabby reality," as Freud once called it. They are part of the same psychical reality that lives in dreams, daydreams, art, and visions. Myths, as productions of the emotional movements and of the imagination of nations, are as important for their psychological understanding and often even more significant than the economic state, social organization, weapons, tools, and other parts of the material civilization of the same nations. The psychological evolution of the psychical reality of a man, for instance the understanding of his dreams or of characterological features, of his behavior, thoughts, and impulses, is as significant as how much money he makes, what job he has, and how many children he has —parts of the material reality.

The two essential considerations decisive for the preference of the Christ myth are first, the object of these essays, which is the psychological understanding of the origin, character, and development of the collective sense of guilt; and secondly, the higher psychological significance and impact of the Christ myth compared with that of His life as a historic person. To these two reasons a third has to be added: the unity, the consistency, and the continuity of the point of view, the coherence of the construction. We looked at myths as the appropriate material for our psychological inquiry and we hope that the mythical clue will provide such insights also within the region of early Christianity. Consistency of treatment is demanded not only by consideration for the architectural structure and style of this book, but by the more important fact of the coherence and congruity of the idea of its immanent material. The two legends are really a single one, the story of the crime and punishment of mankind, of the first sin and its expiation. It is the same folklore material that shapes both myths, "such stuff as dreams are made of."

The myth of the Fall of Man and the myth of the death and redemption of Christ form a single unit. Only very narrow-minded historians and theologians have to draw a sharp demarcation line between the mythical worlds of Judaism and Christianity and only those who zealously confess Jewish or Christian belief see a clean and sharp cut between the stories of the Old Covenant and of the New Covenant. We deny that there is any such boundary between the two phases. There is not even a caesura for persons who listen perceptively to the great lines of the melody of evolution. A single stream of events is perceptible in the myths of Adam and Christ. I shall endeavor to prove that there is a single story unfolding in them, that they form an invisible unity and a whole and that their sequence has the significance of consequence.

Christ is not only the successor of Adam, not only another son of God, but the same in a higher mythical sense. Adam is not only the precursor and herald of Christ, but His earlier form. He fails where the other succeeds, but they both have to grapple with the same problem. Their story is a single one, comparable to those modern novels that do not present the history of an individual person, but of several generations, for instance Emile Zola's treatment of the family Rougon-Macquart. We shall follow the less visible side of the interrelation of the mythical figures later on; here only the most conspicuous features, as they appear in Christian doctrine, will be mentioned: Jesus Christ is the last man, the "heavenly" Adam (I Corinthians 15:49) as opposed to the first or "earthly" Adam (Romans 5:12-21; I Corinthians 15:21, 22, 45-49). The first Adam brought death upon all mankind; Jesus Christ, the "last Adam," redeems all mankind from Satan, from death and from sin. "For as in Adam all die, even so in Christ shall all be made alive" (I Corinthians 15:22). The first Adam listened to the voice of the serpent, which had a most disastrous effect; the last Adam did not listen to the voice of Satan and did not sin. Whoever believes in Jesus will "put off . . . the old man and . . . put on the new man" (Ephesians 4:22-24). The parallelism that Saint Paul drew becomes a central part of Christianity. Pascal declares:[3] "Toute la foi consiste en Jésus-Christ et Adam." The comparison of the first and second Adam and their vicissitudes led the early Fathers to an astonishing parallelism of the virgin Eve and the virgin Mary, to the death-bringing tree of the Fall and the life-bringing tree of the Cross."[4]

The psychologist who follows the mythical development from the Fall narrative to the legend of Christ's resurrection sees an indivisible and organic unity. The myths presented here are psychologically so intimately tied together and interrelated that they follow each other with the inevitability not of a Greek but of a Jewish tragedy. This our concept, the Fall and Redemption myth as one, is the most important factor in giving priority to the Christ myth over

[3] *Pensées sur la Religion*, XVI, 2.
[4] Irenaeus, *Against the Heresies*, I, 16.

an historical treatment, which in our psychological sense
would be barren.

We tried to show why for the purpose of this exploration
the mythological figure of Christ is more important than the
historical. Alongside and behind those rational and well-
considered reasons there are certain intangible factors that
make the figure of the historic Christ incompatible with
the analytic treatment of the problem to be dealt with. It
is very difficult to characterize the nature of these aspects
within a scientific framework. They will appear by inference
in the following interlude, which is meant half-seriously.

Hollywood has in this De Millennium discovered the
Bible and the Ten Commandments and it is only a question
of time before it will make a biographical film of His life
on earth. To tell the truth, I despair of Hollywood, but
there are perhaps still some film writers with imagination
and daring in France and Italy who might not shy away
from a serious treatment of a religious theme. One of them,
we imagine, would have an amusing and at the same time
pathetic idea. How would it be to show the historic Jesus
transported to New York, or to depict some high-society
New Yorkers encountering the historic Jesus in Galilee? In
this age of science fiction it does not need even the imagina-
tive power of Dostoevski, who saw Him in that famous
conversation with the Grand Inquisitor.

The modern script writer would perhaps daydream an
initial scene in the club car that brings some commuting
middle-aged executives, vice-presidents, and manufacturers
from Grand Central or Penn Station to their suburban
homes. He would show how they board the train, greet each
other, exchange the usual phrases, joke, and make themselves comfortable. They are discussing the case of a rich
Jewish corporation lawyer who is trying to buy almost a

hundred acres in Katonah to build a house for his family, and the measures that have to be taken to keep the community Jew-free. Someone has called the lawyer "a kike" and an assistant-to-somebody just remembers the funny definition that a kike is the gentleman who just left the room. Charlie Brown, vice-president of an industrial concern, wants to tell what took place the other day at a stockholders' meeting when a Jewish banker—then it happens. The five-thirty they all take to go home is suddenly changed into a time machine à la Wells and transports them two thousand years back, landing them in Palestine. For a few minutes they become contemporaries of that carpenter's son and migratory preacher. Yet they maintain their personal identity as individual members of the community of Stamford, Katonah, or Darien, hard-working and hard-playing, churchgoing, hundred-per-cent Americans who maintain the American way of life.

The gentlemen look at that carpenter's son Jesus, observe his manners, and listen to what he says. All these successful gentlemen, junior and senior executives, who had walked down Madison Avenue swinging their attaché cases an hour ago, suddenly understand Aramaic. The miracle has caught the men in gray flannel suits unaware. They do not know what happened to them and confuse the Galilean landscape with the local woods that they daily cut through on their way from home to board the Central or the New Haven train. They now see a young man with reddish, curly hair, hollow cheeks, deep eyes, and a Semitic nose. His raiment reminds them somewhat of the kaftan of an Eastern Jew whom they have once seen on Madison Avenue from the taxi taking them to Grand Central Station. That man—undoubtedly a "kike"—has a kind of strange shawl around his shoulders. It hangs down from his shoulders and it has some kind of long fringes at its end. He seems to pray because he is kneeling. On his arms and his forehead are leather straps with odd little boxes. The vice-president of a Manhattan bank vaguely remembers having seen such a strange combination of boxes and straps on Jews when he passed by a synagogue once and happened to glance into the window. He decides that he has to speak with his senator. This cannot go on; the Immigration laws have to be changed. Such immigrants are highly undesirable.

The gentlemen hear with horror that this Jew speaks with utter contempt of Gentiles and collectors of the government, that he forbids his disciples to preach the kingdom of God to non-Jews, that he calls the Jews "the salt of the earth" and dares to assert that salvation comes from them. They witness a strange scene: a Greek woman falls at his feet and begs him to drive out the devil from her little daughter. He refuses her brusquely and asserts that he is sent only to the children of Israel: "It is not meet to take the children's bread, and to cast it to dogs." (But this is a monster, a chauvinistic Israeli!) The gentlemen listen with growing indignation: the man calls those who are persecuted blessed; he caters to the poor and he proclaims that it is easier for a camel to go through the eye of a needle than for a rich man to enter the Kingdom of Heaven. But this man is a dangerous revolutionary red. He ought to be exterminated like a cockroach! The company he keeps are all proletarians, and unsavory characters. The whole rabble should be investigated by the FBI, taken to Ellis Island, and deported. The government is too soft to Communists and Jews. McCarthy was right!

These or similar emotions and thoughts are awakened and voiced by the junior and senior executives whose train is miraculously taken to Palestine instead of Katonah,

Darien, or Stamford. (If the script writer of that film thinks
of box-office success, he would, it is true, take the suburban-
ites first to the house of the proconsul at Jerusalem and let
them enjoy the spectacle of some orgies between Roman
officers and voluptuous Syrian women.)

The picture presenting the encounter of the commuters
of the five-thirty with the historic Jesus is to be followed by
another series of pictures showing Him in New York, in
1957. The time machine of the script moves on a two-
sided street. It also takes people from the remote past to
the present. After a short intermission in which only the
noises of the moving train are heard, the film shows the
rabbi Jehoshua of Nazareth suddenly transported to the
streets of New York in the late afternoon hours. He wanders
on Broadway and creates something of a sensation. He is
lonely—as lonely as only a man can be and not a god—
and He wants to find a synagogue in which to pray. The
City of New York impresses Him as little as the City of
Jerusalem when He, a provincial, first came from Galilee
to the metropolis.

He enters a church because the building reminds Him
in some vague way of a temple. In the twilight He sees men
and women kneeling, recognizes something that resembles
an altar; but then He shudders with horror. He sees pictures of gods in the temple, presenting a young woman with
a child, a man, apparently a shepherd, with a lamb in his
arms and other men with tiaras on their heads. The pagan
abomination! Pictures and statues in a synagogue! And
what does it mean that in every corner of this temple there
is a blasphemically sculptured man hanging on a cross?
What is there so unusual in Jews being crucified? That is
an everyday occurrence. And why should a crucifixion be
presented in the temple? Do these pagan Romans put it up

as a mockery of the many thousands of Jews who were crucified? He sees the priest conduct all kinds of puzzling ceremonials, speaking an unknown language. Is he praying? But the Gentiles do not pray. They merely babble, using vain repetitions (Matthew 6:7). He realizes that the priest is speaking Latin and finally understands that all resistance in Palestine had been in vain. The Romans have conquered the world and Caesar is its emperor. When He walks to the exit of the church, His heart is full of grief. What has happened to His people? Have they again been brought to Babylon? Have they again been deported and dispersed in a foreign country?

In His wanderings He arrives at another building. He recognizes over its portal the star of David and its architecture seems for a moment familiarly oriental. Here at last is a synagogue! But the men wear no prayer shawls and no cover for their heads. The rabbi recites from the Torah roll, but what he says can scarcely be understood. It is not Aramaic. It is not Samaritan either. The sacred service is held in another language! What is that? Are those Jews? They are not dressed as Jews are and they do not behave as Jews do. Are they observing the Law? "Think not that I am come to destroy the law, or the prophets. I am not come to destroy, but to fulfil. For verily I say unto you, Till heaven and earth pass, one jot or one tittle shall in no wise pass from the law, till all be fulfilled" (Matthew 5:17-18). No, these are not His people. They are not Jews. They are perhaps members of a heretic sect that has abandoned the Lord. He runs away in horror and despair.

Crossing Broadway and walking on a narrow side street, He enters a small and shabby house because He has seen in the lighted windows Jews in prayer shawls, the phylacteries on their heads and arms. They pray, but even their services,

their very pronunciation of the sacred words, all their
manner and gestures are foreign to Him. They are so different from His people! He does not feel at home with them.
Neither in the Christian churches nor in the synagogues of
Reformed Judaism could He detect any trace of His religion. Here with the poor, orthodox zealotic Jews from East
Europe was at least a refuge, a touch of familiarity.

The next picture shows the historic Jesus leaving New
York, walking at sunset to His destination, in search of His
people who confessed with Him: "Hear, Israel, our God is
the Only One!" The figure of the historic Jesus slowly
changes into that of the Wandering Jew. There is an aura
of the grotesque and of the pathetic around the lonely
figure.

The following picture, a kind of epilogue to the sequence,
shows a mountainous scene in Poland during the second
World War. The Nazis have caught three Jews and hanged
them on trees. The branches of the tree resemble the crossbeam of the cross. Stripped naked of all clothes, the middle
figure, the young rabbi of a neighboring city, changes slowly
into the figure of the historic Jesus, hanging for hours in
torture. It is dark. The rabbi cries: "I thirst." The storm
troopers abuse and mock him. Their guns and bayonets
slowly take the form of the spears the Roman soldiers carried on Calvary.

The final shot shows the club car a few minutes after that
vision had transported the men in gray flannel suits to the
places where the Saviour lived. All is again ordinary and
everyday life continues. They have some whisky and soda
and are in a jolly mood. Their conversation has turned to
memories of the time of "that bad man in the White House"
and of his Jewish friends. Something has dawned on Charlie
Jones, the junior executive: "Say, isn't the name Roose-

velt—? Jesus Christ, maybe that bastard was a Jew himself!" At this moment the conductor opens the door of the
car and says: "Next station Katonah!"

I would like to preface the following new interpretation
of the Christ story by trying to justify its treatment, comparing the method used with the one applied in the case
of the Fall myth. In the analysis of the narrative of the
second and third chapters of Genesis, only a segment of
the story was used as material. We cut the biblical tale into
two halves and considered only the second half or rather a
certain piece of this half, namely the text presenting the Fall
of Man. The whole preceding description of the Creation of
the World, of Adam and Eve, of the Garden of Eden, was
separated and left aside, as if it did not belong to the other
part. So important dramatis personae as Eve and the Serpent were not considered. Cut to the bones, the material to
be subjected to analytic investigation was limited to the
single scene of a forbidden tree and of Adam—or rather of
primeval man—eating of it.

I tried to justify this dismemberment by pointing to our
purpose: to discover the primal tradition of the Fall story.
We noted also that this early mythical material was fused
later on with other myths and so closely joined that it appeared to form a coherent and continued story. It cannot be
denied that the selection of that small part of the Fall story
strikes the reader at first as artificial and arbitrary, but he
will not forget that the process of blending different mythological strains about which we tried to conjecture was not
less artificial and arbitrary.

In the following analysis of the Christ myth I shall proceed in the same manner, dealing only with the part that
presents the crucifixion and resurrection of the Saviour. It
has to be admitted that a division as daring as this seems

even more arbitrary than the severance of one small part of the Genesis tale from the whole. Yet the separation and selection of the last act of the great tragedy can again be justified by the aim of discovering the significant features of the myth and of connecting it with the Fall story. But is not such an artificial partition in this case much more objectionable than in the treatment of the Fall story? The mythical character of the Adam story is obvious to everybody—with the exception of theologians—but the gospels of Matthew, Mark, and Luke present reports of historic events or at least reports of events in historic times. They belong to an age that already knew objective written records and in which historians gave full statements of the happenings.

We shall not waste time and energy in arguing this point, but rather turn the attention of the critical reader to the purpose we previously mentioned. We explicitly stated that we preferred in this treatment the mythical aspects of Jesus' biography to the possible historic elements. We are interested only in the mythological face of the figure of the Saviour. It must be permissible to the analyst to choose one part of the myth and neglect the others if he pursues a certain end and we selected the most important part, the story of the Passion, of the suffering of Jesus on the Cross.

Myths are built like the old cathedrals we admire: they were built through hundreds of years. Many generations worked on them and left their signs in their architecture. The observer who casually looks at the Strassburger Münster or the Cathedral of St. Stephen in Vienna sees, it is true, only a very impressive monument of perfect architecture, without being aware that it is the result of the efforts of successive generations. In the examination of ancient myths and of those great old cathedrals one part is often the object of the historian or the art scholar.

It cannot be our task to stratify the different parts of the Christ myth, but it is easy to recognize the ancient elements of the biography of Jesus and to differentiate them from the more recent ones. The pattern of the myth of the young god, son of a god and a savior, was given. The old tradition transmitted from one generation to the other the tragic tale of the death of this young god, Attis, Osiris, Adonis, Tammuz, Dionysus, or Orpheus, of his tortures and of his resurrection. Deutero-Isaiah's prediction of the servant of the Lord as well as other stories in the Old Testament shows how similar myths once existed in a different form in ancient Israel. The god who was a culture hero became the Saviour, the Messiah in the imagination of that small nation that was impoverished, deprived of its independence, and oppressed by its enemies. The recent features of Jesus' biography, especially His trial before Pilate and other incidents, filled the gap that the mythological tradition had left. It is obvious that this old tradition continues to live in the story telling of the suffering of the young god, of His crucifixion and His resurrection. These are Jewish variations on an old mythological theme of the peoples on the shore of the Mediterranean.

In the stratification of the Christ story the tragic fate of the Son of God is certainly the oldest piece. It carries the time mark of ancient traditions that were modernized to fit the situation of the Jews in Palestine in the first century. To use a comparison: it is as if the fairy tale of Hänsel and Gretel were to be transformed into a story of two children in New York in the home of an evil foster-mother who let them starve and so on. We are not at the moment concerned with the changes and transformations of the Christ myth under the influence of that Jewish fanatic and Roman citizen called Paul, nor with the concept of Christianity of

Saint Augustine. We shall not discuss the possibility that these transformations often amounted to deviations and aberrations from what Jesus preached. A historian once spoke of a Paulinic heresy of Christianity. These elaborations and distortions are organic developments of the Christ story.

We are interested only in a single aspect of the mythology of Christianity: in the sacrificial death of Jesus on the Cross and His resurrection and in the obvious and the less visible connections of the Passion tale with the Fall story.

CHAPTER XXI

TO LET THE PUNISHMENT
FIT THE CRIME

IN DEALING with the Fall story we behaved as though we were detectives in a prehistoric mystery story. The problem we had to solve was not the usual one found in that kind of literature: not who done it, but what was done. A long line of investigators, theologians, biblical scholars, anthropologists, and finally psychoanalysts have carried on a great deal of examination of that primeval crime. Criticism of the text, research into the sources of the tale, comparison with many myths of the ancient Orient and with folklore of savage people have provided many clues, some of which were very useful in our own investigation. Yet the problem of the nature of the original crime was not solved by the deductions at which those scholarly detectives arrived. Their interpretation, for instance that the Fall of Man concerns the obtaining of forbidden sexual knowledge and refers to the nature of sexual intercourse and later of incest, does not tally with certain facts. At a special occasion Sherlock Holmes remarks:[1] "I ought to know by this time that when a fact appears opposed to a

[1] Arthur Conan Doyle, *A Study In Scarlet*.

long train of reductions, it invariably proves to be capable
of bearing other interpretations."

In following a novel line of investigation we arrived at
a clue we considered of paramount importance: the secret
significance of the forbidden tree. We hear from experts[2]
of mystery fiction that its foundation is the failure of the
reader to perceive the essential value of facts. Such lack
of understanding is to a great extent determined by the fact
that clues, although clearly produced and without ambiguity, are exhibited separately and inconspicuously, often
unconnected. There are several methods of concealing and
camouflaging the real significance of clues. Their presentation within the story is one of the serious problems of the
writer. We tried to show how the Jehovist and his predecessors who told the story of the Fall dealt so successfully with
that problem that almost two thousand years of investigation
did not fathom the true nature of certain clues concealed
in the narrative.

What are clues? Traces of guilt that the criminal leaves
behind. Their existence is seldom proof of guilt that has to
be deduced from the understanding of their significance.
The word "clue" derives its connotation in this context
from the clew of thread that Ariadne, daughter of Minos,
provided for Theseus, who is safely guided by means of it
to find his way out of the Cretan labyrinth. With the help
of this thread that he fastened at the entrance of the mysterious building the hero got away with murder, namely
with the slaying of the Minotaur. Is it accidental that the
bull-headed, man-eating monster, the Minotaur, is himself

---

[2] R. Austin Freeman, "The Art of the Detective Story" in *The Art
of the Mystery Story,* edited by Howard Haycraft (New York, 1946),
p. 15.

a kind of totem god? Is the Theseus myth not another animal totemistic version of the original crime of primordial age?[3] That may be; as it is, the word "clue" was later on generally used in the sense of a guide to the solving of a mystery or problem. Has the clue of the concealed significance of the forbidden tree the evidential value we attributed to it? Can it be applied to make us find the exit from the intricate, labyrinthian story of the Fall?

The construction of the detective story follows certain patterns: first, the statement of the problem generally contained in the telling of the story, then the inquest with correct clues and false trails (in the case of the Fall mystery the many exegetic attempts and interpretations of almost twenty centuries). The investigation usually arrives at an impasse. A novel line of investigation follows in which new suspects appear or facts already presented appear in a new light. Then the denouement, the discovery that means the completion of the inquiry; then the declaration of the solution.

The climax is the sudden recognition of a number of hitherto uncomprehended facts. The conclusion, says our expert,[4] must "emerge truly and inevitably from the premises, it must be the only possible one, and it must leave the competent reader in no doubt as to its unimpeachable truth." Is this the case with the conclusion that we reached in the reconstruction of the original nature of that primordial crime? Is the conclusion we suggested the only one, is it inevitable? It is not for us to decide. If we are allowed to express a doubt, it does not concern the correctness and

---

[3] J. G. Frazer compared the Minotaur with the Phoenician Moloch to whom children were sacrificed. *The Golden Bough,* "The Dying God," p. 14.

[4] Freeman, *op. cit.,* p. 13.

inevitableness of the solution, but the possibility of proving it. In other words: the possibility to demonstrate the evidence in such a manner that every reader has arrived at the conclusion "It must be that" and "It cannot be different." This task is in mystery literature generally performed by the last part of the story, which follows the denouement and brings proof of the solution by analysis and exposition of the evidence. Whatever we could provide of such analysis was produced in the preceding chapters, which present the body of evidence at our disposal.

The case is not only difficult. It is, considering its prehistoric character, unique. It does not only present the greatest mystery story of mankind, but also its first crime story. We cannot hope to secure more evidence coming forth from still undiscovered sources. The only possibility at our disposal is to search for internal evidence proving that our construction is correct. This kind of evidence can be provided by the analysis of the Christ myth. This might sound paradoxical since it seems to indicate that a mystery can be solved by introducing another mystery. But that is not as nonsensical as it appears. One can crack two nuts better than one when one presses the two shells against each other. It is in this sense that we approach the central problem of Christology.

The attempt at such mutual illumination will appear more legitimate to the reader when he remembers that we have previously followed the parallel between Adam and Christ. To mention only the doctrine of Paul: sin and death entered into history through Adam whereas righteousness and life have entered by Christ (Romans 5:12 ff.). Another comparison with reference to death and resurrection appears in I Corinthians 15:21-23, 45-49. Adam and

Christ represent to Paul the two separate origins of the life of the race. Christ is called "the last Adam" because at His coming (I Corinthians 15:28, 45, 47) the new and final order of humanity will be established. Here we find a connection in the relation to Adam's transgression by which all men died. Only Jesus who also died that shameful death on the cross was resurrected. Although He was without sin He died a death of punishment and thus provided by His atonement redemption from death and inherited sin alike. Adam's sin divided men from God; Christ's vicarious sufferings and dying united them with their Father.

There are many theological theories about Christ's sacrificial death on the cross, but its primal character cannot be dubious. Christ took the sins of all men on His shoulders and died atoning for them. The atonement theory has its central point in the condition of reconciliation by which man returns into complete communion with God. Words closely associated with atonement and often used by theology are ransom, propitiation, and penance. Jesus Christ, although sinless, died atoning for all sins of mankind, as if He had committed those sins, especially the crime of Adam, the "original sin." The "last Adam" was subjected to the punishment that the first Adam deserved, was vicariously punished as if He were the criminal Himself. It is in the sphere of the problems springing from the penance of punishment of Christ that we are searching for the inner evidence of our conclusion with regard to the nature of the crime of the first Adam.

The Old Testament proclaims, "Whoso sheddeth man's blood, by man shall his blood be shed." Here is the oldest law given in the Holy Scripture, but that unwritten law existed long before Moses. It is older than Jahveh. Primitive society punished crimes on the principle of the law of talion, the principle of equivalence in punishment. The *lex talionis* is perhaps originally connected with the instinctive movements of the person who is hurt by another and attempts to make the aggressor suffer a similar hurt. Blow for blow. The way from this primitive reflex to law-giving is a long one, but savage and more advanced societies react to crimes essentially as a boy who was hit and hits the aggressor at the same place. This system of vengeance prescribes that the punishment should be exacted with the same kind of weapon and in the same manner as the crime.

The famous *lex talionis* had already been operating among the Babylonians almost two thousand years before the Mosaic Law. The code of King Hammurabi decrees:[5] "If a man has struck his father, his hand one shall cut off. If a man has caused the loss of a patrician's eye, his eye one shall cause to be lost. If he has shattered a patrician's limb, one shall shatter his limb. If a man has made the tooth of a man who is his equal to fall out, one shall make his tooth fall out." The same strict retaliation is to be found among people at an even earlier stage of development than the Babylonians. Among many savage tribes the thief loses eye or hand, the adulterer may be castrated, the perjurer loses his tongue. Hobhouse[6] quotes an example of exact retaliation carried out with grotesque literalness: a man had killed another by falling on him from a tree. The criminal is himself put to death by exactly the same method —a relation of the deceased solemnly mounting the tree and descending upon the defender. When a man among the

---

[5] Kohler and Pleiser, *Hammurabi's Gesetz* (1904), pp. 195-197.

[6] L. T. Hobhouse, *Morals in Evolution* (London, 1951), p. 74, quoting Howitt Frazer, *Tribes of N. S. Wales*.

Australian Whayook wounds a fellow tribesman, he has to present himself to the sufferer for a similar wound.[7] We can pursue the idea of life for life, eye for eye, from ancient Babylon, Egypt, and Israel to traces it has left in our own morals. Gilbert and Sullivan's *Mikado* proclaims the law of talion in his solo:

> My object is sublime,
> I shall achieve in time;
> To let the punishment fit the crime,
> The punishment fit the crime.

In the course of a long development the underlying principle of talion assumed different and sometimes curious forms. In some cases the punishment seems to be out of all proportion to the crime committed, much too cruel. Other variations of the principle are difficult to understand, if considered from our modern viewpoint. They are explicable only by taking into account the particular social and religious conditions in which they originated.

Is the principle of the law of talion also discernible in the Christ myth? Does the punishment fit the crime also here? Is the penance adequate to the sin? Christ's painful and shameful death should atone Adam's sin. The punishment He had to suffer was the one the first sinner should have undergone. A law that has such deep roots in the human urge to retaliate, a desire for vengeance that had found an almost instinctive and unchanged expression for many millennia could, of course, not disappear. It must have kept its validity also in the age of the Saviour.

We know what the first crime of primitive society was: the killing and eating of the brutal and despotic father of the horde. Even when we assume (which is likely) that no

[7] E. M. Curr, *The Australian Race,* Vol. I, p. 339.

punishment followed the deed in that early Paleolithic Age, we have to believe that societies punished murder of chieftains and heads of families according to the law of talion. Was Jesus in His voluntary and vicarious part as archsinner and universal criminal punished in this way? He was murdered as was the father of the horde in the primal crime, but He was not eaten as was that chieftain of the primal band. The penalty imposed upon Him or the punishment that He suffered for the sin of Adam shows features that decidedly do not correspond to the conditions of that oldest law and are not to be met with in the primitive societies in which it is valid.

Except the death penalty itself, nothing in the passion of the Christ myth seems to be analogous to the primal crime for which the Saviour atones in His vicarious suffering. Compare, for instance, the punishment Prometheus in the Greek myth has to undergo for his outrage against Zeus. To be chained on a rock, his liver daily to be eaten by vultures—here are certainly characteristics of a barbaric kind of penalty. In the story of the Greek hero we still breathe the air of a mythological age. And is that not the same with the terrible punishment of Sisyphus, of Tantalus, of Ixion? In those myths also, it is true, the cruel sufferings of those primeval heroes and criminals seem not to bear the character of the law of talion—or do we not understand them enough?—but we do not doubt that the punishment fits the crime even though we do not recognize how. At all events, it fits the character of Greek mythology.

There is nothing "mythological" or "mythical" in the punishment Jesus had to undergo on Calvary. It was a definite hill and, it seems, a well-known place of execution. Its name, which means "skull," has nothing to do with the skull of Adam, which is often painted lying on the foot of the cross in sacred pictures.[8]

The penalty to which Jesus submitted Himself is supposed to be the punishment and atonement for Adam's sin. Yet that punishment, utterly brutal and revolting as it was, is not mythical, but was the customary one with the Romans. The scourging and mocking of the condemned was nothing unusual. As a matter of fact, scourging was always inflicted on criminals before their crucifixion. The Christ myth certainly does not follow the ancient tradition of the primitive law of the talion. Almost all in the report of the events at Golgotha is time-conditioned, which means that it is according to the habits and customs of the Roman province of Palestine whose Jewish inhabitants were subjugated by Caesar to such an extent that they could not even inflict their way of punishment on criminals. Jesus was not stoned nor strangulated as the Jewish law would have demanded. And Pilate said to the Jews, "take ye him and judge him according to your law." The Jews had to make the humiliating confession that they could not do that because they had been deprived of the right to inflict the death sentence. The story of Jesus, including that of His preaching and His trial, carries the earmarks of contemporary history with accuracy of data, with names of historic persons and real places.

Should we now drop the attempt to find the law of talion, the principle of eye for eye, tooth for tooth valid in the Christ myth? We would then, of course, have to admit failure because we started the inquiry with the expectancy that it would lead to an indirect proof of our hypothesis on

[8] Fredric W. Farrar, *The Life of Christ,* new ed. (New York, 1894), p. 616.

the original crime. If the law of talion has lost its validity
for the age of the Christ myth, no internal evidence for our
construction can be found in it. If no such body of evidence
can be produced, our conclusion was perhaps incorrect and
we were misled by false clues. Our construction and reconstruction threaten to collapse before our eyes. We who
are fallen from grace have to have that evidence. We cannot
rely on faith which is, according to St. Paul (Hebrews
11:1) "the substance for things hoped for, the evidence of
things not seen."

CHAPTER XXII

WE LET SOMETHING SLIP

WE HAVE to admit that the law of talion seems to have lost its validity for the age of the Christ myth. The crime of Adam is, of course, punished—or, as we had better say in this case, atoned for by the death of the incarnated self-sacrificing God, but we take the death penalty for granted. The way of execution, namely crucifixion, is the contemporary and usual capital punishment for grave crimes and has no visible connection with the nature of the offense. Nor can we detect that scourging and abusing, the tortures of the victim on the cross, correspond to the character of the sin Adam had committed. We have thus at least temporarily—until someone comes along to correct us—to assume that the insults and injuries, the mocking and the agony on the cross are features of the myth that are without connection to the motif of the young dying and resurrected god.

A second consideration will tell us that the primitive law of talion must have undergone many decisive transformations since it emerged in the first forms of elementary societies as their most instinctive reaction to crime. From its earliest crude shape it developed into more complex and complicated measures of punishment and new ways of wreaking vengeance upon criminals. The time of Tiberius, of Pontius Pilate, and of the Sanhedrin was many thousands of years advanced from the phase of primitive retaliation. It was, as a matter of fact, already the age of decadence and decay of the Roman civilization and of the old Jewish tradition. There were not only new measures of punishment for crimes, but also new kinds of crime, unknown or not conceived of as such at the low levels of social evolution for which *lex talionis* was fully valid. In accordance with changing social conditions the old law was subjected to many transformations, but beside and beyond them, novel principles of punishment appeared.

We failed to take those changes into account when we explored the Christ story in search for the old forms of retaliation. We made a second mistake: the early myths themselves that had been transmitted in oral tradition did not remain unaltered in those communications. They showed in their later and elaborated forms the influence of the newer concepts of a progressed civilization, not satisfied any more by the simple and unrefined ways of punishments and penalties. The legends and stories of ancient times changed thus, not only in their form, but also in their content. Latent tendencies that had been alien to oral traditions or to early fixations made themselves felt and affected their original shape.

Comparative history of religions has shown us to what an astonishing degree the essential features of the destiny of Christ resemble those of Attis, Adonis, and other young gods who were killed and resurrected. The Christ myth is, so to speak, a much younger edition of this old religious motif, elevated to one of the most sublime moral heights mankind has ever reached. The inference is that the ancient tradition of a young god who dies, is resurrected, and becomes the savior was in the Christ story adapted to a certain actual situation, put into the frame of a historical and local reality, acted out in the milieu of Galilee at the time of the Roman emperor Tiberius. It is only the difference of the external circumstances, the new milieu, that prevents our recognizing in the new melody an elaborated, newly instrumentated, and harmonized variation of an ancient folk song.

I venture to guess that even the whole myth of the dying and resurrected god who was the lover of the great mother-goddess had originally another form, and that the legends of Adonis, Attis, Osiris, Tammuz, and their counterparts as they were told in Phrygia, Greece, Egypt, and Asia Minor present secondary elaborations of an earlier tradition. In those original tales, young gods die a violent death as punishment for their rebellion against the father-god. Their death is the penance for their transgression, originally for the murder of the old god who appears either as Zeus, as Ormuzd in the Mithra cult, or in the totemistic form of a wild boar in the myth of Astarte and Adonis. The mythical theme appears, therefore, first as a tradition of the terrible penance a rebellious and incestuous son-god has to suffer for the murderous assault against the Lord of the world. The law of talion—a violent death as punishment for murder—still had its full validity.

Can we guess how the myth developed later on and arrived at the form with which we meet in the Mediterranean area? The resurrection or reincarnation of the young god belongs not to the original myth theme. It emerged later as an expression of the recurring rebellious tendencies against the tyrannical and vengeful old god. It was also a manifestation of affectionate and admiring feeling toward the young son who had to pay the supreme penance for such pardonable transgressions as an outbreak of hate against a severe despot and of sexual desires for his mate. These trends of defiance, long repressed, became victorious and demanded expression in the myths that had described the suffering of the young god who had been so cruelly punished. He was resurrected, became again the lover of Isis or Cybele, of the mother-goddess, and ascended to Heaven at the side and sometimes in the place of the old god.

The rescue and resurrection of the dead god—often with the very active help of the mourning goddess—is thus a manifestation of the same rebellious feelings that had been responsible for his attack against divine authority, a revival of the ferocious emotions that led to the crime for which he was killed. In many myths the succession of violent death and triumph, punishment and elevation gives the impression that victory was paid for by self-sacrifice or penalty. The hero or savior undergoes punishment and then attains his end—for instance, he is killed or suffers great tortures and then is resurrected and becomes god, replacing god-father. Since this is the goal he wanted to reach by his crime, you can say, he repeats his sacrilegious act after having paid the penalty for it.

This is a hypothesis difficult to verify because the development of myth formation sketched here occurred in prehistoric times. The sequence: murder of the primal godfather—violent death of the son-god as punishment for his atrocious deed—triumphant resurrection of the young god who appears as liberator or savior—recurs in so many variations of the myth that it presents good circumstantial evidence for my assumption, for which conclusive proof is not available.

As a late descendant of many Oriental legends of this

kind, the Christ myth follows these very same lines, differing only in that the original transgression is not committed by the sinless son of God, but by Adam. Yet Jesus Christ takes the penance and atonement for this primeval crime on His own shoulders. He is killed, resurrected, and ascends to heaven where He sits at the right hand of godfather. A telescopic view of the development of that myth motif presents the following picture: its first phase shows a hero or representative of the tribe who is a liberator and frees his people from a despotic and brutal overlord or oppressor, or kills a monster, often a feared and ferocious beast, as Mithras slays the sacred bull. This hero is a benefactor of men. The creation of men is often ascribed to him, as it is, for instance, to Prometheus. This savior is in most cases cruelly punished for the outrage against the superior god or father. At the end he is resurrected from death, freed from torture and released from agony as Prometheus and Hercules and triumphantly ascends to heaven.

There is an interesting and illuminating analogy to the phases of this development in an area very remote from that of the myths: in the symptomatology of neuroses, especially of the obsessional neuroses. We observe there that the first obsession ideas have the form and the purpose of a defense or protection against forbidden aggressive and sexual impulses. These ideas show the moral reaction to incestuous, savage, and destructive tendencies and have often the character of atonement or punishment to which the patient subjects himself. This initial phase has the mark of warding off socially undesirable impulses and is slowly replaced by another one in which the symptoms assume the character of compromise actions. In these later formations, the defense against the forbidden drives and the drives themselves are blended. The ratio of mixture is different in individual cases and varies with the duration of the illness. The longer the symptoms of this kind persist, the more energetically they develop into actions or thoughts in which the rejected aggressive or hostile strivings win the upper hand. The forbidden impulses finally recur, often with surprising force, from the subterranean vault into which the repression had banned them.

Here is a typical instance: a patient of mine had a bizarre compulsion; he had to measure with his hand the distance from the doorknob of his room to the head of his little son. The strange, often camouflaged gestures to which the mysterious inner demands compelled him were repeated innumerable times. Their origin became clear through psychoanalysis: once, when he violently opened a door, he had slightly hurt his little son, who accidentally stood near the knob. Very shortly after that accident, he developed that strange ceremonial of rehearsal in which he convinced himself that he could not hurt his son when he opened or closed a door. The compulsive symptom had the obvious character of a measure of defense or protection against unconscious impulses to harm his son. Since the child grew, he had to convince himself more frequently that the boy's head was still below the doorknob. In measuring the height of the growing child whom he put under the doorknob, he sometimes became impatient with the boy and taking the measurement was often done in a harsh manner. Several times he treated the reluctant boy rather roughly in pushing him here and there. In his eagerness to measure the distance, he was once so fidgety and impatient that he pushed the boy's head so hard toward the knob that the child began to cry. In this detour, the original impulse returned from repression.

The compromise symptoms of the later phase of compulsive symptomatology seem to present aggravations of the atoning or punishing measures or actions. They appear especially in the beginning in the form of intensifications or complications of the defense against, or punishment for, the forbidden impulses. But such increased severity of the penance heralds simultaneously the transition to a release from the pressure and to the breakthrough of repressed forbidden tendencies. In the formation of myths, this phase corresponds to a period in which the punishment of the hero or criminal becomes more drastic and severe. Injury is accompanied by insults, his tortures become agony. But then the hour of triumph is approaching.

Another form of this transition is characterized by derision and mockery inflicted on the suffering god. We think immediately of the mockery of Jesus Christ, upon whose head a green wreath of thorns was twisted and in whose trembling hands a reed scepter was placed. The soldiers of the governor put an old scarlet robe on Him and, kneeling down, shouted with mock salutation: "Hail, King of the Jews!" Is that derision, this mocking display, still part and parcel of the punishment? Does it have only the function of sharpening the pain, to degrade the victim, adding insult to injury? When the Roman legionnaires sneered at Him hanging on the cross, when they wrote on the board above His head the inscription, "This is Jesus the King of the Jews," it was certainly done to ridicule and shame the incarnate son of God.

But is there something else in this derision? Does it only mean to aggravate His suffering? Here something announces itself that eludes us. Something in this scene has a remote resemblance to a scene of futility and mockery in other myths, especially that feature of the thirsty sufferer. We now remember what it reminds us of: the myth of Tantalus in Greek mythology, of the Greek king punished in the nether world. He has to stand up to his chin in water, under branches laden with fruits, but whenever he tries to drink or eat, the water or fruits withdraw from his reach. And there is that other myth of King Sisyphus, condemned forever to roll a heavy stone up a steep hill, only to have it roll down again when it was reaching the peak. What are the common traits in those scenes of these royal criminals in Hades and Jesus Christ at Golgotha? The element of derision is obvious and so is the aggravation of punishment.

But the mocking frustration has also a positive element, one could almost say, an acknowledging or respectful note. This other aspect is contained in the "almost" character of reaching the goal or accomplishing the aim for which those condemned suffer cruel punishment. Jesus Christ became almost the King of the Jews as that tablet mockingly announces, Tantalus almost reached the desired water and fruits, and Sisyphus nearly succeeded in placing the rock at the top of the hill. The brutal display of frustration that ridicules the failure of a deed at the same time admits the courage and superhuman will power of the criminal who is a could-be-hero. This treatment does not deny his superiority though it derides and mocks him. It does not assert that his zeal was worthy of a better cause. It was the best cause.

The sarcastic display of His failure and frustration is not only an intensification of punishment, but also a perverted kind of glorification. The two sides of this ambivalent attitude toward the criminal show themselves again in two-sided actions. The soldiers, putting a crown of thorns upon Christ's head and a reed in His right hand, knelt before Him saying, "Hail, King of the Jews!" and then they spat upon Him and took the reed, and smote Him on the head.

In this case it is only one step from the ridicule to the sublime and this step leads from derision to reluctant acknowledgment, from sneering rejection to unwilling acceptance. In the scornful demonstration of a failure that almost reached the aim of a great adventure, a reluctant recognition of its near success is concealed. This *à peu près* character in the shameful exposition of the criminal's undertaking can form an appropriate transition to a later development in which his rebellious action is celebrated as the daring deed of a hero, of a liberator, or even of a savior.

This long excursion led us to the discovery of an unrecognized phase of ancient punishment, particularly of the secret meaning of some obscure traits of the Christ myth. Yet it did not provide any information about the presence and validity of the law of talion in the execution on Calvary. Our impression increases that the ancient law that makes punishment equivalent to the crime cannot be applied in the interpretation of the Passion story. The Christ story seems to remain outside the realm for which that archaic principle of retaliation is valid and is apparently also in this respect unique among myths. The incarnated son of God, who carries the burden of Adam's sin and suffers the penance for it, is not treated according to the *lex talionis*.

The secret meaning of Adam's atrocious crime was that he killed and devoured the primal father, God-father, who appears in the distorted saga of Genesis as a tree totem. That ancient code would demand that the primordial deed should be repeated in the punishment of the culprit. The penance should be a reproduction of the original crime, inflicted as punishment in every feature. We would expect not only capital punishment of Christ in His victorious role, but that He would be devoured by the murderers. If that archaic principle of retaliation were applicable to the second Adam, the sinner should not only be killed, but also eaten and His death should be somewhere connected with a sacred or worshiped tree.

When, just a minute ago, we imagined the nude, bloody body of the Lord nailed to the cross, we must have thought something that now eludes us. Yet it was knocking at the door of our mind, asking for attention. It was something that had an important bearing on that impression. The thought cannot be isolated any more. What was it?

Soberly and rationally considered, the Christ myth boils down to the following: a person is executed for the crime another man has committed. Christ is crucified as penance for Adam's sin. The gospels tell the story of the first judicial murder. But we do not want to quibble nor to examine whether there was a miscarriage of divine justice. We wish to know the relation between the sacrificial death of the innocent victim and the crime of the real killer. We want to face this problem only and not the music of the spheres.

We are here, it seems to me, still in the atmosphere of the mystery stories. Is it not appropriate to remember a special situation from one of these? "What's that you were saying?" the detective asks Gracie Allen in S. S. Van Dine's *The Gracie Allen Murder Case* in the midst of her chatting, when she had inadvertently revealed some important clues. "How should I know?" she answers, "I wasn't listening." It was just small talk and Gracie had not paid attention to what she was saying. The same process can, I assume, also be observed in the area of one's own thoughts. "What's that you were thinking?" we could ask ourselves, and we could answer as Gracie did: "How should I know? I wasn't listening."

In this way, perhaps some significant clue had slipped our attention. Maybe we missed something important when we probed into the secrets of the vicarious penalty of the Lord. Our investigation, though consciously undertaken and comprehensive, has perhaps overlooked some less palpable connections. The thought that eluded us concerned the cross on Calvary and the tree in the middle of the garden of Eden.

CHAPTER XXIII

THE CROSS AND THE TREE

IN THE study of the rich material on the cross and crucifixion in comparative religion, a part of that lost thought—its tailpiece, so to speak—re-emerged like a will-o'-the-wisp. It did not spring up from speculation, but from the material itself. It was not suggested, nor implied; it is explicitly stated in the ancient sources. The intimate connection between the first sinner and Jesus Christ does not only mean that mankind became sinful with Adam and was released by Christ ("For as in Adam all die, even so in Christ shall all be made alive" (I Corinthians 15:22). The comparison between the two is continued into the details of the Fall and of the Redemption in tradition, in service, and in folklore.

The Tree of Life is frequently contrasted with the cross. The cross is considered the true Tree of Life, for instance in the Mass on Good Friday. The very cross is the holy tree: "The one tree noble above all, no forest affords the like of this in life, in flower or seed. Sweet the wood, sweet the nails, sweet the weight it bears." The origin of the cross in tradition is sometimes directly traced back to the tree in the middle of the garden of Eden.

In one of those stories, Seth, a son of Adam, acquires

seeds from that tree. That portion of the tree had a miraculous history. It became the famous rod of Moses that
turned into a serpent to confound the Egyptian magicians.
It struck the rock in the wilderness so that it gave forth
water. It became a beam in the great temple built by
Solomon the Wise. It passed, in time, to the carpenter's
shop of Joseph, the foster father of Jesus, and from him it
was acquired by Judas, the betrayer, who turned it over to
the Roman soldiers who used it, in the end, for the cross
upon which they crucified Christ.

A similar genealogy of the cross is presented in another
story in which the dying Adam asks his son Seth to
secure for him oil of the tree of mercy from paradise. The
Angel Michael refuses Seth entrance into paradise, but
asks him to look three times through its open gates. The
first time Seth saw the Garden of Eden and in its center
a tree of wondrous beauty upon which five thousand different kinds of fruit grew. The second time he saw this tree
despoiled of fruits and denuded of leaves, with a hideous
serpent coiled about its trunk. The third time Seth saw
the tree rising to heaven, covered with leaves and fruits.
The serpent had vanished. On the crest of the tree, Seth saw
a child of wonderful beauty.

Archangel Michael explained the vision: the first sight
showed the condition of man before the Fall, the second
presented the tree after man had fallen into sin, and the
third the beginning of salvation for mankind. Michael gave
Seth a branch of the Tree of Life. Seth planted it on Adam's
grave, which was on the summit of Golgotha. The branch
grew into a beautiful tree. A beam from it was used for the
cross on which the Saviour was crucified. The mysterious
significance of the Tree of Life, continued into that of the
cross, appears in the vision that closes the drama of religion.

The Tree of Life is in New Jerusalem: "In the midst of the street of it, and on either side of the river, was there the tree of life, which bare twelve manner of fruits, and yielded her fruit every month: and the leaves of the tree were for the healing of the nations" (Revelation 22:2).

Through ancient Christianity, the interpretation of the cross as the Tree of Life is common. It is the symbol of the cross in the old covenant (*lignum vitae* = *lignum crucis*). Augustine[1] considered Christ the fruit of the tree of life and Origen presents the equation Tree of Life = Cross = Christ. We shall not accumulate here instances from poetry and art[2] for the identification of or substitution for the Tree of Life and the cross. Only a single instance should be added, chosen from the abundant material gathered by Mrs. J. H. Philpot because it beautifully illustrates the last development of the connection between the first and the second Adam and the significance of the tree within it. The ancient church had devoted the day before Christmas to the memory of Adam and Eve and it was customary in many parts of the continent to give at Christmas a dramatic presentation of the story of the Creation and of the Fall, connecting it with the Nativity. From this celebration arose the Paradise plays that were familiar to the Middle Ages from the thirteenth century onward. Here is the place of the well-known legend that the cross of Christ was fashioned from a tree that had sprung from the chip of the Tree of Knowledge. It served as the link between the celebrated events and tied together the memory of the Fall and of the birth of the Redeemer.

[1] *De civitate*, 1331.
[2] Compare, for instance, H. Heras' "The Tree of Life," *The New Review* (April, 1944), XIX, No. 112, p. 281, and Romould Bauerreis, *Arbor vitae. Der Lebensbaum und seine Verwendung in Literatur, Kunst und Brauchtum des Abendlandes* (Munich, 1935).

The central scene of the Paradise play was sometimes the one in which a single tree, laden with apples and decked with ribbons, was carried to the stage by an actor. In this way the apple-bearing tree became the recognized scenic symbol of Christmas. The scene was connected with the early legend of the church that all nature blossomed at the birth of Christ who, in the words of Mrs. Philpot, "Himself, according to the fanciful symbolism of the time, was the very tree of life which had once stood in paradise." We recognize here, of course, the origin of the familiar custom of the Christmas tree that was traced back in Germany to the beginning of the seventeenth century.

Professor J. Konrad Dannhauer, a celebrated theologian of the eighteenth century in Strassburg, quoted by Mrs. Philpot, expressed his indignation about that custom as follows: "Among the other absurdities with which men are often more busied at Christmas than with the Word of God, there is also the Christmas or fir tree, which they erect in their houses. They hang it with dolls and sweetmeats and then shake it and cause it to shed its flowers. I know not the origin of the custom, it is a child's game. Far better were it to lead the children to the spiritual cedar, Jesus Christ."

Mrs. Philpot wonders at the "fanciful symbolism" that saw in Jesus Christ Himself the tree of life. The scholarly professor uses in his polemics against the Christmas tree that very symbolism in speaking of the "spiritual cedar, Jesus Christ." Each in his own way failed to recognize that what is now a spiritual comparison or fanciful symbolism was once for the mind of the ancient Orientals much more. It was once no empty metaphor, but reality. It was no arbitrary figure of speech in which a phrase that ordinarily means one thing is used for another, to suggest a likeness between the two, when Jesus Christ was called the Tree of Life. In comparisons of this kind, to be found as far back as in the myths and the rituals of ancient Mesopotamia, lived the memory of an age in which the totemistic god was conceived of as a tree. Jahveh says: "I am like a green cypress. From me thy fruit will be found." Jahveh was once in days He Himself has forgotten a tree like the baalim of the tribes who were neighbors to the Israelites.

We recognized in the analysis of the Fall myth that this was His primitive shape, which He exchanged later for that of a human and superhuman god. The first sin was committed against Him when He was still a tree-god. What does it mean that Jesus Christ is now compared with a cedar? Nothing else than that He too is sometimes conceived as a tree and is hailed as the cedar like Tammuz who was the lover of the Mesopotamian goddess, Ishtar. As king of the Jews, He is compared with the Tree of Life as was the king in the Gilgamesh epic in other texts and hymns, a few thousand years before Him. His worship is thus regressively expressed in terms of the tree-totemistic cult. Calling Him the Tree of Life would mean calling Him the son of god, the tree-totemistic god.

In comparing Jesus Christ with a cedar, the old suppressed idea re-emerged. Here, as so often in the evolution of human civilization, phases of a relatively late period bring to the surface once more something that had been long submerged. The later Christian fathers, likening Jesus Christ to the Tree of Life, revived a concept that had been dormant for many centuries, a concept of the primitive tree worship of which we discovered traces in the Fall story. In connecting the ancient tradition of the first sin with the sacrificial death of the Redeemer on the cross and in tying the Tree of Life to the cross, the Church, without being aware of it, expressed the tragedy of mankind in the language of tree totemism. Do we ourselves know that we, too, unconsciously fall back into tree worship when we stand around the Christmas tree?

At this point many problems that have resisted the efforts of researchers emerge. Choosing from them is irksome. Should we pursue the thread leading from the Tree of Life to the cross that finally became a symbol of the Saviour Himself? Should we try to explore the mystery of salvation on the cross? Is it our task to find out why the crucifixion of an Essene rabbi in some corner of an insignificant province of the Roman Empire shook the world? But did we not start from the unsolved question of whether there are features in the Passion that confirm the archaic law of talion?

At this moment the intermittent light of that elusive thought emerges again and beckons us to follow it. Will it lead us astray? There is something mysterious and highly significant in the kind of punishment, penance, or atonement suffered by the Saviour on the cross. It must have a secret meaning that He hung on the beams of the cross. The translation of the Passion into the language of tree totemism and the equalization of the Tree of Life with the cross seem to open a new avenue for the explorer as if here were an undiscovered track.

Voices around us try to discourage the attempt at inquiry and, strangely enough, they come from two opposite sides. The one is heard from the representatives of religion. They declare that the Church has entirely solved the mystery. We are told that we have to accept this solution. It is contained in the works of the great Fathers of the Church. The answers we are searching for are there given in plain, easily understood terms in catechism lessons. Only one premise is necessary: faith. We know that he that believeth shall be saved, but we cannot oblige. Like Faust, we profess: The message I have heard, but faith is lacking.

On the other hand, religion declares that not all of that mystery can be solved by the human mind. A part of it, an unsolved portion, is beyond the power of human reason and will always remain impenetrable to man. And not to man only. What does Charles Wesley's Passion hymn say?

> 'Tis mystery all! The immortal dies!
> Who can explore this strange design?
> In vain the firstborn seraph tries
> To sound the depths of love divine.
> 'Tis mercy all! let earth adore.
> Let angels minds inquire no more.

Since we are very much lower than the angels, we need not heed that solemn warning. We can dare enter where they fear to tread and to inquire.

The other warning voice is that of sweet reasonableness or rather of sober rationalism. It is not as high-sounding as that of religious argument, but it is persistent and awakens an echo in ourselves. It refers to the fact that the crucifixion of Christ was nothing extraordinary, that it was a customary punishment usually inflicted on slaves and non-Romans from the days of the Punic Wars on. Did we not hear from Josephus that after the capture of Jerusalem "there was not enough room for crosses nor enough crosses for bodies"? Crucifixion was certainly to the Romans the most humiliating punishment besides being, as Cicero said, the most cruel and hideous of all tortures. But just this most degrading and agonizing death became the redemption of the world, the glory of mankind. The infamous figure of the condemned, hanging on the cross, has been converted and that humiliating death became a symbol of resurrection and salvation. The Jews require a sign and the Greek seeks after wisdom, Paul writes to the Corinthians (I Corinthians 1:22), but "we preach Christ crucified, unto the Jews a stumblingblock, and unto the Greeks foolishness; But unto them which are called, both Jews and Greeks, Christ the power of God, and the wisdom of God." The utterly humiliating punishment turned into triumph. The tree that became the cross is the theme of a thousand hymns:

> O tree of beauty, tree most fair,
> Ordained those holy limbs to bear.
> Gone is thy shame, each crimsoned bough
> Proclaims the king of glory now.

We are inclined to believe that there was a Rabbi Jehoshua of Nazareth among the thousands crucified by the Romans. Perhaps he died crying with a loud voice: "My God, my God, why hast thou forsaken me?" With this consideration we arrive at the critical point: the historical Jesus died the death of a thousand Jews, criminals and innocents. What made His death distinguished from the others? What turned that agonizing hanging on a wooden post, surmounted by a crossbeam, into the most adored scene? What changed that cross into the favorite symbol of millions of people? For our analytic exploration the problem of whether there was a historic Jesus is not important. We deal here with the Christ myth, with the problems of Christology. We want to find out what is the occult meaning of the very crucifixion and by which emotional dynamics it was made possible to turn the most infamous death into the glory of salvation.

The way to the solution of the problem is paved by the recognition that in the myth of the Fall and in the Christ's Passion the tree of life and its prehistoric prototype, the tree totem, have been resurrected in a disguised form. In

times long forgotten, at the epoch when the tradition of the
Fall was fixed in written form and at the time the Gospels
reported the crucifixion of Christ—in a past beyond oblivion—trees were worshiped as gods by the Mediterranean
people, and also by the tribes later on called the Hebrews.
Not only were prayers addressed to them, they were hung
with votive gifts. The sacred date palm at Nijran was adored
and hung with fine clothes by the Arabs at an annual
feast. The people of Mecca hung upon a certain tree animals, weapons, garments, eggs, and other gifts. With the
ancient Phoenicians and Canaanites trees were esteemed as
gods and honored with libations and sacrifices.[3] The natives
of the Vindhy, an island of India, until lately offered human
sacrifices to trees. In Egypt the sycamore is hung with jars
and fruits and in Greece the tree sacred to Artemis was
hung with the weapons of the chase. The ancient Egyptians,
Babylonians, Greeks, and the tribesman of our time hang
gifts upon trees. They are destined for the trees, are gifts
to the gods embodied in the tree, which is supposed to be
a divine person or a god.

At this point that thought which eluded us before and
whose contours we dimly perceived steps into the limelight.
It leads to a new concept of the hidden meaning of Christ's
death on the Cross, which is a late descendant of the totem
tree, exactly as the gifts ancient Oriental people and primitive tribes attributed to sacred trees. Christ on the Cross
is, so to speak, a recent reappearance of the human sacrifice brought to the Father-God. This sacrificial character
of the crucifixion is not contradicted by the fact that it was
the Roman form of capital punishment for grave offenses.

[3] Compare Robertson Smith, *Lectures on the Religion of the Semites*
(3d ed., 1927), p. 185 and passim; and the article on tree worship in
Encyclopedia of Religion and Ethics (Edinburgh, 1921), XI, p. 448 f.

This form was perhaps itself a transformation of an ancient sacrifice to the gods.

Another aspect of the crucifixion becomes transparent when the light cast upon it by the novel concept spreads into a new direction, namely to the form of the punishment or atonement. When we want to understand the concealed meaning of Christ's hanging on the Cross tree, we have to follow that forgotten, ancient idea of sacrifice to the sacred tree to its consequences. Christ is united with the tree, the animistic tree god. The most primitive way of such a fusion is to cling to the object, to become one with it by cleaving to it, to adhere to it until one becomes inherent. What takes place in crucifying Christ is—expressed in tree-totemistic terms—the union with His Father. It is the plastic realization and fulfillment of His saying that the Father and He are one. This is in a sense the translation of the great mystery of His death into the language of the unconscious. In His dying on the Cross, He was united with His Father, "for the tree . . . is . . . man's life" (Deuteronomy 20:19).

CHAPTER XXIV

THE UNCONSCIOUS MEANING
OF CRUCIFIXION

BUT DIDN'T we overreach ourselves in this interpretation? Our inference that Christ's voluntary and self-sacrificing death has also the character of the union with the Father cannot be confirmed by the Jewish tradition, out of which Christianity grew. Such a community with God was certainly also aspired to by the Jews, but it had other forms of expression and never took the shape of the idea of full incorporation. This concept belongs rather to the circle of the mystic religions of the Hellenistic era. Not even the Jewish mystery cults of the Essenes, of the Therapeutae, hold a view whereby that most intimate union with the Father, that "to be in God," is possible for man.[1]

God can be approached only spiritually. It is true that the Scripture says: "But ye that did cleave unto the Lord your God are alive every one of you this day" (Deuteronomy 4:4), and advises, "love the Lord thy God, and

[1] Compare the discussion in Joseph Klausner's *From Jesus to Paul* (New York, 1943), pp. 492 ff., and A. Deissmann, *Die neutestamentliche Formel "In Christo Jesu,"* (Marburg, 1892), and Bouset-Gressmann, *Die Religion des Judentums im späthellenischen Zeitalter* (Tubingen 1926).

that thou mayest obey his voice, and that thou mayest cleave unto him, for he is thy life" (Deuteronomy 30:20). It is significant that the Talmudic Haggadah asks about it: "Is it possible for a human being to 'cleave' unto the divine presence?" and answers that it is only possible "to cleave unto the attributes of the Holy One, blessed be He" (Kethuboth 111b). Klausner[2] calls that view of a mystic union a pagan belief. We know that the idea of "being swallowed up in God" existed in the Hellenistic circles with which Paul came in contact. It is very likely that the apostle of the Gentiles extended the belief in cleaving to God in the Jewish sense to the concept of a mystic communion. In Paul's writings the expression "being in Christ" (or "in the Lord") occurs again and again.[3] It is meant almost literally in the sense of the mystery cults of the time: "I am crucified with Christ: nevertheless I live; yet not I, but Christ liveth in me . . . (Galatians 2:20).

We can see at least the possibility of a concept of Christ's union with the Father by means of crucifixion, of an idea developed in late Jewish times, under the influence of the mystery cults.

We return to the discussion of the ambiguous character of penalty in late myths, to the double face of mythological punishment. I stated that in some myths the punishment and the realization of the forbidden wish coincide, form a strange unity. This compromise character of the mythical penance for an outrage against a god can be even better understood in the analysis of some Greek myths than in the death of Jesus Christ on the Cross.

A digression into Greek antiquity and its myths of savior

[2] *Ibid.*
[3] In the Epistles, 164 times.

figures similar to the figure that Christ was for the Jews
is at this point the more permissible because it shows the
ubiquity of the dynamics operating in the legends of other
civilizations. At the same time it will disclose the concealed
resemblance of all those myths of a god or hero who is
cruelly punished and then elevated. That unconscious
circle, beginning with a great crime or sin against the highest God, atoned for by terrible tortures and resolving in the
union with this God, is a course characteristic of a certain
phase of myth development. We endeavored to prove that
even in those highly developed forms of punishment the
primitive law of talion, insisting that the penalty fit the
crime, survived and remained valid.

When Ulysses visited the Underworld, as Homer tells us,
he saw three penitents, suffering great anguish. There was
the giant Tityus, Son of Earth, bound fast as he lay
stretched upon the ground, while two vultures, one at either
side, tore at his liver. There was Sisyphus condemned eternally to roll a "pitiless" stone up a hill, from whence it invariably rolled down, and Tantalus, who stood neck-deep
in a pool of water that ever receded as he sought to drink
of it, while a wind tossed out of his reach the many fruits
that hung just above his head.

What was the sin of Tantalus? There are different versions of it. The one tells that the hero asked the gods to a
banquet and served them flesh of his own son Pelops,
whom he had cut in pieces and cooked in a boiler. Zeus,
perceiving the deception, restored the child to life. In another version, Tantalus is said to have stolen the nectar
and ambrosia, the food of the gods, and to have given it
to his friends. The punishment in this case would well fit
the crime, since Tantalus is "tantalized" when he cannot

satisfy his thirst and hunger although the water and the fruits seem to be so near. Tantalus aspired to a life similar to that of the gods and dared to be like them. In the words of Athenaeus: "Being a man insatiable in his desire for enjoyment, he asked that he should live after the fashion of the gods."[4] Tantalus' sin, according to this version, springs from the same motives as that of Lucifer of whom Isaiah (14:13) had said, ". . . thou hast said in thine heart, I will ascend into heaven, I will exalt my throne above the stars of God: I will sit also upon the mount of the congregation." This same motive Adam had, or at least Jahveh suspects him to have: "Behold, the man is become as one of us, to know good and evil: and now, lest he put forth his hand, and take also of the tree of life, and eat, and live for ever" (Genesis 3:22).

We see here the nature of the crime and its motives. But we also see that the punishment fits the crime. The sin was to eat the food of the gods (originally to eat them), the motive was unlimited ambition and the wish to be like them. The realization of this wish was possible only by incorporating them. The punishment is a display of the futility of this wish, a demonstration of its eternal frustration. A side glance at the latest analytic interpretation of the Tantalus myth is perhaps mildly amusing: H. A. Bunker suggests[5] that in the background of this myth is "the theme of oral frustration at the hands of mother." "It is," says this psychoanalyst, "hardly necessary to point out the praedipal fantasy here depicted" (p. 356). It is not necessary because

[4] Jane Ellen Harrison, *Prolegomena to the Study of Greek Religion,* 3d edition.
[5] Henry Alden Bunker, "The Feast of Tantalus," *The Psychoanalytic Quarterly,* XIX, 1952, No. 3, and "Tantalus, A Praedipal Figure of Myth," *The Psychoanalytic Quarterly,* XXI, 1953, No. 2.

it would be mistaken. The mythical crime concerns, in reality, the eating of the Father-God. The version of Tantalus serving his own son to the gods is in reality a reversal, similar to that of the Bible in which Abraham has to sacrifice his son to Jahveh.

Tityus and Prometheus have to undergo similar punishments. An eagle—in Tityus' case two vultures—eats on their livers, which each night grow again. The liver is in Greek thought the organ in which passion dwells. Thus the punishment concerns the seat of forbidden desires, but this is a secondary interpretation. The vulture and eagle are not only birds sacred to Zeus, but originally Zeus himself, god-father in his totemistic form. Bunker justly remarks that the punishments of Sisyphus and Prometheus have common features, including what he calls "a common eternal undoing." (Prometheus' liver grows nightly, Sisyphus' rock rolls down again eternally.)

According to the law of talion, the oral frustration must be a punishment for eating forbidden food. If Prometheus is eaten by eagles and Tityus by two vultures, they have eaten something that was tabooed. They are punished by being eaten because they committed a crime in eating what was forbidden. This conclusion is in the sense of that archaic principle of retaliation, as inevitable as the fact that a person who has eaten something has an upset stomach. We know what was in an earlier tradition the outrage of those sinners: they have devoured the old god. Thanks to the analytic method of interpretation, we arrived here at the reconstruction of a Greek counterpart to the biblical Fall story. In the Prometheus myth and in the Tityus myth the original crime or sin is the same as Adam's in the Bible; however, the harmed and outraged god appears not in the shape of a tree totem, but in that of an archaic totemistic animal (eagle, vultures) that was worshiped thousands of years before Zeus became god. The law of talion also pervades other ancient myths. In the Sisyphus saga the penitent has to roll an enormous stone up a hill, from whence it always rolls down. If our supposition, our "Hilfshypothese," as the German scholars would call it, is correct, Sisyphus' crime must have been to roll that stone until it reached the peak of the hill, to pile that rock on the hill. At first, this does not seem to make sense, or as little sense as what S. Reinach calls the *"puériles et contradic-toirées"* explanations of the mythologists.[6]

Yet there are some almost unnoticed features of the Sisyphus myth that might shed a new light on the saga and help us discover its concealed meaning. The myth tells us that Sisyphus was "the craftiest of men" and was even "as wise as a god." He had abused that endowment of almost divine knowledge and was thus terribly punished by the gods. Casually, in an aside, so to speak, we learn that he founded Corinth, and that was his crime or sin. There are, of course, several versions of the tale, but we venture an interpretation faithful to the principle that the punishment must fit the crime. Sisyphus' crime is the same as that of the children of men who planned to build a city and a tower whose top may reach unto heaven. The Lord came down to see the city and said: ". . . this they begin to do: and now nothing will be restrained from them, which they have imagined to do" (Genesis11:6).

Men wanted to reach heaven. They were guilty of that crime that the Greek called *hybris* or *hubris,* of conceit and of haughty presumption directed against the gods. And

[6] *Cultes, Mythes et Religions,* II (Paris, 1906), p. 90.

thus was Sisyphus. Is it accidental that the myth calls him
a master builder and attributes to him the foundation of
Corinth? It seems Zeus liked the building of skycrapers
as little as Jahveh the building of that Tower of Babel.
Both gods considered the construction of high buildings an
infraction of or intrusion upon their privacy. The Sisyphus
myth must originally have had some features analogous to
the Genesis tale of the building of the Tower of Babel. Only
in this way can we explain the special kind of punishment
the king had to suffer in Hades, where he tries eternally
to roll a stone uphill and always fails. If the designing and
building of a house or a tower reaching to heaven was the
outrageous crime of Sisyphus, the myth that shows him
rolling a stone up the hill depicts his action in a displacement to a symbolic detail. S. Reinach has brilliantly shown[7]
that the ancient King of Corinth is depicted as carrying
on his normal pursuit in the underworld. Reinach explains
Sisyphus' difficulties in the transportation of rocks to the
height of Acro-Corinth. The oldest meaning of the myth
that had perhaps the more direct concern with stone worship—we will remark on it—was very likely changed and
adapted to a more progressed level of civilization that already knew the building of houses or cities.

If we can trust our opinion—or if you like, our prejudice
—about the persistent equivalence of crime and punishment, this same transformation and evolutional adaption
should be discerned also in other myths whose original
meaning is obscured and made unrecognizable by secondary
elaboration that superimposes a new content on their primal
one. It is a process similar to that which archaeology has

[7] "Sisyphe aux enfers," *Rev. Arch.* 1903, p. 111. Albert Camus calls
Sisyphus "l'homme absurde" in *Le mythe de Sisyphus* (Paris, 1946).

found in the excavation of the cities of ancient civilizations, for instance of old Troy, where several newer cities were built on the very place on which the old settlements had stood before they were destroyed by fire, water, or conquest.

This secondary elaboration can easily be constructed when the content of the myth obviously carries a distinct time mark. Here is an instance: Ixion, son of Phlegas, King of the Lapithae in Thessaly, had murdered his father-in-law and abused the pardon of Zeus by trying to seduce Hera. The indignant Zeus bound the criminal on a fiery wheel that spun unceasingly through the air. The "time mark" is here implied. The invention of the wheel belongs to historical time. The oldest wheels known to us are, according to Ralph Linton,[8] at the royal tombs at Ur. The axle, fixed to a cart with a wheel, was known in Sumer by 3000 B.C. According to the principle of talion, the eternal revolutions of Ixion bound on the fiery wheel must be in intimate connection with his crime against Zeus. The mythologists explain the story with the practice of carrying a blazing revolving wheel through the fields that needed the heat of the sun. Thus the wheel must, according to the explanation of the mythologists, have appeared at first as the earthly image of the sun. But the sun was originally a god, for instance the Egyptian Ra, Surya in the Hindu Vedas, Helios in Greece. The punishment of Ixion is, therefore—at least in one version—comprised of being incorporated into the celestial body of the sun god, i.e., of Zeus.

It is likely that this interpretation refers only to a secondary elaboration of the myth. The eternal revolving of the wheel was perhaps originally a symbolic presentation of Ixion having unceasing sexual intercourse whereby the fiery

[8] *The Tree of Culture* (New York, 1955), p. 114 f.

wheel substitutes for the vagina within which Ixion moves.
In this case our formula according to which the forbidden
wish is in the myth fulfilled, but changed into torture,
would be confirmed: Ixion is condemned to have eternal
sexual excitement. (It is remarkable that this interpretation
is not to be found, as far as I know, in literature. There is
perhaps an allusion to it at a place that is very remote from
analytic theories: Benjamin Disraeli, later Earl of Beacons-
field, wrote as a young man in 1837 a burlesque satire,
"Ixis in Heaven." In it is a funny scene in which Jupiter,
who almost catches his wife with Ixion, asks Apollo to
bring him a wheel of his chariot. Here is the following
dialogue. "What shall I do tomorrow?" inquired the God of
Light; "Order an eclipse," replied Jove. "Bind the insolent
wretch to the wheel; hurl him to Hades; its motion shall be
perpetual." "What am I to bind him with?" inquired
Hercules. "The girdle of Venus," replied the Thunderer.
The passage seems to prove that the young writer Disraeli
had an unconscious understanding of the concealed meaning of Ixion's penalty.)

We are too little aware that the punishments in a single
myth can have different forms, multiple manifestations.
Such a variety serves to demonstrate the reinforcement or
aggravation of penalty. Its occurrence can also be explained
by the transformation of the punishing gods in the myths.
The eagle that eats the liver of Prometheus is God in his
early prehellenistic, in his totemistic form. The form of
punishment is transformed or complicated according to
the changes of religious ideology. What does it mean, for
instance, that Prometheus is chained to a rock as punishment for his crime? At first, the character of this penance
appears obvious. Prometheus was a prisoner on this rock

exactly as is a modern criminal, let us say Dreyfus on Devil's Island, or in a different position, Napoleon on Elba. Yet it would be a grave mistake to compare this modern form of punishment with that in the Greek myth. There the penalty is meant quite literally. The archsinner Prometheus is not banned on an island, but in material reality is chained on the rock.

We understand well that this is a most cruel and drastic form of penalty, but we cannot imagine how it too should fit the crime committed by this culture-hero. I now return to the point of departure to this too lengthy digression, to the comparison of the particular fate of Prometheus with that of Christ. The Greek half-god is chained on the rock from which he is freed later, to be reconciled with Zeus. The Jewish Saviour hangs on the Cross from which He is resurrected and reunited with His Father.

Does such a comparison not sound fantastic, even sacrilegious? Several scholars, for instance Karl Kereny,[9] compare Prometheus to Christ. Both are saviors of mankind and both have the most painful fate of men. Prometheus is in many Greek versions considered the great benefactor of man to whom he gave art, craft, and culture. Some describe him as a god, some as Titan. The common features of their destiny, the similarity of their fate in the most humiliating penalty, and the final reunion with the father-god were often discussed. The one common element whose significance is neglected by most mythologists is the simi-

---

[9] Karl Kereny, *Prometheus, das Mythologem der menschlichen Existenz* (Albae Vigiliae, 1946). More often Prometheus is compared with Adam and his myth with that of the Fall of Man. Compare for instance Walter Headlam, "Prometheus and the Garden of Eden," *The Classical Quarterly*, April, 1934, and the Ph.D. thesis by Elisabeth Locker-Euler, *Philosophische Deutung von Sündenfall and Prometheus Mythus* (Heidelberg, 1933).

larity of the punishment both gods suffer, the one being bound to the rock, the other nailed to the cross. The punishment consists in this enforced and helpless hanging on the rock or the cross in agony without hope of being freed.

The clue of the tree—and the cross is but a tree—in its secret significance as a totemistic god served us as *leitfossil*. This leading idea let us recognize that in the crucifixion Christ is most intimately united with the tree god. Through being hanged on it He became one with God-Father. The Lord appears in the Christ myth in a double form: in the center of the sacred story as Jahveh, the spiritual Father in the superhumanlike form of the Almighty, and in His most primitive forgotten and obsolete shape as tree totem. The fusion with the sacred tree is presented as penalty, executed by such mechanical means as hanging and nailing. The last act of the holy tragedy, following the execution of the sinless Christ, is His ascension to Heaven and His reunion with God-Father.

That other sufferer and savior, Prometheus, is bound to the rock by Zeus as Christ was nailed to the cross with the permission of Jahveh. The similarity seems to end suddenly at this point. The rock on which Prometheus hangs, suffering agony, cannot be compared with the Cross. Here is an inanimate piece of stone, there a sacred symbol. But the rock was once in the primitive mind as little inanimate as the tree.

We cannot and we do not want to discuss here the prehistoric stone worship with the same extensiveness as the tree-cult of the ancient people and of the savage tribes of our time. It must suffice to state that the worship of stone, of which important traces remained in altars and monuments until the present time, was once observed everywhere in the Paleolithic Age. Its universality in prehistory can be studied in the documents to be found in the textbooks of comparative religion and of archaelogy.[10] Stone pillars have been objects of religious veneration in Greece since prehistoric times. Arthur Evans discovered several in the great prehistoric palace at Cnossus in Crete. They usually have cut in them the sacred sign of the double ax, the symbol of the Cretan deity afterwards called Zeus. Prometheus, bound on the rock of the Caucasus, is incorporated by Zeus, who was a stone god in his prehistoric shape.

We note that the highest god in the Prometheus myth is represented in three forms: as Zeus, a superhuman but humanlike god, as the eagle devouring the liver of Prometheus in his animal-totemistic character, and as stone totem in the role of the rock on which the savior is bound. Prometheus is celebrated as the wisest half-god and teacher of mankind, as Sisyphus is the craftiest builder, as Tantalus is the most clever, and as Hercules is the most powerful half-god. Those criminals and archsinners are in the popular imagination "heroes rather than evildoers," as Bunker correctly says.[11] In many versions they appear not only as benefactors, but even as saviors of mankind; Prometheus, in some versions of the myth, even as their creator.

The first sinners—we include Christ also in this group because He Himself, though sinless, took the original sin on His shoulders—have thus a double function within the myth and the following legend tradition. They are rebels against the highest gods, the fathers, whom they defy and whom they want to replace and they free mankind in teach-

[10] A good survey of stone worship is to be found in the article in the *Encyclopedia of Religion and Ethics*, XI, p. 864 ff.
[11] Henry Alden Bunker, "Tantalus," *The Psychoanalytic Quarterly*, XXII, 1953, No. 2, p. 168.

ing them all that is worth knowing or achieving. They are
gods themselves or half-gods, sons of gods, and have as
such superhuman and divine qualities. Even Adam as the
son of Jahveh is, in the late Jewish tradition, conceived as
being worshiped by the angels and endowed with divine
power and wisdom. Thus is the second Adam, Jesus Christ.
As Prometheus brought men the fire and Sisyphus taught
them to build houses, Adam was the first to teach them
agriculture.

We asserted that the penalty that those gods and culture
heroes have to suffer is slowly changing its character into
victory and triumph. Here the law of talion operates in the
opposite direction: the crime repeated after its atonement
fits the punishment. Prometheus ascends to Olympus and
Christ is resurrected to sit at the right side of the Father.
The aim of their ambition is fulfilled after their rebellion
and outrage against the supreme god has been paid for by
the most torturous penalty.

According to the double role of those mythological
figures as terrible sinners and as saviors the character of
their deed appears alternatively as the most condemnable
outrage and revolt and as the most praiseworthy and celebrated action, as the greatest benefit for men. Adam's eating
of the forbidden tree is interpreted by late commentators
(Kant, Schiller, Hegel, and many others) as a liberating
deed, leading men from the state of savages to culture and
paving the way of mankind to civilization.[12] Prometheus
and Hercules were often celebrated as culture heroes and
benefactors of mankind. It seems that on a long detour the
freeing and liberating character of that crime of parricide

---

[12] Compare the discussion of the different philosophical interpretations
in Elisabeth Locker-Euler's book.

and deicide returns from the repression. After a long interval, man sees the positive side of the original revolt against
the gods. Aeschylus considers Zeus a cruel despot and feels
sympathy for Prometheus bound. This great tragic hero
protests to the end against Zeus: "Behold me, I am
wronged."

No such defiance is to be expected in Jewish view of
the relation of Jahveh and man. Besides Lucifer, only
Adam revolts against the Lord. This primal man has in
Milton's *Paradise Lost* a vision of man's future and marvels
at the good resulting from his sin, especially the coming
of Christ:

> . . . full of doubt I stand,
> Whether I should repent me now of sin
> By me done and occasion'd, or rejoice
> Much more, that much more good thereof shall spring.

That famous "Paradox of the Fortunate Fall" was followed through Christian history by A. O. Lovejoy[13] who
remarks that the Fall "could never be sufficiently condemned and lamented, and likewise, when all its consequences were considered, it could never be sufficiently
rejoiced over." The Church itself, which traces the downfall of mankind to Adam's sin, celebrates it in that magnificent, paradoxical piece of liturgy, "Exultet," on the Eve
of Easter. Since the guilt of the first sinner brought redemption to us all, it is called blessed or fortunate.

In that most solemn Catholic service, the original sin
is apostrophized: "O Felix Culpa."

St. Francis de Sales declared in his *Essai de l'amour de
Dieu* (1616) that Adam's sin served to excite and provoke
the benevolence of God. "Therefore the church, in a holy

---

[13] *Essays in the History of Ideas.* (Baltimore, 1948), p. 283.

excess of admiration, exclaims on the Eve of Easter 'O sin of Adam, truly necessary' . . . Of this truth we can say 'We should be lost, if we had not been lost'; that is to say, our loss has been our gain, since human nature has received more gifts of grace from its redemption by its Savior than it would have received from the innocence of Adam, if he had persevered in it."[14]

[14] Quoted by A. O. Lovejoy, *op. cit.*, p. 295.

CHAPTER XXV

THE FIRST AND THE SECOND ADAM

WE STARTED from the statement that the Fall myth and the Christ story form a single indivisible unit in the sense of a saga of crime and punishment. The first Adam commits the deed, the second atones for it with his death. The best way to demonstrate the unity and coherence of the two parts of the sacred story is to present their main features in the form of a comparison and confrontation. A first attempt of this kind was made nineteen hundred years before our time by St. Paul. But the doctrine of the Apostle of the Gentiles was built in the service of his Christology and our inquiry has the character of a criminal investigation. In this sense we have to take the sacrilegious liberty of treating the first and the second Adam as though they were one person. We can justify such a seemingly arbitrary attitude when we refer to the Gospels, which testify that the Son of Man took the sins of mankind upon Himself and suffered penance for them. He is, to use the expression of a British theologian,[1] the "Sin Bearer." Our criminal investigation moves in an unusual direction. It searches for evidence of the character of its crime through inquiry into its

[1] F. W. Dillistone, *Jesus Christ and His Cross* (Philadelphia, 1953), p. 66.

punishment or atonement. If the punishment fits the crime, it must be possible to conclude the nature of the offense by the scrutiny of the penalty.

The first result of our investigation, contained in the preceding chapter, was that Christ in His crucifixion was killed in such a way that He became one with God-father, with the tree-totemistic manifestation of the primitive deity. This is meant in its physical sense: the body of the redeemer is united with the body of the tree god. We understand that in the corporal character of that punishment a kind of mocking or sarcastic wish fulfillment is contained, as though it realizes the desire to become one with the father, to take His place. Christ is, so to speak—and that is more than a turn of phrase—"swallowed up" by the tree on which He hangs. That was perhaps the first and crudest shape of the mythological tradition that is the concealed background for the Passion. The young son-god is not only killed by the avenging father or his representative (for instance, the Semitic Adonis by a wild boar), but eaten.

If the nature of the first crime was such as we assumed, we would expect, according to the law of talion, that the punishment would have some other very definite features besides this one. It is, of course, impossible to construct an accurate, precise, and detailed counterpart of the crime within the procedure of the punishment. The changes in the religious and social evolution as they reflect themselves in the tradition will influence the shape and form of the later myth and will, through elaboration, distort the original congruity. One of the means by which the censorship succeeds in making a primary connection unrecognizable would be to put a time interval between two elements that are originally simultaneous. The strong conservatism—you can call it better the tenacity of tradition—expresses itself nevertheless in letting some inconspicuous details slip into the story, pointing to their original simultaneousness. Such neglected and unobserved features revealing a traditional connection can be brought to light in the analytic exploration of the Passion.

We expect as counterpart of the tradition of the original crime the following fundamental traits of the punishment or penalty suffered by the sinless second Adam: the tree that appears in the Eden story was a totemistic god and as such sacred and forbidden. The counterpart in the penalty of the second Adam should also be a god or tree worshiped as sacred. According to our reconstruction, the first crime was the murder and the devouring of father by prehistoric man, in reality by the gang of his sons. The repetition of that crime in the punishment has to be that the murderer is himself killed and eaten by his people. The main motive of the atrocious prehistoric deed was the ambitious wish to replace the father, to be he, in the biblical tale to become Jahveh. The corresponding ambition of the second Adam should be exposed and condemned.

If we can prove the existence and expression of those basic trends in the saga of Christ in His role as atoner, we could state that we succeeded in providing unambiguous internal evidence for the fact that our reconstruction of the nature of the first crime was correct. The Tree of Life that stands in the middle of the Garden of Eden is the center of this analytic exploration and of this book. It is, so to speak, the center of the newfound-land that this voyage of discovery is describing. That fateful tree served us as the *leitfossil* that we followed from the prehistoric ages to the dawn of civilization until we found its remains in the crosses and in the Christmas tree. In the narrative of the Fall of Man, the sacred tree is the last representative of that tree

god. The reverence for it, the taboo surrounding it, the prohibition to touch or eat it, are the last vestiges of the belief
that a god is in this tree or rather that a god is the tree—in
other words, Jahveh in His previous, now obsolete shape.
But that has been carefully suppressed for many millennia.
When the story of the Fall is written down, Jahveh is already
the God of the Heaven and "the earth is my footstool."
There are scarcely any memories left that He too was once
worshiped as a tree. He does not like to be reminded of
His humble beginnings since He has arrived, a parvenu
among the Semitic deities. Yet His family tree shows that
His ancestor was that tree we meet within the Garden
of Eden.

There is a direct though subterrranean connection between that tree of life, the animistic god, and the beam of
the cross. That sacred tree on which Christ was crucified
has its roots in the soil from which that plant in paradise
sprang. We heard of the old Christian legend that relates
the genealogy of the cross, made into a mystical poem by
Giocomo da Varaggio in the thirteenth century. A branch
taken from the tree of life was planted on the tomb of Adam
by his son Seth and grew into a tree from which Moses
obtained his magic rod. The wood of this tree was used
by Solomon for his temple. Finally, the executioners of
Jesus cut from it the material for the making of the cross.

The sign of the tree became the sacred symbol for the
early Christians, who saw it in all intersecting lines in
everyday life, in nature and in art.[2] At the beginning of the
3d century, Tertullian writes (*De Corona* 3): "At every
step, at every movement, at every coming in and coming
out, in putting on our clothes and our shoes, in the bath,
at table, in the evening, lying down or sitting, whatever

[2] "Cross" in *Encyclopedia of Ethics and Religion,* p. 328.

we assume, we mark our foreheads with a little sign of the cross." The early Christians had to defend themselves against the charge of the pagans that they paid adoration to the cross as to a god. Yet the great mass of Christians attached to it a divine character. They used the sign as a form of exorcism. It was supposed to work miracles. One of the most ancient crosses found in a Christian tomb in Rome had the inscription, "Crux est vita mihi; mors, inimice, tibi." (The cross is life to me; death, o enemy, to thee.)

Many churches possess among their miraculous relics alleged fragments of the cross. A legend tries to explain this abundance. It relates that these fragments not only can miraculously heal diseases, but can be reproduced and multiply themselves indefinitely. According to a Roman Catholic archaeologist, P. Didron, the cross is more than a figure of Christ; it is in iconography Christ Himself.[3] "Thus a legend has been created around it as if it were a living being . . ." It became the object of a veritable cult. The same writer, P. Didron, admits,[4] "The cross has received a worship similar, if not equal, to that of Christ; this sacred wood is adored almost equally with God Himself." Here the circle has come full round from the totemistic tree worship to the cult of the cross, from the tree of life to the tree of salvation.

Whoever studies the history of religions—the plural is intentional, since he who knows only one religion knows none—will get certain impressions about the gods and the objects of worship. A telescopic view of their parts shows that none of the gods was in power longer than a few thousand years. The oldest religions we know, for instance the worship of Egyptian gods, changed their character and

[3] *Histoire de Dieu,* 1843, p. 351.
[4] *Ibid.,* p. 412.

with this change altered the concept of their gods within five thousand years so radically that the old deities would scarcely be acknowledged any longer after three hundred generations. Gods come and go as in the vision the saint saw in Flaubert's *Tentation du Saint Antoine.* The small sequence of time during which each of them rules appears to their short-sighted worshipers an eternity. There is even a slow rise and decline observable to the biographer of the gods, a tiding of the waves of their worship. From an animistic cult to the totemistic religion and to the worship of a human and superhuman deity is but a step of eight thousand years, a mere fraction of the time during which Homo sapiens inhabited this planet. It is a span of civilization that can be bridged within two generations under the influence of missionaries with savage tribes in this rapidly accelerated phase of evolution.

We studied the history of the tree worship from its animistic beginnings to the phase of tree totemism, traces of which we still discovered in disguised form in the Genesis myth of the Fall. The tree god became the tree of life and as such first the dwelling place of a Semitic god, later his symbol. As such, it was revived in the form of the cross on which the Saviour died. By and by, the cross became the symbol for Christ. It was not only worshiped as the crucifix, or as the cross with the body of Jesus nailed upon it, but in its proper form without any annex.[5] As such, it finally evolved as the object of adoration.

[5] F. W. Dillistone, who shows the multitude of meanings the cross has adopted in many centuries, asserts that "when Christianity has lost touch with the cross, it has grown weak; when it has renewed its contact, it has renewed its strength." (*Jesus Christ and His Cross,* Philadelphia, 1953, p. 11.)

The scholar who observes this development will, if he is unbiased, state that the lives of the powerful and dreaded gods of ancient times follow a downward course. At the same time, a displacement from the original shape of the deity to one of his emblems or symbols takes place. Such an emblem becomes not only the representation of the religious idea, but often of the god himself. Sometimes, as in the case of the cross, it can even replace the deity. It is remarkable that the symbol receives all worship originally devoted to the god: "Hail cross, thou only hope of man!'" says the hymn of the Catholic church, sung on Palm Sunday and Good Friday: "O sacred wood, most royally empurpled, how beauteously thy stem dost shine. How glorious was its lot to touch those limbs, so holy and divine . . . Balance sublime upon whose beam was weighted the ransom of mankind."

A visitor from Mars would have great difficulty in discerning between the cult of a totem pole of North American Indians and the prayer before a cross. Not initiated in the eternal verities of the church, he might confuse the pious Christian with a fetish worshiper.

The second point I have to make is the most important with regard to the internal evidence to be produced. It concerns the event at the Last Supper that provided the origin for the central rite of the Christian Church, the Eucharist. The four passages dealing with the Last Supper (Matthew 26:26-29; Mark 14:22-25; Luke 22:15-20; I Corinthians 11:23-26) report that Jesus on the evening before His arrest, during a meal with His disciples, took bread and pronounced a blessing over it—or a thanksgiving. The bread was distributed to the disciples with the words, "This is my body." Jesus took the cup, and having given thanks, He gave it to them and said: "This is my blood of the new testament, which is shed for many." Paul has the addition, "Do this . . . in remembrance of me" after the words, "This is my body," and "as oft as ye drink it," after the words about the cup.

It is not my task here to describe the development of the Last Supper to the Eucharist of the Church nor to enter into the difficult discussion about the mystical significance of that center of the Mass in which the wafer and the wine are each time transubstantiated into the body and the blood of the Saviour, who remains simultaneously in heaven. We are concerned here with the significance of the scene of the Supper at the time of Passover, which Christ celebrated together with His pupils. No one who knows the literature on the subject will doubt that in the Eucharist the ancient totem meal is revived. In the primitive totem meal a sacred animal, a substitute for God, and generally forbidden to be eaten, is consumed by the whole tribe. In this ceremony, all members of the clan get into communion with God or the primeval father by incorporating him in the most literal sense, by the collective eating of his flesh and drinking of his blood. In the sacrament of the Eucharist, which inherited all essential features from the old totem meal, the Christians sanctify themselves and obtain identification with Christ, with the Son-God instead of the God-Father.

But what does it mean that the Saviour Himself offers His flesh and blood to the company of His disciples? In the scene, the Godhead seems to be twice present: once as the host of the sacramental meal and again as the food. We understand that here is a new development as it evolved from the primitive ritual of the totem meal. Robertson Smith and Freud[6] have shown us that, in the course of many centuries, the prehistoric ceremonial has taken different forms. The sacred animal was first eaten by the tribesman as commemoration of that atrocious murder. Later, the animal was sacrificed to the God, who eats it, together with his worshipers, and renews the union with them. Then follows the anthropic sacrifice in which a man was personifying the deity.

In the Last Supper and in the rite of the Eucharist that developed later from it, the son of God offers Himself as victim. He does not only sacrifice His life, redeeming the company of brothers from the original crime, but He also offers His flesh and blood as atonement for the cannibalistic, gruesome devouring of the primal father. In the sense of the *lex talionis,* this has to be considered the most important part of the evidence that the original sin was the devouring of the terrifying father of the antediluvial horde. The horror-filled scene of the paleolithic phase is re-enacted here. However, it is no longer the body of the primeval father, but that of the son, which is eaten in the communion. In the Eucharist celebrated in our churches the law of the prehistoric jungle survives, with the alternatives of eating or being eaten. Christ offering His flesh and blood to His community renews His penitence and redemption whenever that highest scene of the Eucharist is re-enacted. With Him and through Him, all mankind confesses its guilt of the crime, whose memory cannot be effaced and which haunts all men. The original meaning of Christ's sacrifice is still transparent when the Lord feeds His faithful people and gives them life: "Except ye eat the flesh of the Son of man,

---

[6] *Lectures on the Religion of the Semites* (2d ed., London, 1894), and *Totem and Taboo* (New York, 1950).

and drink his blood, ye have no life in you." Charles Wesley's hymn expresses the symbolic meaning with which the Eucharist became charged:

> Author of life divine,
> Who hast a table spread,
> Furnished with mystic wine
> And everlasting bread,
> Preserve the life Thyself hast given,
> And feed and train us up for heaven.

The last piece of internal evidence can easily be produced, because we can refer to the records of the Holy Scripture itself. The Genesis narrative does not leave any doubt about the nature of the impulse that impelled Adam to his nefarious deed. The Lord God Himself declares: "Behold the man is become as one of us, to know good and evil . . ." The son's efforts to put himself in the place of the Father-God began then and there and never ceased. The Son of Man, who took the guilt of the first Adam upon Himself, offered total atonement for the original sin in sacrificing His own life, attempting to appease His divine Father. The fateful ambivalent character manifests itself in the act of fullest atonement; it produces simultaneously the repetition and the fulfillment of that most ambitious desire. There is a characteristic hesitancy in Jesus to declare Himself as the Messiah, but at the end He proclaims the coming of the Kingdom of Heaven. He becomes the Son of God, then God Himself beside Jahveh, or rather in place of Jahveh.

Before we turn our undivided attention to the conclusions for which we are bound, the comparative view of the Fall and the Passion story, we have to remind ourselves that we cannot expect a full congruity of the two myths, since they belong to different phases of religious and social evolution.

We also have to take into account that their relationship is not simply that of crime and punishment. Christ, the sinless second Adam, does not repeat the original crime, but atones for it. His sacrificial death does not mark the breach of man with God, but man's reconciliation through His vicarious end, voluntary suffering and death.

It is obvious that we cannot restrict our reconstruction to the report of the Gospels, but have also to consider the later legends and traditions. The following presentation has to be dogmatic, since the material for the conclusions drawn here has been described and psychologically evaluated in preceding chapters. The circumstantial evidence produced there is partly from the area of comparative religion and prehistoric research, partly of the nature of internal evidence.

Here are the essential results of our new interpretation of the Fall myth, compared and contrasted with our interpretation of the Christ story.

The Fall Myth	*The Christ Myth*
Primeval man murdered the father of the primitive horde whose image became, many thousands of years later, the model for God.	Jesus Christ is the son of God. He is murdered.
The primeval father was eaten by the gang of brothers.	Jesus Christ is eaten in the Eucharist by the Christian community. In eating the Host and in drinking of the chalice, the flesh and blood of the Saviour is incorporated.
Primitive man wanted to incorporate the primeval father to obtain his power. The strong-	The Christians identify themselves with Christ in the act of the Eucharist.

est motive for the parricide
was the desire to take possession of the superior qualities of
the father and to replace him.

The eating of God-Father is
presented in the Genesis tale in
tree-totemistic language. Re-
gressing to the primitive tree
worship, the tree of life appears as the early representative of the Semitic God.

Jesus Christ dies on the cross,
which is a late descendant of
the tree of life. The cross became later an object of adoration as once the sacred tree
(of life) had been.

The murder and eating of God-
Father became the original sin,
which is shared by all men.

Christ took the sins of all men
and atoned for them by His
death by offering Himself as
sacrifice and thus redeeming
all from guilt.

This is, in bold outline, the state of divine affairs as they
appear in the Fall myth and in the Christ myth in our interpretation. It demonstrates the connection and cohesive-
ness of the manifest content of the two myths, but also their
inner relation. In our interpretation, the real character
of that primal crime becomes transparent, ascends from
the depths into which the repression of many millennia has
banned it to the surface of conscious recognition. The redesigning and re-evaluating of the mythical material that
was the premise of the analytic exploration took its departure from a single neglected, misunderstood element:
from the concealed significance of the tree in the middle of
the Garden of Eden, which was replaced by the cross in the
Garden of Calvary. It seemed to us that the historians of
religion and the mythologists, the exegetes and biblical
commentators did not do justice to the—in more than one
respect—central place of that fateful tree within the myth.
They did not see that tree for the wood of whose pulp

many thousands of books and papers about the two most important myths of mankind have been created.

A hypothesis such as the one presented here cannot be proved; it can be made only probable, since it is based mostly on internal evidence. It is not for me to evaluate the scope and limits of this new concept. If this pioneer attempt should succeed in reaching its aim, it cannot fail to cause ferment in the research area of comparative religion and of the history of human civilization. Such revolutionary changes cannot be immediately expected. The process of fermentation is a gradual one and takes a long time in a substance as tough and resistant as the interpretation of the Holy Scriptures. Also, this truth will be "allowed only a brief interval of victory between the two long periods when it is condemned as paradox or belittled as trivial" (Schopenhauer). The last test for my hypothesis is whether or not it advances our insight into the history of civilization. The Tree of Life, too, is known by the fruits it produces.

CHAPTER XXVI

THE SEXUAL RE-INTERPRETATION

THE NATURE of the first sin was clarified in our analytic exploration. While most commentaries agree that crime was an act of disobedience toward Jahveh, the character of the act itself remained unknown. Only relatively late, with the introduction of the allegoric or symbolic interpretation, was that disobedient offense conceived of as sexual. To arrive at such an interpretation, certain psychological premises have to be assumed. One of the decisive factors leading to that reinterpretation must have been a tendency to conceal the real character of Adam's transgression. No doubt the attempt was made here to camouflage the meaning of the Genesis tale, to hide the barbaric and crude content of a primal tradition reporting that terrible catastrophe of primordial ages. The idea that man had once, and more than once, been disobedient and defiant against the Lord was still imaginable to the ancient Hebrews. The idea of God's murder and incorporation had already passed over the horizon of the people.

How did the reinterpretation of the old myth come about? Let us for some moments return to the comparison of the criminal interrogation and to the view that the Genesis tale is a mystery story. No one will doubt that it is a crime story, the story of the crime of crimes. In our comparison with fiction, we remarked that in this story the criminal was identified, but that the real nature of his crime remained unknown. Let us now search for a modern counterpart of that crime or mystery story in order to compare the introduction of the sexual interpretation in the tradition. We imagine that on a lonely farm, on which live the old farmer, his wife, and a hired man, a similar crime is committed. (No allusion to Eugene O'Neill's drama, *Desire Under the Elms*, is intended.) The old farmer is killed and the authorities do not doubt that the young farmhand is the murderer. During the inquest, the hired man denies the deed, but admits that he had, at the critical hour, sexual intercourse with the farmer's wife.

Something similar to that must have happened with the primal tradition as it is reflected in the late interpretation of the Genesis narrative by Paul, Augustine, and the Fathers of the Church. The repression of sexual tendencies, increasing with asceticism of the Jewish Christians, favored, of course, the development of such a concept. But the decisive factor in the disavowal of the nature of the original sin was the impossibility of admitting the murder of God-Father. As a very diluted and comparatively unimportant remnant of the original version of the crime remained the feature that Adam's offense was an act of disobedience toward the Lord.

Compared with the original character of the crime, forbidden sexual intercourse was a minor offense. The process of substitution and distortion leading to the present concept of original sin is to be explained as the result of the combined effects of two emotional powers. The one pulled the inquiring mind away from the recognition of the real character of the deed; the other pushed the inquiry into the direction of forbidden sexual activity.

There are only two crimes punishable in the most primitive societies: parricide and incest. These two crimes became the two taboos of totemism. They produced the prohibitions against eating the sacred animal and marrying within one's own clan. Freud points out that the two taboos with which human morality begins "are not on a par psychologically."[1] Sexual desires divide men. The new social organization of the brothers, each of whom wanted the women of the father, would have collapsed in a struggle of all against all, had not the law against incest rescued its fragile structure. Besides emotional factors, the prohibition of incest had a powerful, practical basis.

The protection of the totem animal or the prohibition against killing and eating it was entirely founded on emotional motives. In it the original crime was unconsciously commemorated and its repetition in its displacement to the totem animal was forever prevented. A covenant with the father allayed the burning sense of guilt and a kind of reconciliation with the father was attempted in the totemistic system that respected his life even in his substitute, an animal. The brothers thus gave a promise "not to repeat the deed that had brought destruction on their real father."[2]

It seems to me that in this brilliant discussion Freud does not consider an emotional factor of paramount impact for the beginning of primitive morality. I do not mean the element of remorse, because he mentions it as exhibited by

[1] *Totem and Taboo,* p. 144.
[2] *Ibid.*

the murderous brothers in the treatment of the animal, a natural and obvious substitute for their father. I mean rather the powerful superstitious fear of retaliation that emerged in the individual members of the gang. The father had actually been eliminated and as Freud says, "in no real sense could the deed be undone." But this is valid only in material reality. Death belongs to the category of conscious thinking. For our unconscious there is no such thing.

The eliminated father was not dead for the sons of a paleolithic age. He was only absent and could at any minute return as he did return in their dreams, in hallucinations, in moments of tension and superstitious fear. There was always the possibility that he might visit his anger upon them and take bloody revenge on them for what they had inflicted on him. We imagine that here in the anticipation of imminent retaliation is the origin of death fear. In my view, the share of that lingering fear of retaliation is not considered by Freud in his magnificent construction of the beginning of primitive totemism. In Freud's thesis, the first attempt at a religion is based on the first taboo of totemism, that "upon taking the life of the totem animal."[3] As mentioned earlier, Freud underestimates in this context the supreme importance of the cannibalistic feature, which I consider the most significant factor of the totemistic system. This evaluation is based on more than the analogy of the paleolithic caveman or jungleman with the infant at the stage of primitive oral development.

I said previously that the first death fear of prehistoric man can perhaps be traced back to the reaction of instinctive fear of physical retaliation from the dead father of the

[3] *Totem and Taboo*, 1950, p. 144.

horde. Comparison with the emotional life of children and neurotics, especially of borderline cases, leads us to assume that the character of that early death fear must have been different from what we experience as adults. That fear must have had a tone that can scarcely be reproduced in our civilization. Only in the reconstruction of early childhood experiences and in analysis of symptoms of our neurotic patients can we sometimes find something comparable to the nature of that early fear. We encounter there a kind of death panic of nightmarish character. Something horrifying and terrible that is nameless and alien emerges from the dark. A dread emerges that cannot be faced because it is as out of this world in which we live as monsters in the anxiety dreams of early childhood. It is much worse than death fear in the usual sense. It is fear of being utterly destroyed physically. In short, it is the fear of being eaten, which we now encounter only in fairy tales. The "spook" of cannibalistic death fear, alien to us, is perhaps the most decisive factor in the reshaping and remodeling of the old mythical tradition at a phase of progressed civilization to which the idea of eating God was utterly abhorrent. Yet, so great is the conservatism or the tenacity of old myths that a trace of the ancient cannibalistic tradition could still sneak into the biblical tale as the substitution displacement of eating of the tree.

The second factor in the reinterpretation of the Fall story amounts to a sexualization of its meaning. We cannot recognize any longer all the tendencies that brought about such a new concept. Should we therefore object to an inquiry into this replacement? Can we exclude it as having no proper bearing, as (to use the legal terms) incompetent, irrelevant, immaterial? Certainly not. The sexual conception of the original crime is part of the official record, of the Genesis tale. It cannot be that it was originally of minor importance and was magnified out of all proportion to its significance later on. We cut the discussion short by asserting that sexual desire for the women who were the father's possession, sexual envy and urge were perhaps the most impelling motives for the primordial parricide. The disavowal of the real nature of the atrocious crime paved the way to its reinterpretation as a sexual transgression, especially since the sexual wishes of the brothers could not be realized, and remained unconsciously alive. As manifestation of a tendency to make woman—or rather her sensual lure—responsible for the deed, Eve appears now as seducing man, an obvious projection.

The return of the repressed sexual desires led thus to a reinterpretation of the old myth, a changed conception in which the most important motive of the crime reappeared as its real nature. We cannot know which transformations in the moral codes of the Jewish tribes contributed to the reshaping of the Fall story and we are unable to determine when and how the transformation of the original saga was performed.

Instead of indulging in sterile hypotheses about the process of reinterpretation, it will perhaps be more helpful to trace the new concept back as far as possible. The story of the Fall of Man, based on a very old Semitic tradition, written down not later than perhaps one thousand years before Christ, was, of course, known to the Jehovistic writer as to all Hebrews. Its significance for him was not greater than that of other myths, telling about the early history of his people. The writer or writers who faithfully, though not without changing and interpolating, gave the tale its shape, would have been flabbergasted had anybody told them that this very story would be considered the cornerstone of religion. They would have been amazed at the view that Adam's transgression was the source of the sinfulness of all men and that his and Eve's fall infected mankind with an inherited taint. Nothing was further from their minds.

It sounds paradoxical, yet it is true, that the narrative of Adam's Fall was considered the beginning of evil and misery for men, that his punishment was taken for granted, but that the myth had not the unique impact it had obtained later on. Here was the story of the breach of a taboo. It implied a stern warning not to disobey Jahveh. It was, perhaps later on, told also as explanation for the first emergence of sin and death, but even as such an "etiological" myth it was far from implying an inherited guilt and the origin of general sinfulness.

Let me use a comparison: many German, English, American, and even Japanese children are told the details of a little boy's misbehavior, the story of slovenly Peter who did not want to comb his hair nor eat his soup. The tale makes a great impression upon small boys of a certain age. Let us now assume the possibility that the pattern of slovenly Peter is not only used as a warning example, but that that naughty boy obtains a place similar to that which Adam has in Christian theology and that one or the other of his childish misdeeds is considered the original sin. After nine hundred or a thousand years the misdemeanor of "Struwelpeter," who was certainly a rebellious and disobedient boy, is quoted as the source of original sin. The religious authorities state that by his misdeeds all mankind is contaminated by an inherited guilt, including the embryo in its mother's womb. The chance that the story of slovenly Peter will be considered the Fall of Man by future generations is not greater than that the narrative of Adam's transgression in the third chapter of Genesis was conceived as original sin by the contemporaries of the Jahvistic writers.

The story of Adam's Fall was originally a myth like others, an episode from the past of the Israelitic tribes, a narrative like that of the Deluge, of Abraham, Jacob, Joseph, and his brothers. If people later on saw any moral in it, it was perhaps that of a warning against disobedience towards God. Many other stories, some of which were transmitted to us as were those of the Tower of Babel, of Sodom and Gomorrah, and others from patriarchal times, hinted in the same direction. Here was a tradition not more important than others, living for many thousands of years and not considered anything special, "a just-so story" of the Hebrews that had no claim for special interest.

How did that ancient tradition of an old outrage against the tribal god become one of the turning points of religion? And what were the properties of that ancient myth, ancient already at the time it was first written down, that made late generations see in it an original crime to which all mankind became accessory after the deed? And how did it come about that that act of transgression against Jahveh was conceived as sexual intercourse although nothing in the original tradition referred to such a character? Those are questions for whose answers scholars of comparative history of religion, of Bible exegesis, and anthropology have prepared an abundance of material without making us understand which psychological processes produced these changes. Without insight into the emotional dynamics that operated in that transformation, it remains mute and unresponsive.

There is in the original tradition no trace of an interpretation that the knowledge of good and evil concerned sex. It is only to modern scholars that Adam and Eve appear as babes in the wood of Eden to whom the serpent tells the facts of life.[4] There was no moralizing tendency in the original tradition; certainly least of all the idea that the disobedience of the ancestor of all Israelites was of the nature of sexual intercourse. Such a puritanical view with regard to sexuality was as utterly alien to the mind of the ancient Hebrews who knew the tradition of a primal Fall as it would be to the members of a primitive tribe of Central Australia. An Israelite of the time when the tradition was first put in writing, let us say a soldier or a shepherd almost three thousand years before our time, who might hear the story interpreted in this way, would perhaps not know what the speaker was talking about. Maybe he would suspect that the speaker was teasing him ("Ain't you funny?") or he would consider him insane. What could that tale of eating fruit from the forbidden tree have to do with sexual intercourse? Did the tradition not explicitly say that Adam ate of the tree tabooed by Jahveh? He would have

[4] Many American and German commentaries still consider the sexual meaning of the Genesis tale an original tradition. Here are two instances. Robert Gordes comes to the conclusion that the phrase "Knowing of good and evil" concerns "sexual consciousness." ("The Significance of the Paradise Myth," *The American Journal of Semitic Languages and Literatures*, LII 1936, 2). Hans Schmidt asserts that the Fall story tells about the emergence of sexual desire in Adam and Eve: "Das Wissen, das ihnen fehlt, ist das Wissen um die Besonderheit ihres Geschlechts." (*Die Erzählung von Paradies und Sündenfall*, Tübingen, 1936, p. 21.)

thought it most unnatural if Adam and Eve had not had
sexual intercourse together. Most likely he would have
agreed with Anatole France's view that of all sexual aberrations chastity is the strangest. The concept that the Fall of
Man was of a sexual nature and the condemnation of sexual
desire—of "concupiscentia," as the Fathers later called it
—were as remote to the thought of the Hebrews as to any
other ancient Oriental people. Not the slightest trace of a
concept that the Fall of Man consisted in sexual intercourse
between Adam and Eve can be detected in the rabbinical
literature until shortly before Christ.

How foreign that Paulinic concept had been originally
to the rabbinical mind can, for instance, be seen by the
fact that R. Jochanan B. Chanina thought that Cain and
his brother were born to the first couple before the Fall.
The motive of the tempter in bringing about the sin of
Adam and Eve is almost always envy since Satan should
worship Adam with the rest of the angels. Legends of this
kind appear in the Treasure Cave, the Act of Philip, in
the Apocalypse, and so on. In certain rabbinical writings
the prevailing explanation of Satan's (the Serpent's) action
is his desire to possess Eve. Only in the time immediately before our era is the sin sometimes conceived as a
sexual one, namely as intercourse between Satan and
Eve.

Even tracing the general sinfulness of mankind back to
Adam was of a very late date. No hint of such an idea
can be discovered before the time of the apocryphal writing. To find the source of the sinfulness of later generations
in Adam's transgression was altogether foreign to the
prophets. Adam's deed seems to have been without conse-

quence for posterity. The Jahvistic compilers treat Adam's transgression not as the most important catastrophe, but as the first of a series of disobedient acts against Jahveh, the fratricide of Cain, the increasing bloodthirstiness of Lamech, the general depravity calling for the Deluge, and so on. Apart from the third chapter of Genesis, no distinct reference to the Fall is to be found.

Only in a much later period, near the time of Christ, the story of the Fall became a subject of theological speculation. According to Sirach 25:23 as to haggadic writings, the idea of the Genesis narrative is to explain how man lost the immortality for which he was constituted. The writer of second Esdras, who was a contemporary of the terrible national events of A.D. 70, speculates on the origin of evil in the world: "A grain of evil was sown in the heart of Adam from the beginning and how much wickedness has it brought forth unto this time, and how much shall it bring forth till the time threshing comes" (4:30).

That grain of evil was supposedly in Adam before he was tempted. It was, if not the source, the cause of the Fall. Man has two things that God has given him, the wicked heart and the law. The "cor malignum" is thus part of Man's natural constitution as he was created by Jahveh. The rabbis of the following time elaborated that theory of a conflict between that malicious part and the good spirit of man.[5] Some rabbis thought that the Lord regretted that He had created the evil spirit ("yetzer" in Hebrew) in man.

[5] Compare Arthur Silver, "A Rabbinical Theory of Instinct" (*Psychoanalysis*, 1955, p. 3), and Henry Enoch Kagan's article, "Fear and Anxiety" in *Judaism and Psychiatry*, (ed. Simon Noveck, New York, 1956), pp. 45 ff.

Thus Rabbi Abbaha reflected:

> God said:
> I made a mistake to create
> The evil yetzer in man;
> For had I not done so,
> He would not have rebelled against me.
> (*Genesis Rabbah* 274)

Certainly a conclusion of truly divine and irrefutable logic!

Much later many rabbis identified the evil impulse with sexual desire, not considering the sexual drive itself evil, but its abuse. The sexual urge was thought not only an essential part of man's equipment, but also the source of great happiness. Was it not written that God saw everything He had made and considered it good? Query: Was it also good that the evil impulse was created? Answer: Yes, were it not for that impulse, a man would not build a house or marry a wife, beget children, or conduct his business affairs (*Genesis Rabbah* 98). In consequence, some prayed for the will to evil and it was delivered to them:

> The prophet said to them:
> Know, if you destroy this one,
> The world will come to an end.
> They improvised it for three days
> Then they sought a new-laid egg
>   in all the land of Israel
> And not one could be found.

Although the idea that Adam's Fall is to be considered the origin of evil is present in the century preceding Christ's birth, there was no agreement about it among the rabbis.

To some, Cain's crime or the fall of the angels appeared as the first sin, while the tale of Adam told only of a transgression. One of the earlier rabbis commenting on Adam's deed went so far as to say that it was an event for which we ought to be grateful, since, had it not occurred, we would not be in existence.

On the other hand, as Judaism grew older it was more and more generally believed that Adam was responsible for the death of his descendants. The pessimistic writer of second Esdras (A.D. 80-150) addresses himself to Adam: "This is my first and last saying that it had been better that the earth had not given thee." When it had given him, it would have been better to have restrained him from sinning. "For what profit is it for all that heavinesses and after death to look for punishment? O thou Adam what hast thou done? For though it was thou that sinned, the evil is not fallen on thee alone, but upon us all, that came of thee. For what profit is it unto us, if there be promised us an immortal time, whereas we have done the works that bring death" (7:46). But the writer of the Apocalypse of Barach, who represents the same circle of ideas, declares that although Adam did sin first and bring untimely death upon all, every man is his own Adam (54:15, 19).

Those were, so to speak, tentative Judaic views of the first century about the Fall; here appears the idea of an inherited depravity or guilt. The Paradise story no longer explains the entrance of death alone, but also of an inherited tendency to sin. The New Testament just touches on the subject without going into discussion of it. Jesus, the highest authority of Christianity, never mentioned the story of the Garden of Eden. Neither Christ nor His apostles ever referred to the first sinner. It is as though the Lord did not know him from Adam.

A Syrian Jew from Tarsus was the first who conceived of the story of the Fall as one of original sin and of inherited guilt from which Jesus Christ redeemed us. St. Paul definitely asserts human sinfulness is connected with Adam's transgression in that passage of the Epistle to the Romans. He says that "by one man sin entered into the world, and death by sin; and so death passed upon all men, for that all have sinned." The connection between Adam's sin and that of his descendants is perhaps conceived as the seminal existence in Adam of his posterity. The doctrine of original sin taught by St. Paul was elaborated by Irenaeus, Origen, Tertullian, and brought to its final orthodox shape by St. Augustine. Irenaeus emphasizes that the Fall was the collective deed of the race. In his later years, Origen taught a doctrine of inherited corruption, introduced by Adam. He asserts that there is an inborn stain, defiling every man and requiring to be cleansed away in baptism. This idea he associated with the Fall of Adam with whom the race forms a unity. Tertullian teaches that every human soul is "a branch" of Adam, reproducing his qualities, including his corruption.

The doctrine of original sin thus evolving and developed by some Fathers was crowned by Augustine, who asserted that our nature committed sin in Adam and sin involved guilt. Hence, even the unbaptized infants incurred damnation. Adam's fall has introduced the depravity in human nature so completely that fallen man is unable to will what is good.

There is no necessity to follow the doctrine of the original sin through patristical literature. It should only be emphasized that the nature of that sin was more and more defined as sexual, originating in concupiscence. The doctrine of original sin, especially in the form conceived by Aquinas, became the official teaching of the Church. According to the decrees of the Council of Trent, the Fall caused loss of original righteousness, infection of body and soul. According to the Church, this sin is transmitted from generation to generation.

Thus it came about that Christianity conceived of the original sin as a transgression against the Seventh Commandment, saw an indelible flaw or weakness inherent in the structure of human personalities in concupiscence, and made yet unborn children accessories after Adam's crime. The history of the idea of original sin certainly reflects the pitifulness and the folly of men.

It is remarkable that the many theologians of different creeds who attempted to reconcile Freudian precepts with Christianity and Judaism, for instance Harry Emerson Fosdick, R. S. Lee, N. P. Williams, Rabbi Joshua Loth Lieberman, and others accepted the libido theory of Freud and find in it a scientific confirmation of the Fall myth. To quote only two instances: Dr. R. S. Lee states[6] with reference to the Fall story that the superego type of religon "condemns . . . basically indulgence in sex and defiance of the primal father. In consciousness they will not appear as crudely as this, but in derivative form nevertheless, adultery and disobedience will tend to rank high in the list."

Dr. Lee, Vicar of St. Mary the Virgin, points to Freud's *Totem and Taboo,* saying that "the primal father of the horde exacted complete sexual abstinence and obedience. . . . So the primal father-God asks chastity and obedience."

[6] *Freud and Christianity* (New York, 1949), p. 166.

Freud's reconstruction of prehistory is here accepted, but with the aim of finding in it again that sexual interpretation of the Fall story—everything, rather than the unheard-of idea that the biblical story reports that primal men killed and ate God-Father and that religion is in its essential features a reaction to this primordial deed. N. P. Williams, fellow and chaplain of Exeter College, Oxford, goes even further. He notes[7] resemblances, sometimes slight and superficial, sometimes astonishingly exact, between the idea of "concupiscence as it appears in Jewish and Christian thought and the Freudian concept of libido" and emphasizes the bearing of the libido theory upon the problem of original sin. He notes "in passing the remarkable fact that this conception should twice in the history of thought have been developed by men of Jewish blood, once in the Palestine of the second century before the birth of Christ and again in the Vienna of the twentieth century after it." Nothing wrong with that except the fact that it is not sexual transgression or unchastity, but a much more serious crime which in Freud's theory constitutes "the primal sin."

Recently William H. Roberts wrote in an article that "the Christian doctrine of original sin, even of total depravity, is paraded as a present scientific discovery of the libido" and justly says that the new trend that "tries to prove that Freud was a religious man verges on farce."[8]

[7] *The Ideas of the Fall* (London, 1927), p. 68.
[8] "Analysis and Faith," *The New Republic,* May, 1955. The Jewish religious view about Freud's theory is perhaps represented by Henry Enoch Kagan "Fear and Anxiety," p. 52), who asserts that "the only really anti-Judaic thought of Freud was his philosophy about the instinctual wickedness and evil of people. That is not Jewish." The rabbi of Mt. Vernon, New York, mildly says he "would not hold Freud's atheism too strongly against him." Though Freud said God was an illu-

We endeavored to show how late Judaism and Christianity reinterpreted the Fall story as a tale of sexual intercourse between Adam and Eve. This new concept had the result that the original nature of the primal crime of man was made unrecognizable and its significance camouflaged by sexualization of the biblical narrative. Its primal meaning was such that it would necessarily have endangered and even annihilated the foundation of Jewish and Christian belief. A modern religion whose tradition tells that God-Father was killed and eaten is impossible. That original meaning was sidetracked so successfully that it could not be found again.

We cannot end this discussion on the original sin without pointing for the last time to the internal evidence of the code of primitive retaliation. If Adam's crime had been a sexual one, the penalty that Christ vicariously undertook to suffer would have been of a sexual nature in its crude or derivative way. Oedipus, who commits incest with his mother, appears at the end of the myth with his eyes gouged out, a transparent symbolic substitute for castration. But Christ in His part of "blameless sinner" was crucified; His blood is drunk, His flesh eaten in the sacrament commemorating His glorious atonement of the original sin. Through the smoke screen of the sexual interpretation of original sin, its cannibalistic nature is still recognizable in the character of Christ's penance. There is no blinking the fact that it tries—alas, in vain—to atone for the bloody deed in the infancy of mankind, but that in the penance the crime is repeated. The Service of the Lord's Supper, authorized by

sion, he, during his entire life, bravely tried to find a technique to cure man and lift him out of his wickedness. "But Freud handicapped his efforts by his unfounded theory of the instinctual complex of evil." Freud would have enjoyed that.

the Church of South India, says: "O Almighty God, our Heavenly Father, who hast accepted us as thy children in thy beloved son Jesus Christ, our Lord, and dost feed us with the spiritual food of his most precious Body and Blood, giving us the forgiveness of our sins and the promise of everlasting life."

PART FOUR

MAN, THE MORAL CLIMBER

The little earth God's stamped in the old way
And is as odd as on creation day.
He'd have got on better, Lord, had you not let
Him have that merest glimpse of heavenly light
Which he calls reason, using it at best
Only to grow more bestial than the beasts.

MEPHISTOPHELES, Prologue in Heaven. *Faust*.

CHAPTER XXVII

THE APOSTLE OF THE GENTILES

A HISTORIC short story, inserted into the novel *Sur La Pierre Blanche* by Anatole France, introduces Gallio, a highly educated Roman aristocrat who was nominated governor of ancient Greece and resided in Corinth. Gallio takes a walk in the garden of his beautiful cottage and discusses with his friends the present situation and the future of the Roman Empire. Some complain at the loss of the old virtues and hope that the young prince, who was just completing his sixteenth year and was known as modest and full of pity, would bring about an era of happiness when he became emperor. The hope of the world rests in that son of Agrippina, called Nero. The friends believe in the future of Rome although some of them doubt that Jupiter and Juno will always remain in power. A Greek philosopher, Apollodor, asserts that the regime of Jupiter approaches its end and Prometheus will be his successor. Gallio is rather inclined to believe that Hercules will succeed the son of Saturn.

The discussion is interrupted by an official who calls Gallio to the court before which two Jews appear as prosecutor and defendant. The head of the synagogue accuses another Jew of speaking each Saturday against the Mosaic

law and asks the proconsul to protect the privileges of the
children of Israel against the obnoxious preacher. The proconsul reluctantly goes to the tribunal while his friends
express their regret that this stinking and ignorant race, the
scum of the earth, had been permitted entrance into Roman
and Greek cities.

The proconsul returning tells them that the issue was as
unimportant and ridiculous as possible. The Jews accused
a very ugly tent-weaver called Paul or Saul of atheism. This
Jew had tried to persuade his coreligionists to worship their
God in a way supposed to contradict their law. Since it was
an argument about words or a difference of opinion about
details of the Jewish law, Gallio had decided it did not
concern him and left the shouting and fighting crowd. He
speaks full of contempt of those Jewish quarrels about
trifles.

By an odd accident Gallio had become witness to an
argument that decided the future of the world. He had
pondered the possibility that Hercules might become the
successor of Jupiter. The shadow of the god who will be
Lord on Earth and in Heaven had passed him by. Gallio
had not the slightest notion that the divine figure took the
shape of a Jew who was crucified in another, less important
Roman province a few years ago, and that that contemptible
tent-maker had just now announced the coming of the
Saviour.

With the discussion of the part and the personality of this
Paul, who appears as an episodic figure in the gracious story
of Anatole France, we abandon for the first time the area
of general psychology and move to the field of exploration
of the emotional life of an individual. Until now we were
occupied with the research into productions of nations and
masses, with the myths of people. In this part we are inter-

ested in the processes of a myth-maker. It cannot be denied
that here is an inconsistency in the architectural style, a
deviation from the plan. There is no sufficient justification
for this faulty architecture. I can only plead mitigating
circumstances. The first is that Paul of Tarsus is the only
real, undoubtedly historic person to appear in the great
drama of religious evolution we present. The person of
Jesus Christ can be conceived as a mythological figure,
while the figure of Saul the Pharisee has nothing mythical.
It is a man of flesh and blood, even of a "thorn in the flesh"
and of hot blood. The second factor to be brought forward
is Paul's importance in the foundation of the new religion.
Paul was not only the first and the greatest missionary of
Christianity, but almost its founder.

It was justly said that the only Christian who ever lived
had died on the cross. World history is little concerned with
the biography of this rabbi, and not much more with his
sayings and teachings—only in what the imagination of his
disciples and apostles made of them. Let us compare the
significance of this Galilean preacher with the character of
the Jewish Messiah who preoccupied his people at the time
before Christ and during His lifetime. The Messiah was in
the thought of the contemporary Jews a kind of glorified,
elevated Judas Maccabaeus. He was the hero of all hopes
of his people who daydreamed of him, believed in him,
and were convinced that he, chosen by Jahveh and endowed
with superhuman powers, would defeat the Romans and
free the nation. After that victory, which was conceived as
the great deed of national liberation, peace, glory, and
justice would rule in Israel, whereto all nations of the world
would look for guidance. What became of this Jewish hope
and daydream? It has vanished as the snow of yesteryear at
the Scopus mountain. Nothing of it has survived. A few

isolated attempts to revive it were fantastic and utopian and doomed to perish. Another Messiah, one not concerned with national and political aims of the Jews, had conquered the world.

Paul was not interested in the person of Jesus, whom he had never seen except in his "mind's eye" on that road to Damascus. Only three events of that sacred life preoccupy that pious Jew of Tarsus: the Last Supper, the Crucifixion, and the Resurrection. It seems he considers all other events of Jesus' life—His miracles, His activities, and even His sayings—as of minor interest. Even His teachings are rarely and almost casually mentioned by the greatest apostle of Christianity. Only the figure of Christ, the Christology, or as we would prefer to say, the mythology of Christianism, is the point on which all thoughts and religious emotions of Paul are focused.

Only by reasoning, daydreaming, and fantasying about the final destiny of Christ as the "firstborn Son of God" did Paul arrive at his concept of a new religion. Did he think of a new religion when he first went out to speak of the crucified Jesus in the synagogues? Certainly not. Nothing was further from his pious mind, that could tolerate neither compromise nor concessions. He had most ardently studied the law with Rabbi Gamaliel in Jerusalem, and had developed an intensive hatred against those who had not obeyed it fully and to the letter. He hated especially those Essenes who confessed a faith he considered an aberration of the law, if not its perversion. Yet this man became not only the most ardent missionary of the new belief, he was much more: he was the builder, the architect, of what we now call Christianity, which is, in most of its essential features, his creation. That is true to such an extent that one can boldly assert that it had little in common with Christ.

A learned theologian asserts that Paul "organized Christ out of the Church," and seriously raises the question whether our churches of today are those of Jesus or Paul.[1] Paul, the mystic, brought the dying and risen Christ in conflict with the teaching and preaching Christ. Not what He said and did was decisive, but His death and resurrection, which brought salvation to mankind. What mattered was the "hanging upon Calvary of the emaciated figure of the ribbed Christ with the blood oozing from his pierced hands and sides and thorned brow."[2] Had this event and the resurrection not taken place, Christ, whom Paul transformed by interpolation and interpretation into the "only Son of God," would have been unable to redeem men, and would have had to leave them doomed to eternity.

The third factor in the decision to deal with Paul's personality within this investigation is the fact that the mystery of his conversion is still unsolved and tempts the curiosity of the psychologist to unravel it. In spite of innumerable attempts at explanation we still do not understand how the Christ-hater became the most ardent apostle of the crucified Son of Man. That great experience on the road to Damascus is still a psychological secret.

The bearing of that conversion upon the problem of the collective guilt feelings is obvious since it was Paul who first drew the conclusion that Christ's death was a ransom, and should atone for the crime of the first Adam. To return to a comparison that will illustrate the part of Paul within the investigation: it is as though, within a mystery story, the detective, eager to solve the crime, becomes intrigued by the strange behavior of the main witness: a witness used first by the attorney for the prosecution and then by the

[1] Desmond Shaw, *Jesus or Paulus* (London, 1945), p. 36.
[2] *Ibid.*, p. 80.

attorney for the defense—so to speak, a puzzle within the
enigma. We would like to follow this thread.

The last but for us most important factor is the kind of
psychological material presented by the development of the
apostle. In his inner struggle a good portion of the religious
evolution of mankind appears, in a sense recapitulated,
reflected in an individual life in rapid abbreviation. There
is the furious hatred against the Galilean and his followers,
then the death of the accursed heretic—one would almost
say his immolation. This is followed by increasing unconscious guilt feeling which, under the active support of
emerging admiration and love, produces the conversion of
Saul. The overwhelming guilt feeling results in full identification with the victim of the persecution.

The following analytic attempt does not aspire to analyze
what made the great man tick, suffer, and act. This writer
will be content if he succeeds in casting a new and surprising
light on some facets of the psychological enigma of Paul's
personality. He was a Jew of the tribe of Benjamin, living
in Tarsus, and a Roman citizen. In the acts of Paul and
Theda, he is described as "of a low stature, bald on the
head, crooked tights; handsome legs, hollow-eyed, had a
crooked nose, full of grace." We have reason to assume that
he must have suffered much under frustrated sexual drives.
This man had seizures of a hysteric or hystero-epileptic
type in which he spoke "in an unknown tongue unto God."
He speaks of his emotional disturbance as "a messenger of
Satan" and "a thorn in the flesh." In those attacks he suffered the tortures of the damned, all the terrors of annihila-
tion, but enjoyed visions given only to those whom the
Lord had called.

Argumentative, quarrelsome, a master of the art of making enemies and of making himself disliked, most sensitive

and suspicious, intolerant and stubborn, sharply logical, often with a twist and turn of arguing later to be called talmudic, eloquent, stubborn as a mule, of a brilliant mind given to singleness of purpose and with an unique moral courage, he was ready to endure unlimited sufferings if he had to stand his ground and fight for his convictions. A conservative of most violent temperament and a hateful rebel preaching love of all men. Arthur Schnitzler once casually remarked that every nation in its pure characteristic traits is essentially unlikeable, the German as well as the French, the English as well as the American, and that only the individual can reconcile you with marked national peculiarities. This is perhaps too sharply expressed but it has a core of truth. Paul of Tarsus had in his personality a combination of the marked characteristics of the Jewish zealot in the diaspora, some of the worst and some of the best.

Only a few words on the outlook and the early training of Paul: he spoke Greek and Aramaic, he declared himself to be "an Hebrew of the Hebrews" (Philippians 3:5), but also emphasized his Roman citizenship, which he had from his birth (Acts 22:28). He was a child of a very strict Jewish home, well read in the history, the hopes, and the destiny of Israel. He went—perhaps when he was fourteen or fifteen —to Jerusalem to study with famous teachers. He boasts that he had "profited in the Jews' religion above many my equals in my own nation, being more exceedingly zealous of the tradition of my fathers" (Galatians 1:14). That Pharisean Jew, Saul, had absorbed all teachings of the synagogue, not only at the feet of Rabbi Gamaliel, but also in his native city of Tarsus. Tarsus was a Cilician city in which many gods were worshiped. The Romans, who were much more tolerant in religious things than other conquerors, had no objections to foreign cults.

Among them the worship of young gods who were beautiful youths, and had also died young as saviors, had a particularly great attraction for the imagination of the Mediterranean people of that period. The principal god of Tarsus, Sandan, was a figure of this type of dying and reviving deity. They had all been killed either by a wild beast, by being hanged on a tree or tied to a rock, or had been torn to pieces—Adonis, Attis, Osiris, Zagreus, Dionysus or Bacchus—only the names were different; their myths were almost the same. The Jewish boy who was told their stories had the impression that he heard variations on a single theme. Also, the ritual of those cults was very similar: there was mourning and lamentation, crying and other expressions of grief at the season when the young god was supposed to have died, and jubilation, joy, and triumph when he was supposed to have risen again and to have victoriously ascended to the gods.

The initiation rituals of young men into the mysteries of those religions were secret; but everybody knew that the novices were thought to die and be reborn in identification with the young god, and were resurrected with him. The young Jew Saul, born and bred in Tarsus, where some of those cults had their own places of worship, was of course as aware of their existence and meaning as a boy from an orthodox Jewish family who visits a public school in Manhattan is aware of Christian observances. He was repelled by the pagan superstitions, which appeared to him as stupid and despicable, but in his conversion and afterwards those old disavowed impressions from his childhood returned to his mind and memories of what he had heard and seen of those strange cults were fused with the rumors and messages of the death and resurrection of the young rabbi from Nazareth. Especially one of those cults is likely to have unconsciously occurred to the young Pharisean who had that shattering experience near the city of Damascus.

When, in the gracious story of Anatole France, the proconsul Gallio returns from the Basilica of Corinth, where he contemptuously dismissed the case of the Jews of the synagogue and of the other Jews who are followers of a certain Palestinian rabbi, he tells his friends about their trifling quarrels. From the confused talk in which that Syrian Jew answered his accusers, the proconsul got the vague impression that that tent-weaver worshiped Orpheus under some strange name he had forgotten. Perhaps he meant Adonis or Attis over whose sufferings and death the women cry.

The cults of several of those young gods spread from Asia over the whole Orient and were also brought to Rome and her provinces, as Vittorio Machioro[3] and André Boulanger[4] convincingly showed. Judea and the neighboring countries in the last century before Christ were filled with believers in Orpheus' death and resurrection. Tarsus was one of the centers of that barbarian worship. A comparison between the Orphic theology and the Christology of Paul shows remarkable resemblance. According to Orphism, Zagreus, the young son of Zeus, is torn to pieces and killed by the Titans. Zeus calls him back to life and he takes him to Heaven.

The Christians of the first centuries were well aware of those striking resemblances of the Greek and Jewish myths. Justin Martyr assumes that the ancient poets had obtained knowledge of the future advent of the Saviour through prophets and invented the myth of Zagreus to make the Saviour Himself into a myth and to persuade Christians to doubt Him. Demons had invented the passion of Dionysus,

[3] *From Orpheus to Paul* (New York, 1930).
[4] *Orphée* (Paris, 1943).

but did not dare to create one thing: the Crucifixion. Justin adds that the demons introduced the story into the very country where the Saviour was born. He also notices that the story of Zagreus was widely accepted by the Hellenistic Jews and explains the popularity of the pagan myth by the fact that those shrewd demons substituted Zagreus for Christ.

The Orphic communion had the following elements: the human soul suffers from an inherited sin, but can be delivered from it by attaining divine life. New birth is achieved through communion with the dying Dionysus or Zagreus. For Orphism as for Paulinism, the aim is to deliver the souls from the burden of the flesh and to bring them into contact with God. Compare those essential features of Orphic belief with Paul's doctrine. Christ died in order to free mankind from the Adamic sin. Deliverance is attained by men through dying and being born again with Him. The body is the seat of sin. In being born again sin is destroyed in the body. The center of the mystery religions was to become similar to a god. The divine nature their worshipers had attained was sometimes expressed by the name attributed to them, which is nothing but the name of the deity. The neophytes of the Dionysus cult were called Bacchi as those of the Christ cult were called Christians.

According to the Orphic concept, mankind inherited an original sin from the murderous deed of the Titans, a sin from which each soul must be purged. During its earthly life, mankind has to serve sentence for the sins of the Titans who had torn to pieces and devoured Zagreus, son of Zeus and Persephone. Athena rescued the heart of the boy, which Zeus swallowed. Zagreus was reborn as Dionysus, child of Zeus and Semele. Mankind arose from the semen of the Titans, who were struck by the lightning of

Zeus. That myth is similar to those of Negro-Australians, American Indians, Bushmen, and Eskimo and Zulu tales to be found in Andrew Lang's comparative work.[5] In Orphic theogony the myth of the swallowed god appears three times. First Kronos devours his children, then Zeus swallows Metis and Phanes, and then the Titans devour Zagreus. The savage character of that myth is obvious.

It cannot be our task to delineate how the combination of the Jewish traditions and of the doctrines of the mystery religions influenced the Christology of Paul. The character of the result of the different determined factors is not ambiguous. Seen from a merely historical view, Christianity is, to quote V. Machioro's words, "an enormous Greek hero cult devoted to a Jewish Messiah." Another aspect of Paul's christology is more important for our inquiry. Although in a veiled and delusional form, Paul arrived at the sources of the original guilt.[6]

The Parisian criminals call conscience *"la muette."* Also mankind tried for many thousands of years to silence the signals of conscience emerging from unconscious depths. In the message of Paul the conscience of mankind obtained a voice. Formulated in the delusional shape of an evangel, Man confessed here his original guilt.

[5] *Myth, Ritual and Religion* (2d ed., London) I, p. 295.
[6] Compare Jacob Taubes' "Religion and the Future of Psychoanalysis" (*Psychoanalysis,* 1956/4).

CHAPTER XXVIII

DYING ANOTHER MAN'S DEATH

WHAT happened? How did Saul the Christ-hater and Christ-baiter become the Christ-lover? The analytic interpretation that follows has, as far as I know, no predecessor in literature except Hanns Sachs' promising but unfinished attempt at Paul's characterization.[1] It cannot be denied that the interpretive attempt presented here has a provisional character, justifiable only by the very limited space granted to it within this book in which the figure of the apostle plays only an episodic part.

The following is an attempt to penetrate at least in some decisive points the psychological wall surrounding the mysterious change to which Saul was subjected. The experience to which he attributed his conversion is clearly described in the ninth chapter of the Acts. Saul was one of the most zealous and active persecutors of the Church in the making. A fanatic Jew, he "made havock of the church, entering into every house, and haling men and women committed

[1] "At the Gates of Heaven" in *Masks of Love and Life* (Cambridge, 1948). Limited space does not allow me to give a critical survey of books on Paul's life, a *bibliographie raisonnée*. It should be mentioned that from the extended literature on Paul studied for this chapter, Albert Schweitzer's *The Mysticism of Paul the Apostle* (New York, 1955) was especially helpful.

them to prison." Saul, "yet breathing out threatenings and slaughter against the disciples of the Lord," went up from Jerusalem to Damascus, to bring the heretics back. When he came near Damascus, suddenly a light from Heaven shone around him and he heard a voice saying "Saul, Saul, why persecutest thou me?" Jesus told him who He was and added, "It is hard for thee to kick against the pricks." When Saul, trembling, arose from the earth, he saw no more. He was brought into Damascus where he remained three days "without sight and neither did eat nor drink." It is known that he then became the Apostle preaching Christ, the "Son of God," in the synagogues, and how confounded the Jews at Damascus had been who had known him as the destroyer of the Christians, and who now planned to kill him.

One is tempted to reconstruct or to guess at what the inner process was that took place in this tortured man when one considers his past history and certain features of the time after the conversion at Damascus. When one adds the insights psychology has gained into the unconscious dynamics of pathological phenomena, especially of hysteria and epilepsy, one will get a hypothesis which, if it does not hit the bull's eye, reaches its neighborhood. The scarcity of biographical and pathological data of course makes the result of this attempt at analytic reconstruction doubtful; but my impression is that it comes closer to the historic reality than previous scientific endeavors of a similar kind.

I would like to preface the analytic interpretation of Paul by some remarks on fanaticism and enthusiasm. The two emotions are obviously akin and have an especially high intensity of feeling in common. They both have, it seems to me, to make an effort to suppress or drown opposite feelings. Enthusiasm has to ward off unconscious doubtful and aggressive tendencies directed against its object, and fanaticism has to reject trends of attraction to the object or cause that is fought and attacked. In the idea of enthusiasm we emphasize the positive, constructive side. Love for a cause or a person is a necessary ingredient of that emotion. We connect with fanaticism a critical note and see in a fanatic a person who is carried away by his beliefs beyond reason. While we in general consider enthusiasm as something desirable, we are inclined to frown upon fanaticism. The reason for this is that fanaticism does not denote only an extraordinary zeal or passionate partisanship for a cause, but also an equal or even more ardent rejection and repulsion of any different attitude or viewpoint.

Singleness of purpose is common to enthusiasm and fanaticism, but the first includes all appropriate things in its circle; the other excludes or rebuffs all that does not strictly belong to its sphere. The term "enthusiasm" has a positive, socially welcome tone—sometimes slightly ironic or condescending when we, for instance, smile at youthful enthusiasm—whereas the expression "fanaticism" has a by-character of rejecting, of ejecting hostility, of exclusiveness and narrow-mindedness. Although the two emotional manifestations are as dissimilar as only parts of the same kin can be, they have besides zeal or ardor other properties in common, for instance loyalty and long duration.

It is difficult to associate the term fanaticism with an emotion that is short-lived and almost as hard to imagine enthusiasm for a cause lasting only for hours. It would be paradoxical to think of those emotions as fleeting and easily changeable. It is impossible to attribute to them an attitude similar to that of a certain woman about whom the Viennese writer Karl Kraus once remarked that she was faithful today to one man and faithful tomorrow to another. Yet there are sudden breakthroughs of disappointment and disillusion in enthusiasm, as there are unexpected disenchantments and dissociations in fanaticism. There are also sudden or gliding transitions from the one to the other; possible changes from enthusiasm to fanaticism, and, although more rarely, from fanaticism into enthusiasm.

It happens frequently that both manifestations are present in the same person, as though he had a Janus head whose one side is turned this way and the other the opposite. Finally, there is the frequently observed case of a turnabout in which a person is first enthusiastic, or even fanatic about a certain cause and then the opposite. In most of these cases, the turning point is brought about by a conversion, by a reversal of conviction, sometimes connected with a character transformation of the person. It is easy enough to say —and some theologians said it—that Paul's conversion means a transition from rigid fanaticism for Judaism to loving enthusiasm for the new religion of Christ. The ambiguity of these terms becomes obvious when you consider that it is possible to apply them the other way around.

In many cases of sudden conversion an intensive doubt, or even a rejection of a certain cause, is followed by an upsurge of passionate belief in it. The fanatical and persecutory zeal of Paul, his cruel and murderous wishes and hate for the Nazarene offenders and blasphemers neared their highest point when he, heading a group of men, went out to bring many of those criminal heretics, bound, back to Jerusalem. The message that Jesus, whose disciples he persecuted, had been crucified reached Paul two years after its occurrence. He had also heard many tales of the Saviour's resurrection. Still breathing slaughter, he thought many times of that crucified man and called his hateful image up. On the road to Damascus the inner situation suddenly changed. What had happened? We have only the descrip-

tion of Paul himself as the testimony of a highly introspec-
tive person, but his description is necessarily restricted and
its value diminished by the fact that the most important part
of the experience occurred in an epileptic or hystero-
epileptic attack. In the seizure he, so to speak, died with
Christ; or, as he would say, "in Christ." That is, he had
identified with the man in whom so many Jews saw the
Messiah.

At first Paul's hate for Christ had reached its peak and
resulted in a vivid image of the Galilean. He seemed to see
Him hanging on the cross with blood oozing from all His
body, with the crown of thorns, in all His misery and last
defamation and shame. But then it was no longer an image,
produced by an act of thinking, but a vision, or better, a
delusion in the sense of a pathological phenomenon, in
which a person seems to be as real—I mean materially real
—as the next man on the street. The vividly expressed
murderous wish against the preacher who had declared himself the Son of God was replaced by the inner image of His
death.

Then came the full identification with that dead man on
the Cross in a vision. He saw, in his hysterical attack, Christ
as a Divine Being, radiant, all-powerful, with full knowledge
of the secrets of the heart; not merely as a Jewish Messiah,
but as exalted. Christ, conceived thus as a deity, spoke
to him.

In that full identification Paul became this crucified
heretic, in a sense, body and soul. It is obvious what determined this change from the cruel and sadistic into the
masochistically suffering. In this reversal we have to recognize not only the operation of unconscious moral powers, of
the forces that bring about an atonement for one's own
cruel tendencies. There is also here the intensity of repressed

feelings of love and admiration for that crucified young
heretic—powerful emotions returning from the depth of
the repressed. Yes, one can assert that this love turned the
scales, decided the outcome of the unconscious conflict.

We cannot know if this reconstruction of the emotional
processes during Paul's hystero-epileptic attack is psychologically correct. The similarity of Paul's description to
the account Dostoevski gave of his own seizures is remarkable. If it is permitted to follow the analogy to the psychology of the attack, we would arrive at the conclusion that
both neurotic men experienced in these seizures their own
death in identification with another hated and loved person.
Freud's interpretation[2] of Dostoevski's neurotic seizures is,
to a great extent, also valid for the case of Paul of Tarsus.

Perhaps the indirect proof of this concept is to be seen
in the behavior of the new apostle or, as we had better say,
of the newborn Paul. I do not mean in the fact that he went
out to the synagogue to preach Christ, but in what he said
and how he said it. He speaks of himself as though he had
lived and died in Christ, and as though he had been resurrected in Him. Only died with Him? "Know ye not, that
so many of us as were baptized into Jesus Christ were
baptized into his death? Therefore we are buried with him
by baptism into death; that like as Christ was raised up
from the dead by the glory of the Father, even so we also
should walk in newness of life" (Romans 6:3, 4). It is as if
—but this "if" approaches the character of full reality—he
had experienced the tortures and the dying of Christ as his

[2] *Dostojewski und die Vatertötung*, Gesammelte Schriften, XII (Vienna, 1934). The problem of guilt and atonement is also the central
motif of the Russian writer. Dostoevski was as Paul "a man with a gift
for religion, in the truest sense of the phrase. Dark traces of the past lay
in his soul, ready to break through into the region of consciousness."
(Freud, *Moses and Monotheism*, p. 137.)

own. The metaphors he uses are more than that; they are
reports of his own vividly felt experience—"whether in the
body or out of the body, I cannot tell"—and have become
only secondarily symbols. He had suffered death and had
overcome the fear of dying, had triumphed over it: "Oh
death, where is thy sting? Oh grave, where is thy victory?"
(I Corinthians 15:55).

The identification with Christ goes so far that he feels
Him in himself, not as incorporated, but also as being Him:
"I am crucified with Christ: nevertheless I live; yet not I,
but Christ liveth in me: and the life which I now live in
the flesh I live by the faith of the Son of God who loved
me. . . . If we be dead with Christ, we believe that we shall
also live with him." Those sentences have to be understood
literally. The final resurrection appears, as Hanns Sachs[3]
has aptly put it, "as a reproduction, enlarged to a grandiose
size, of the experience that every man can find"—but, as
we would add, of the experience of Paul on that road to
Damascus. That "other self" in Paul had tried again and
again to make itself known, but in vain. It could not penetrate the thick walls of loyalty to the past, the devotion to
the law and tradition. When it succeeded in breaking
through all resistances, it was with a forcefulness that did
not allow contradiction any longer. The denied and repressed emotions knocked out everything Paul had learned
to appreciate, and acknowledged only one power, the same
that brought him to feel as one with Jesus: "And though I
have the gift of prophecy, and understand all mysteries, and
all knowledge; and though I have all faith so that I could
remove mountains, and have not charity, I am nothing"
(I Corinthians 13:2).

Many emotions, emerging from the dark underground

[3] Hanns Sachs, *At the Gates of Heaven*, p. 100.

into which they had been banned, worked together to produce that great about-face, but the strongest was love, that is greater than "faith and hope," love for a young prophet he had never seen and who had been crucified by the Romans. Paul does not speak of Eros, but uses the word "Agape," which means love in a desexualized form; but psychoanalysis knows from which hidden sources or deeper sensual desires this emotion is fed. That passion that had boiled up in hate against the new preacher, the Essenes, and the disciples of Johannes, that same zealous ardor of fanatic loathing has been reversed by the sudden emergence of a long-disavowed emotion of longing and belonging to that other rejected world and its priest. In identifying with the victim whom others had killed, but for whose agony and death he felt responsible, the persecutor became persecuted. In the intensity of an experience shared with the loved object, he knew he had to go out to convey to his people the death-conquering mysteries of the Last Supper, of the Crucifixion, and the Resurrection.

Paul's breakthrough to Jesus, the inner uproar produced by the assault of repressed emotions, also brought with it a revival and revision of thoughts long known and kept in the dark: the ideas of Orphic teachings, which now blended with the image of the Messiah as he lived in Hebrew literature and lore. Until then shadows vegetating in the underworld, those ideas gained a new life and significance in the light surrounding the drooping head of Jesus on the cross.

Much should be, but cannot be, said here about the changes in the personality of Paul subsequent to that vision; changes conditioned to a great extent by the reception he found when he told his people about the Messiah Jesus. The Jews could not stand the idea of another god besides Jahveh. Until Paul's death, Jesus was to Jewish Christians not another god, but the first-born of the sons of God who had sacrificed him for the salvation of mankind. Yet the way to deification of this contemporary son of God was opened by his sacrificial death and resurrection. Paul tried, for a long time, to reconcile his own overwhelming experience and the convictions resulting from it with the law. "A Hebrew of the Hebrews," proud of his nation as well as of his mission to the Jews, he desperately endeavored to show them the way to their salvation.

But there came a moment when a decision had to be made, when it became necessary to choose: the law or the faith. Paul could not remain with the Jews believing in God according to their law; he had to return to the Jews and Gentiles believing in Jehovah and in the Lord Jesus of Nazareth. More and more the death of Christ and His resurrection became the pivot of history for Paul. More and more the "new Adam" contrasted with the old Adam. The law has to yield to faith. Jahveh had, without knowing it, given His place to His firstborn son. It is unnecessary to be circumcised. What is needed is to be "baptized in Jesus," which means being reborn with Him and in Him. It presupposes dying with Him first in order to experience His resurrection as Paul did.

The totem meal was also renewed—no longer in the form of a communion in eating a sacred, otherwise forbidden animal, but in eating the God Himself and at His own explicit command. In these two acts the new Christians, and all Christians of future generations, became identified with Christ, renewing the oldest primitive ritual of many thousands of years ago. A ritual that had survived only in a symbolic and displaced form became again a material and "real" action in which the community was united with God whose body they eat and whose blood they drink in the most

Holy Sacrament of the new religion. It is as though an essential part of the process that had once taken place in the brother horde had been repeated in its secondary phase, now displaced to the son figure. Jesus Christ, who appears as the firstborn son of God and His messenger in human form, was a rebel against Jahveh. Anatole France once aptly remarked that there are no victorious rebels. They are transformed into generally accepted and acknowledged authorities. After having atoned for His crime—in the myth the crime of all mankind—Jesus Christ becomes God Himself. The second round was won by the Son-God.

In Paul's conversion experience the world-historic essence of the Fall and of the Christ myth reappeared in individual reproduction. In his vision he again committed that first crime and suffered punishment for it. It is not accidental, but determined by his own experience, that he discovered that the two figures of Adam and Christ are intimately connected. Christ Himself did not mention Adam, but Paul taught that, as sin entered the world by one man, and also death by sin, so again by one man, Christ, was the Fall of Man converted into the Rise of Man, and sin eliminated by the shedding of His blood. If there had been no Fall, the salvation by Jesus, the coming of the Son of God would not have been necessary. In making Christ the antitype of Adam and in declaring that He atoned for the original sin, Paul has laid down the outline of the Christian Fall doctrine. The synoptic evidence shows that Jesus Christ never raised the question of the origin of sin, nor did He allude to the Fall of Adam. Again and again the contrast of the disobedience of Adam and the obedience of Christ is drawn by Paul (Romans 5:19). I Corinthians 15:22 proclaims: "For as in Adam all die, even so in Christ shall all be made alive."

The Fall finds then its predestined counterpart in the

Redemption wrought by Christ in the writings of Augustine, perhaps the greatest man next to Paul in the history of Christianity, and by the other Fathers of the Church. Theology speaks of "the two complementary conceptions," of "the twin focal points which determine the ellipse of traditional theology," of the "two pillars of the Fall and of Redemption."[4] From the theologian's point of view human history begins with Adam and begins again with Christ, so much so that what happens in between occurs within an epoch of darkness. The two great events in the history of mankind, the Fall by Adam and the Redemption by Christ, became the double foundation of the Christian faith. St. Cyril of Alexandria only continues the line, introduced by the great apostles of the Gentiles, "We are all in Christ and the totality of mankind comes to life again in Him. For He is called the New Adam because by sharing in our nature He has enriched all unto happiness and glory, as the first Adam filled all with corruption and ignomy." (Comment in St. John Evang. I.1.24)

Paul's concept of the murder of God is, of course, not mentioned. It was replaced, as Freud said,[5] "by the tenet of the somewhat shadowy conception of the original sin." That conception did not remain shadowy. The Fathers of the Church made it definite and definable: Adam's sin was of the flesh, was a sexual transgression. Later generations of Christians willingly accepted that doctrine, following their priests as sheep the shepherd. Mankind accuses itself of concupiscence instead of murder. The sidetracking to sexuality which was the strongest motive of the primeval crime promised an easing of the collective guilt feeling. By confessing the minor offense one had avoided admitting the

[4] N. P. Williams, *The Ideas of the Fall* (London, 1927), p. 8.
[5] *Moses and Monotheism,* p. 214.

full gravity of the original deed. It seemed that mankind was released through salvation.

The emotional situation before Christianity resembled that in which a festering boil is felt. There is pressure and pain at the places where pus gathers. The unconscious guilt feeling of man thus was painfully experienced. Christianity can be compared to the lancing of the abscess and with it a relief from pressure was felt for a certain time. The deep abscess is still there.

Paul could not penetrate to the core of the Fall story. The true nature of the primal crime remained unconscious, but he pierced the amnesia of mankind at a certain point.

CHAPTER XXIX

THE INVISIBLE GOD

THIS INQUIRY has now reached a point where inevitably the problem arises of why the people of Israel did not accept Jesus Christ as their Messiah. The split of the core of the Jewish people marks one of the decisive turns in the tremendous tragedy that is their fate.

Freud, deeply interested in the destiny of his people, approaches again in his last years the problem that had preoccupied him as a child and as a young man. He approaches it now equipped with the new instrument of psychoanalysis he had created. The new religion was no doubt a cultural regression as compared with the older religion of the children of Israel. The lofty height of spirituality reached in Mosaic religion was renounced: Christianity is no longer strictly monotheistic and was accessible to many magical and mystical elements. Yet Christianity marked, in spite of all this, a progress in the history of religion insofar as the repressed returns in it. From now on, Freud says,[1] "The Jewish religion was, so to speak, a fossil."

Among the reasons Freud presents to explain why the Jews rejected the new religion, one of the decisive ones is conspicuous by its absence. We are not astonished that it

[1] *Moses and Monotheism* (New York, 1949), p. 140.

does not appear in the vast scientific and theological literature on the question, but its absence in Freud's treatment
is the more surprising because he needed only to make a few
steps more on his way to come to the conclusion I shall
present. He just missed it because, it seems to me, he would
have had to deviate from the course of his inquiry at a
certain point. I do not remember any longer whether that
aspect of the question was mentioned in the many conversations I had with Freud on the problem, but I feel it is my
task to march along on the trail he blazed just before he
reached that critical point. As a matter of fact, there are
two points during his exploration where he missed the
opportunity for such a richly rewarding digression.

In the second part of his book, he compares the Jewish
monotheism with the Egyptian Aton religion of the king
Ikhnaton. He remarks that the sun god of Ikhnaton is represented only by a round disc from which emanate rays. No
personal representation of the sun god has been found.[2]
The king believed that the true god had no form. Jewish
monotheism, which Freud traces back to the Egyptian Aton
cult, is even more uncompromising here when it forbids all
visual representation of its God. It relinquishes the worship
of the sun, to which the Egyptian cult still adhered.

The second opportunity for the digression is to be found
in the chapter entitled "The Progress in Spirituality." Freud
inquires there into the prohibition Moses had given to his
people against making an image of God. The Mosaic religion surpassed that of Aton in strictness. Moses perhaps
meant to be consistent:[3] "His God was to have neither a
name nor a countenance. The prohibition was perhaps a
fresh precaution against magic malpractices." Freud ex-

[2] *Ibid.*, p. 35.
[3] *Ibid.*, p. 178.

plains the profound influence of this prohibition; once accepted, it signifies a triumph of spirituality over the perception of the senses. The consequence of the Mosaic prohibition against worshiping God in a visible form contributed to turning the Jews to spiritual interests and to transforming the religion into one of instinctual renunciation. Freud wants here to cast some light on the question of how the Jewish people acquired some qualities that characterize them.

I am following a side path that branches off at this point. I believe that Freud overestimated the importance and value of monotheism.[4] The idea of the grandeur of the God of the Jews is, in my view, as much—or even more—connected with the character of His invisibility as with His uniqueness. Jahveh is the only God, but He is also characterized by incorporeality and immateriality. Judaism is imageless monotheism. The second consideration that appears of importance to me is the contrast of Christianity with the old religion, especially concerning the belief in the invisibility of God.

Let me preface the following inquiry by quoting the "True Account of Celsus, a distinguished Roman of the time of Marcus Aurelius.[5] In this first polemic against the new religion of Christianity Celsus, who was interested in the attitude of cultivated Romans toward the new faith, tries also to explain the refusal of the Jews to acknowledge the Messiah. A Jew is introduced who addresses Christ:

[4] Also A. Bronson Feldman emphasized that monotheism represented for Freud the highest peak of ethics that religion could attain and adds: "Now there is not a particle of proof that monotheists reached a higher summit of ethics than the polytheist Greeks, or the followers of Confucius." "Freudian Theology," (*Psychoanalysis,* 1953/4.)

[5] Excerpts from the work of Celsus, who speaks of Christ as a "man who lived and died a few years ago," are quoted in the refutation by Origen, *Contra Celsum.*

"You were born in a small Jewish village. Your mother was a poor woman who earned her bread by spinning. Her husband divorced her for adultery. You were born in secret, and afterward carried to Egypt and were bred among the Egyptian conquerors. The arts which you there learned, you practiced when you returned to our own people and you thus persuaded them that you were God. It was given out that you were born of a virgin. Your real father was a soldier named Panther. The story of your Divine parentage is like the story of Danae. You say that when you were baptized in Jordan, a dove descended upon you and a voice was heard from heaven declaring that you were the son of God. Who saw the dove? Who heard the voice except another who suffered as you suffered? The prophets have foretold that a son of God is to come. Granted. But how are we to know that they referred to you? They spoke of a glorious King who was to reign over the world. You were known only as wandering about with publicans and boatmen of abandoned character. You tell us that the wise men of the East came at your birth to adore you; that they gave notice to Herod and that Herod killed all the children in Bethlehem to prevent you from becoming king. You yourself escaped by going to Egypt. Is this story true? And if it be, could not the angels who had been busy about your birth have protected you at home? When you grew up what did you accomplish remarkable? What did you say? We challenged you in the temple to give us a sign as your credential. You had none to give. You cured disease; it is said you restored dead bodies to life; you fed multitudes with a few loaves. These are the common tricks of the Egyptian wizards which you may see performed every day in our markets for a few halfpence. They too drive out devils, heal sickness, call up the souls of the dead, provide suppers and tables covered with dishes and make things seem what they are not. We do not call these wizards sons of God. We call them rogues and vagabonds."

I have quoted these excerpts from the speech of the Jew because they clearly show the attitude of the majority of the Palestinian contemporaries in the first century toward Christ. Celsus, who had obtained excellent information both of the Christian and Jewish traditions, shows the contrast between the Jewish attitude and the Christian claims. The tone heard here is from the first sentence on ("Can any good thing come out of Nazareth?") to the last, that energetically denies the divine sonship of Jesus Christ, hostile and rejecting. The speech addressed to the redeemer and another one addressed to converted Jews reflect the spiritual atmosphere of hate and contempt toward the new covenant.

The word "regression" that Freud uses to characterize some traits of Christianity in comparison with its parent religion denotes some of the emotional reasons that turned the people of Israel against the new faith. The general term "regression" includes also the slow removal of the idea of God's invisibility. The silent but eloquent retreat from the Mosaic prohibition to make an image of God or of divine things resulted in a development that saw many thousands of pictures, sculptures, and symbols in Christian churches. Jesus is still set forth as the "image of the invisible God" (Colossians 1:15), but no religion can rival Christianity in the multitude of its images. In the French cathedrals of Paris, Chartres, Rheims, and Amiens there are as many as two, three, or four thousand statues; in the cathedrals of Chartres, Bourges, and Le Mans there are four or five thousand figures on stained glass.[6] The Jews must have

[6] A. V. Didron, *Histoire de Dieu* (Paris, 1843), Introduction, p. 1.

conceived of the divine images as a relapse into pagan times, when their prophets raised an outcry against idolatry.

Every great historical religion except Judaism, and Islam following in the tracks of Jewish religion, has attempted to express the legends and myths in images. G. de Alviella pointed out[7] that idolatry is neither a general nor a primitive fact. It is unknown in India in Vedic time. First traces of it are to be found in historic phases of China and Japan. Only exceptional cases are reported among the Jews (the golden calf and the brazen serpent). Even the Roman images representing their gods appeared rather late in their history. Idolatry is equally unknown to most of the peoples who are today considered primitive. Idolatry flourished in the civilized states of Mexico, Peru, and Central America; it was but rarely encountered in the savages of both American continents. Before the spread of Buddhism it was unknown in Japan. Alviella comes to the conclusion that idolatry is but a step in religious evolution, "and it even represents a comparative advance."

Images have magical properties. They give to their possessor control over the original. Savages usually refuse to be photographed or sketched, out of this superstitious fear. Spells used on images and figures were known to the Chaldeans, Egyptians, Hindus, Greeks, and Romans and most uncivilized people of today employ them in the service of black magic. The power to dispose of the original becomes clear when we hear that the Tyrians, besieged by Alexander, chained up the statue of Baal Melkart, to keep the god from escaping to the enemy's side, and according to Pausanias the Spartans chained the statue of Ares to prevent its escaping.[8]

---

[7] "Images and Idols," in *Encyclopedia of Religion and Ethics,* VII, p. 113.

[8] Other instances in J. G. Frazer, *Pausanias* (London, 1898), III, pp. 336 f.

It is certain that Moses created that prohibition of representing human figures or any animate beings as reaction to such practices.

The invisibility of God is an attribute ascribed late in religious development. The narrative of Genesis 3 shows that in early Hebrew belief God was conceived as visibly having intercourse with man. Only later He is thought to be more withdrawn. The invisibility of gods is explained, for instance, in Shintoism by the theory that they have removed themselves further from the earth, so that they are now beyond the scope of human vision.[9] In later times of Hebrew religion the idea occurs that it is dangerous to see Him: "There shall no man see me, and live" (Exodus 33:2); "I am undone . . . for mine eyes have seen . . . the Lord" (Isaiah 6:5); Job complains: "Behold, I go forward, but he is not there; and backward, but I cannot perceive him. On the left hand, where he doth work, but I cannot behold him; he hideth himself on the right hand, that I cannot see him" (Job 23:8, 9).

The Jews at the time of Jesus had reached in their religious development the phase in which the idea of a visible god appeared to them as a blasphemy. When they refused to bow to the figures of the Roman kings, when they died rather than yield to the commandments of their Roman oppressors, it was not only rigid monotheism that they manifested in their refusal. It was the rejection of a concept that an idol, an image, should be conceived as a god. God is invisible and Christ cannot be the son of God because He was visible, walked about, and died. Soon appeared His symbol, the lamb and the dove, in pictures; and finally He Himself was portrayed hanging on the cross in pictures and

[9] W. G. Aston, *Shinto* (London, 1905), p. 32.

statues. What kind of God was it who could be seen by the eyes of mortals? Here was a clear regression to the beliefs of the heathen.

The mystery of the invisibility of God is not fully explained when we, following Freud's remarks, assume that Moses' prohibition against making pictures representing God should protect the Jews against relapsing into magic practices. We heard from Freud that Moses or his followers were even more radical than the priests of the Aton religion who allowed the representation of God in the pictures of the sun and its rays. On the other hand, we learned that the idea of the invisibility of God belongs to a relatively late phase of religious development.

We understand further that the Christian cult of pictures and statues marks a regression to an earlier state at which the gods were represented in images. My father used to quote a little story about the Viennese writer Moritz Gottlieb Saphir, who was his contemporary. Saphir, a sometimes witty but cynical and shallow humorist whose columns were once popular in Austria, was born of Jewish parents, became later a Catholic, and finally turned Protestant. When he was once asked about the reasons for such an astonishing change of religious beliefs, he answered: "First I was a Jew. Then God could see me but I could not see Him. Then I became a Catholic. Then I could see Him, but He could not see me. At last I became Protestant. Now He does not see me and I don't see Him." This cynical information alludes of course to the Jewish idea of God's invisibility, and then to the images and statues of Christ, which are considered lifeless. The final sentence means that Protestantism is, so to speak, the easiest way to arrive at atheism. In that anecdote the regression of Christianity is alluded to in the attack upon the cult of images. What can be seen, can be looked at, can be criticized. The God of the Jews was unknown and unknowable.

It is obvious that the concept of the Invisible God marks a higher phase of religious evolution, and it would be superfluous to present the reasons for the assumption. But when we take for granted those reasons and motives often discussed in theological literature, does it mean that there might not be other determining factors of an unconscious kind, tendencies whose existence had remained unknown, but whose concealed operation led the religious development to such a concept?

We recognize at this point that the question is not answered when we acknowledge the spiritual superiority of the idea of the invisible God. We feel that here are subterranean processes not yet perceived and far from being understood. How can we find a way to approach their character and meaning?

There is a field, very remote from that of the phenomena of religion, in which we encounter similar processes whose nature we have learned to recognize. I mean the psychopathology of a serious mental disturbance called paranoia. Patients who are suffering from this kind of insanity imagine that they are persecuted by certain, and sometimes uncertain, men or groups of men, who have designs on their goods or even on their lives. Another form of this disturbance is apparent in the symptoms of patients who imagine that they are objects of homosexual attentions and even attacks. Many patients develop ideas of grandeur in which they imagine that they have an important mission, will save the world from its ills, and so on. Some patients of this kind are convinced that they are chosen as objects or victims of mysterious antagonists who plan their destruction.

But what have the fantasies and delusions of those psychotic persons to do with the concept of an invisible God?
Little, it seems, but we are using this pathologic material
only as analogy to explain the emotional origin of that religious concept. It is not the content of the paranoic symptoms that interests us at the moment, but the dynamics of
the projection used by these patients. They are in general
mistrustful, secretive, and suspicious toward others; always
on their guard against the imagined evil designs and machi-
nations of their enemies. They observe very sharply all persons around them, trying to guess what these individuals
plan to do against them. By way of projection they feel
watched and observed often by unseen enemies who keep
their plots carefully secret and do not give away their
scheming and evil designs. Paranoic patients are frequently
convinced that mysterious and secret powers try to control
their actions and even their thoughts. They themselves are,
of course, very careful not to show their thoughts, and become extremely cautious, reticent, and reserved in order
to protect themselves. Convinced that every word and gesture can betray them, they have to be always on the de-
fensive against all kinds of dangers and menaces from the
persons who are hostile to them. It is certainly pycho-
logically interesting that many paranoic patients develop
a high sensitiveness to being "stared at," as if the persons
who look at them look them over in an inquisitorial, critical
or aggressive manner, and want to "find out" some hidden
weaknesses or shortcomings.

The analogy with the idea of the invisible God that I
would like to point out revolves around that psychical
mechanism of projection. The unconscious meaning of the
invisibility of God has its roots in the wish not to be seen
or watched by Him, to hide before Him. Instead of the

expression of the desire to be concealed and safe, the concept emerges that He is hidden, invisible, but watches His children, sees all that goes on in the world. Unseen Himself, He knows what men do and think. Instead of the expression of the wish to keep their own thoughts and actions —mostly the evil ones—concealed, appears the conviction that God is secretive and hides His plans, remaining mysterious. The ways of the Lord are proverbially dark. Exteriorizing what takes place within His worshipers by projection, and transferring it to God, a considerable emotional amelioration is reached and the unconscious guilt feeling is reduced.

The process of projection is an archaic mechanism that was originally general, and is by no means restricted to pathological cases. We all can observe in ourselves many instances of such projective techniques that we unconsciously apply. The analogy we presented shows a collective counterpart of the projection in the special case of the evolution of a religious idea.

Many ramifications of the concept of an invisible God cannot here be considered, for instance the fact that something that cannot be easily imagined stimulates imagination. The lure of the female body is to a great extent based on the secret location of the genitals.

A kind of internal evidence for the unconscious origin of the concept of the invisible God is the belief that the person who sees God will die. In this form the original thought—if God sees me (doing or thinking evil, forbidden things) I have to die or He will kill me—recurred in projection. If my hypothesis is correct, it cannot be difficult to discover situations in which the original fear, secretiveness, and desire to hide before God is still evident, situations that present the point of departure for the later development of the hiding of God. The history of religions and of myths can certainly present many instances of this kind. But why go for a search of remote examples when one is close at hand? In the third chapter of Genesis the Lord God appears still in this anthropomorphic shape. He is walking in the garden in the cool of the day. Adam and his wife "hid themselves from the presence of the Lord God amongst trees of the garden. And the Lord God called unto Adam and said unto him: 'Where art thou?'" (Genesis 3:8, 9.) Here the Lord God is still visible and man tries to hide and to keep the guilty feeling secret.

Returning to the theme from which we departed, we now understand that the concept of the invisible God appears rather late in the evolution of religion. It is the result of a projection, made necessary by the increase of unconscious guilt feeling that belongs to a progressed phase of religious development.

It seems to me that Freud passed by the opportunity to point out that one of the most important objections the people of Israel had against the Divine Sonship of Jesus Christ, and later against Christianity in general, was the fact that here God became visible. The Jews insisted that their God and with Him His potential Son would remain invisible. My thesis about the origin of that idea explains not only why the belief in the invisible presence of God was maintained by Judaism, but also why Christianity relaxed and abolished that old Mosaic prohibition to make images of God and sacred things. It is not only simply a regression to paganism and idolatry. With the reduction of guilt feeling by the sacrificial death of the Redeemer, the idea of a manifest incarnation of God was again accessible. The projection discovered here in the concept of the invisibility of God had become unnecessary by the decrease of guilt feeling and, by the confession contained in the Passion of Jesus Christ. God could again become visible. Jesus appears as "the Image" of God and not simply "made in the image." His appearance is the revelation of God. He is said by St. Paul (Philippians 2:6) to be "in the form of God." Here is the renewed image of God who had been invisible for ages.[10]

That Freud did not attribute higher psychological importance to the Jewish rigidity about Jahveh's invisibility is the more astonishing as its significance was emphasized in a book that he admired just at the time when he wrote the last pages of *Moses and Monotheism*. At the end of 1938, R. B. Bardi sent him the novel *The Emperor, the Sages and Death*,[11] which had been published in Vienna a short time before Hitler entered the city. Freud was deeply impressed by the book, which he called "mysteriously beautiful," and wrote a still unpublished preface for it.[12] He saw the writer, an Austrian refugee who like himself lived in London, several times. Mrs. Bardi, who had been a student of mine in Berlin and Vienna, wrote the novel (which had occupied her thoughts for many years) at the end of her psychoanalysis. Freud expressed his regret that I had never told him about my remarkable student who showed such excellent understanding for the insights of psychoanalysis in her novel.

[10] It is significant in this connection that St. Luke traces the genealogy of Jesus from Joseph upward (Luke 3:23-38) and ends with Adam, the "son of God." In connecting the second Adam with the first, the Lucan pedigree "places a son of God at either end of this list of names" (C. S. Cox, *Expositions* (London, 1885), I, p. 27). The Lord God, who was not yet invisible at the time of the first Adam, manifests Himself after a very long retreat in the second Adam.

[11] *Der Kaiser, die Weisen und der Tod* (Saturn-Verlag, Vienna, 1938). The novel is not yet translated into English.

[12] The Preface and unpublished letters of Freud to Mrs. Bardi are in possession of the Sigmund Freud Foundation in London.

The book whose profoundness and beauty of style Freud praised is a historical novel that recalls the time and personality of the German Holy Roman Emperor Frederick II (1194-1250), King of Sicily and Jerusalem. This enlightened and temperamental Hohenstaufer, who was excommunicated by the Pope and accused of heresy, blasphemy, and other crimes, made his luxurious court in Sicily a center of intellectual activity and research, gathering Christian, Jewish, and Mohammedan scholars and artists around him. The Emperor who kept a harem at Lucera often shocked the world.

An episode in Bardi's novel deals with the theme of the unseen God. The archbishop of Mainz baits the Rabbi Benaron, an honored guest at Frederick's Sicilian court. The priest cannot understand why the Jews love their God who has only earthly goods to offer. The Rabbi has to explain why the children of Israel do not believe that the Messiah had already come. He says that they cannot imagine that life would go on as before if the Messiah had already appeared. The Messiah is perhaps God's mystery solved. "Again secret!" the archbishop flares up. The priest points out that the secrecy with which Jewish mentality is filled separates people from each other, while frankness unites them. The Rabbi admits that, but adds that there are things man cannot say even if he wants to betray them because he does not know them. It is not that which is kept secret that is important, but that which is secret before oneself. At this point the Emperor, who witnesses the conversation, asks why the Jews chose that strange God.

Benaron tells a fairy tale of Jewish sages: a beautiful child of a king, heiress of a powerful empire, decided to invite all her suitors to select a husband from among them. The city was festively decorated and many princes with

their retinues from all corners of the world presented their
gifts to the princess. The suitors formed a semicircle around
her as she sat on the throne in the hall. Each prince appeared, preceded by his noblemen. His name, titles, and
country were announced and his rich gifts of devotion were
deposited at the stairs of the throne. When only a single
place in the circle was vacant, penetrating sounds of rams'
horns were heard in the yard. The door opened and two
old men in white attire, solemnly carrying a scroll, entered
the hall. They bowed and called "The Lord." Everything
was quiet. No one appeared. But the young princess got up
from the throne as if she had seen a being. She had raised
her hands as though in joyful surprise but then humbly
crossed them over her breast. She descended the stairs and
pushed the jewels and other gifts carelessly away with her
feet. She stood with raised head but then bowed deeply and
announced, "Thou art whom I choose. Be my Lord." She
took the scroll from the old ones and put her royal seal
on it. The people were told that the queen had become en-
gaged to the invisible Lord. It was no choice; it was being
chosen.

The fairy tale beautifully expresses the uniqueness of
the invisible presence. It is not accidental, but in accordance
with the language of the prophets, that Israel appears here
in the role of Jahveh's bride.

Many peoples know invisible gods but those deities become visible sometimes and can be seen by certain persons.
The fanatic insistence on Jahveh's indivisibility and invisibility was maintained through the ages by the Jewish people.
Whoever sees Him has to die. In the concept, the sinister
and menacing aspects of His majesty are present side by
side with His mysteriousness. Compared with the awe other
nations experience toward their gods, the fear Jahveh

instilled in His people is overwhelming. "Clouds and darkness are round about Him" (Psalms 97:2). So great is the unconscious guilt feeling of the people of Israel that He has to remain invisible because no one can stand to face Him. Christianity eased somewhere that guilt feeling for a short time and God can be seen again: "For nothing is secret, that shall not be made manifest; neither any thing hid, that shall not be known and come abroad" (Luke 8:17).

CHAPTER XXX

THE SPLENDID ISOLATION
OF THE JEWS

IN HIS book[1] Freud follows the development from Judaism to Christianity in the concept of Paul. The new religion confessed the murder of God-Father and atoned it by the sacrifice of the Saviour. The message of Paul of Tarsus was: We have been delivered from guilt since Christ laid down His life in expiation for our sin. One part of the Jewish people accepted the new doctrine; the major part did not, was unwilling to admit that they had murdered God. In Freud's interpretation, the reproach of the Christians would have the following meaning: the Jews do not admit that they killed God, whereas we do and are cleansed from the guilt of it. There is, Freud states, some truth behind the reproach, and he continues: "Why the Jews were unable to participate in the progress this confession to the murder of God betokened (in spite of all its distortion) might well be the subject of a special investigation." I am neither equipped nor competent to undertake this task, but the course of this inquiry has spontaneously led to a point where this same question looms before our eyes. The following para-

[1] *Moses and Monotheism* (New York, 1949).

378

graphs do not pretend to comprise that special inquiry, but to make a psychological contribution that might facilitate it.

Let us first explore Freud's statement that there is a reproach from the Gentiles against the Jews such as he describes. Undoubtedly there is, but Freud did not define its special form, nor the manifest shape it took through the last nineteen hundred years. It has now almost vanished— at least in the civilized Western countries—but it was in full blast during the whole medieval period and caused innumerable mass persecutions and pogroms. It is not so many decades ago that murderous mobs broke into the Jewish quarters in Russia and Poland, killing, raping, and pillaging. The reproach was that the Jews had slain Jesus Christ. In calling the Jews Christ-murderers, the accusation was displaced from its original object, God-Father, to His Divine Son. In a generalized form, that reproach was continued in the accusation that the Jews were in the habit of killing a Christian child at Passover. In this trait we recognize a return to a typical mythological displacement as it appears, for instance, in the Orphic doctrine of original sin: the Titans killed the little son of Zeus, Zagreus. But it was Passover when Christ was preparing for the last supper with His disciples. In the earlier, more primitive ritual accusations there was even manifestation of that terrible charge against the Jews, namely that they ate a Christian child at their Passover meal. Here is the full regression to the cannibalistic concept of the murderous act. Freud was correct in formulating the latent content of that reproach. He could have added that it took, in historical reality, the special form of a substitution displacement, the accusation against the Jews that they had killed and eaten Christ.

The severing of the umbilical cord connecting the new religion with its mother religion was by no means a sudden and sharp cut. The operation was performed late when one part of the Jewish people acknowledged the Rabbi of Nazareth as Messiah. When the earliest Christians saw the Lord in the image of a lamb, the Jews began to consider Him the black sheep of the family. The early Christians were much more aware of the ties that united the new covenant with the old one than the Gentiles of modern times. The Middle Ages looked at the Jews with a mixture of horror and awe. Their survival had been destined by the design of the Lord: they were the perennial witnesses for the Saviour, for His dying and the atonement by His sacrifice. The Jews were not only the object of intense hatred, but also of envious feelings: the Redeemer had come from them.

But what about the Jews? Why didn't they allow themselves the benefit of the confession of that primeval father murder? Why didn't they give up the religious and national isolation that had brought them only indescribable sufferings? History remains mute when these questions are asked, questions raised time and again for two thousand years, renewed in all their sinister and tragic aspects by the atrocious crimes of the Nazis. Sociologic and economic points of view can furnish some surface reasons, but cannot penetrate the core of the problem. History can clarify the external conditions, but only analytic penetration of collective emotional processes can solve the enigma.

The word "confession" means the acknowledgment or admission of guilt. Were the Jews not guilt-conscious before and at the time of Jesus Christ? But we have evidence that it was an age of extreme awareness of guilt. The prophets never tired of accusing their people of their transgressions and had again and again made the sins of the Jews responsible for national misfortune. More than this: the century before Christ was one of the demonstrable phases in history in which a whole people felt guilty. The consequence was that the laws were observed with even greater strictness and conscientiousness. The whole of individual life was filled with measures of undoing one's sins and protecting oneself against temptation, to build even higher the wall against the intruding inner enemy.

The enforcement of the observance of rituals, the increased maintenance of religious service, the minute obedience to the Torah could remind the psychoanalyst of the compulsive activity of neurotic patients, who develop in their symptoms individual measures of defense against repressed impulses. A compulsive patient will be filled with anxiety if he has not followed his ceremonial, if for instance he did not wash each finger separately nine times after having previously washed his hands nine times. This neurotic anxiety can well be compared to the guilt feeling of a religious Jew who has omitted to pray a certain prescribed number of times or to repeat certain ceremonials. But there are in obsessional cases also other obscure guilt feelings, mysterious remorse, as though the patient had committed murder or some other violent act although he knows well that he has done nothing of this kind. The patient has perhaps such intense anxiety of guilt because certain hateful or sexual thoughts had occurred to him that are contradicted by his moral or aesthetic views, or he is bothered by some mysterious commandments or forbiddings that appear as insults to his intelligence or reason. Only psychoanalysis can reveal what is concealed behind such seemingly non-

sensical or incomprehensible ideas. At the bottom of them
are always found repressed ideas, originating in forbidden
aggressive or sexual impulses.

Are the guilt feelings of the Jews in the phase before
Christ in any way comparable to those of neurotic patients?
Are the passionate recriminations of the prophets as the
mouthpiece of their people not well justified and reasonable
once you acknowledge the soil from which they spring,
namely religious faith and loyalty to Jahveh? Were not the
Jews unfaithful to Him, tempted to worship other gods? Did
not many of them really, at one time or another, follow
foreign cults, forget or neglect the religion of their forefathers, and pray to pagan deities? The comparison between
the religious and the neurotic guilt feelings has, of course,
only a limited validity. In both cases the reason given for
the sense of guilt is not the real or deepest one, but only
a distant descendant and replacement for the original cause
that has remained unconscious and cannot be remembered.
We know what was hidden behind those self-accusations of
the Jews: the enormous crime of primordial times that is
at the root of all the guilt feelings of mankind. Compared
with it, occasional disloyalty to Jahveh pales to insignificance although the threads from the original to the displaced
substitute can still be followed in analytic exploration.

But why did the guilt feeling that was so distinctly felt
not result in confession of the crime? In order to understand the dynamics operating here, I would do best to refer
to the relationship between guilt feelings and the compulsion to confess that I have mentioned previously. My analytic theory, based on clinical material, discovered an unconscious tendency I called the compulsion to confess.[2] This
trend had been developed from the elementary urge of

[2] *Geständniszwang und Strafbedürfnis* (Vienna, 1926).

expressing the primal drives. The growing demands of the superego and other factors greatly modified that original urge. The main result of the operation of those opposite powers is a need to confess that mitigates the dark anxiety of guilt feeling but also allows a possibility of expression to the instinctual drives. I pointed out that such a compromise manifestation becomes impossible, if the anxiety is too intense. Instead of confession, unconsciously various acts of self-inflicted or self-stage-managed suffering result.

Many of the analytic insights presented in my book could be transferred with the necessary modifications to the area of group psychology. The understanding of the relationship between the compulsion of confession and the intensity of the unconscious anxiety we call guilt feeling can be used to pave the way to the solution of that problem Freud formulated. The simple answer would be that the unconscious guilt feeling of Jewish people was too intense to allow them its partial release through confession. The fear of God that was put into them for so long, under terrible threats of punishment, was so strong that they did not dare to confess. A child who is too afraid of his father and of his wrath will not confess some naughty action and prefers to carry the burden of his guilt.

We cannot be content with this tentative explanation. Without being properly aware of it we had been gliding into a confusion of guilt feeling and of fear of punishment. It is correct that guilt feeling is in its core social anxiety, and its beginnings evolved from the fear of punishment or fear of losing the love of a dear person, but this fear was later replaced by the fear of the superego. Guilt feeling is, we said, the dark fear at the emergence of aggressiveness, an impulse to commit a forbidden violent or hateful act.

This characterization does not tally with the assumption

we tentatively made that the fear of God prevented the Jews from confessing the primal crime. The danger did not come from without, not punishment was feared nor loss of God's love, but some other unknown, more devastating evil. What was impending was not only a calamity coming from external enemies: no catastrophes such as the loss of national independence, captivity, and dispersion—all these the Jewish people had suffered—but something indefinable and unfathomable born in themselves. Those punishments such as oppression and penalties were certainly painfully and mournfully experienced, yet in a certain sense they were unconsciously welcomed because their severity seemed a foretoken of the coming release. They seemed rather to mitigate the guilt feeling that so often manifests itself in the unconscious need for punishment. The differentiation between fear and guilt feelings, as well as the characterization of the tension of guilt as reaction to emerging hostility, excludes the thought that only immediate awe of the Lord can be made responsible for the fact that the Jews were not ready to confess.

Some other, still undiscovered factors must have determined that outcome. It would be in the spirit of analytic psychology to ask which forces determined the perpetuation of the unconscious guilt feeling rather than to guess what prevented its release. But is the answer not so close at hand that the question itself seems to evaporate before our eyes? The fanatic worship of the Lord, the concentration of all religious zeal, yes, of most thoughts on the Lord, and the survival of the Jewish faith in spite of two millennia of suppression and persecution, present loud enough testimony for the intensity of love for the God of their forefathers. This extreme tenacity, this permanent clinging to the one God, this utter loyalty and absolute devotion—do they not fully explain why that guilt feeling could not be reduced? We realize, perplexed and bewildered, that we return to a point where we had already been a short time ago. We find ourselves in a situation similar to that of a wanderer who lost his way in the woods during a fog and is confused because, in his search for the exit, he arrives again at a certain spot, for instance at a definite tree. (Is it that tree in the middle of the Garden of Eden?)

No, the undivided love for Jahveh and utmost faithfulness to Him do not explain the perpetuation of the unconscious guilt feeling of the Jewish people. The impression of the Gentiles was that the Jews keep a secret, but perhaps they also keep it from themselves? The solution of the enigma of their persistent guilt-feeling is that it cannot be given up nor can it be relaxed or reduced because the aggressiveness and the hate against God-Father is unconsciously as alive and as intense as in the prehistoric age that saw the murder of his earliest representative. In other words, the repressed aggression has to be anxiously kept in its cage, has to be guarded day and night, because the ferocious beast would be dangerous if it broke out. That love and awe of the Lord is a reactive emotion and its tremendous intensity is determined by the power of the repressed rebellious and hateful tendencies. We guessed that it is the danger from within, the fear of the superego, that made the diminution of guilt feeling by confession impossible for the majority of the Jewish people.

Not only the unconscious guilt feeling, but also the intensive hostility, the murderous rage against the Lord of Lords had been perpetuated. Total loyalty to Him could not be lessened because of the risk that the lid would be blown off in an explosion of fury. The Messiah had to come not only to save the people and to expiate for the old crime,

but to save them from themselves and to free them from the
waves of unconscious hate that endangered their existence.
The mightiest bulwark had to be erected against that dread
of their own fiery and vehement impulses. The great elevation of their God, His ascent to the most sublime and highest
levels, covered the temptation of most violent attack upon
His majesty. Nietzsche has written a few lines revealing the
same unconscious motives beneath the loftiness and elevation of the concept of Jahveh in the philosophy of the Jew
Baruch de Spinoza, whom the synagogue condemned and
excommunicated in 1656:

To Spinoza

> Turning to the "One in All" most lovingly
> "Amore dei"—bliss from reason—
> Off with the shoes! Land Holy three times ever!
> But deep beneath that love
> A secret vengeful fire's consuming
> Jew-hate from the Jew-God eating.
> Hermit, did I not find you out?

Herman Melville once remarked that in their hearts men
really hate God.[3] It is to this subterranean rebelliousness
and hate that Nietzsche alludes in the quoted lines. It is
strange that so few psychologists have felt the intensity of
that resentment, hidden beneath the utter devotion to Jahveh. Yet almost three hundred years ago an anti-Semitic
English poet wrote:[4]

> The Jews, a headstrong, moody, murm'ring race,
> As ever tried th' extent and stretch of grace,
> God's pampered children, whom, debauch'd with ease,
> No king could govern nor no God could please.

[3] Quoted in Herbert J. Muller, *The Spirit of Tragedy* (New York,
1956), p. 31.
[4] John Dryden, *Absalom and Achitophel*, I:45.

It is this unconscious rebellious trend that makes a con-
tinual vigilance necessary and that drove piety and reverence toward the God of the fathers to a height not reached
by any ancient people, elevated His stature beyond all
other gods. The slightest transgression of His laws was
treated as though it were a murderous impulse. The result
of such a strong reaction formation, born from the tension
of ambivalence, was an aggravation and intensification of
measures of defense and protection against the assault of
the unconscious aggression against God. On the other hand,
a special ethical sensitiveness and the highest appreciation
of spiritual values formed a Jewish heritage still possessed
by the latest descendants of the ancient Hebrew people.

The following instance, which I owe to Dr. Carl Fulton
Sulzberger, will provide an individual neurotic counterpart
to the dynamics operating in the development of this collective ambivalent attitude. Dr. Sulzberger's patient, a young
man reared in an orthodox family but alienated from Jewish
traditions and an atheist for many years, had after having
received two doctorate degrees chosen a business career, in
which he was successful. Some years ago he considered it
advantageous to suggest a certain business deal to his old
father, who had retired a long time before. A year after this
special enterprise was brought to a successful end, the son,
looking through his correspondence, decided to take all
papers referring to it out of the folder in which they were
and put them on file. While he did that, it occurred to him
that he could now use the emptied folder for other business
correspondence. On the folder's cover were his and the
father's name. While he quickly erased his own name, he
had an intensive reluctance to remove the name of his father.

It became clear in psychoanalysis that the patient could
not erase his father's name because this removal was uncon-

sciously identical for him with killing the father. The wording of curses in the Old Testament in which deleting the
name has the significance of utter effacement had unconsciously returned to his mind and had made it impossible
for him to erase the inscription on the folder. The Jewish
people developed a similar acute vigilance toward the
slightest aggressive impulse against their Father in Heaven.

There were enough racial memory traces of an old tribal
god whose wrath the Jews had to fear. There was His
dreadful threat to visit the sins of the fathers on later
generations. The unconscious feeling of guilt, originating
in the primeval crime, has never left the Jews and was only
partially soothed by the destruction of the temple and other
national calamities. Yet not only that unconscious guilt
feeling, but also the hidden rebelliousness against God, the
mortal deified successor of the primal father, was passed
on from generation to generation.[5] The continued effect of
both contradictory, or rather complementing, emotional
trends are manifested in the vicissitudes of the Jews. Perhaps the most important consequence of the intensive guilt
feeling made perennial by the renewal of the temptation is
that the Jews cannot pardon themselves. Such self-forgive-
ness seems to be the premise of interrupting the circle of
guilt and temptation. There is a profound sentence of Rabbi
Bunam of Pzejbscha who asked: "How can we tell when a
sin committed has been pardoned?" and answered: "By the
fact that we no longer commit that sin."

The perennial and always lingering temptation to repeat
the primordial deed invalidated every attempt of the Jews

[5] Even in psychoanalytic literature that continued ambivalence of the
Jews toward their God has not found any sufficient psychological evaluation. A commendable exception is to be mentioned: Joseph H. Goldner's
paper "Dilemma of the American Jew," *The Jewish Social Service
Quarterly*, XXXI, No. 2, 1954.

to make peace with Jahveh. That subterranean rebelliousness that prevented the breakthrough to reconciliation made
the Jews prefer to bear the martyrdom of terrible sufferings
that was unconsciously conceived as punishment for the
primeval sin, but also for its perpetuation and renewal. They
unconsciously knew that all punishment and penalty they
got from their severe divine taskmaster would not make
them repent and give up their self-willed and obstreperous
ways. Did He himself not call them a "stiff-necked people"?
They obstinately insisted that He should first stretch out His
hand as an expression of forgiveness. There is somewhere
in the Talmud, the collection of Jewish civil and canonical
law, the prescription that not the offender but the person
who has been affronted has first to give the sign that he
wishes to be friends again. That has its good psychological
reasons: it is not only the awareness of guiltiness that prevents the wrongdoer from asking for reconciliation. His
shameful pride also makes it difficult for him to approach
the person he has offended.

The Jews who have, in spite of all awe and worship,
looked at Jahveh as one of their own people, expected such
a reconciliatory gesture from Him also. There is no better
evidence for this proud and defiant attitude than the
Christology of that fanatic Jew from Tarsus who had the
grandiose daydream that Jahveh would send His son and
sacrifice Him for the sins of man, to show His willingness
for reconciliation and His wish to forgive and forget. The
Jew's head was indeed bloody but still unbowed in spite of
all displayed humility and exhibited submissiveness to Jahveh. Did not the suggestion of a covenant between Him
and the Hebrews come from His side?

There are many proofs in the Old Testament, from the
prophets to the passionate protestations of Job, that Jahveh

has to redeem His sinful and rebellious people. Beneath their prayers, their demonstration, and their display of remorse and guilt feeling is sometimes heard the appeal to Him—not a cry for help or mercy, but a reminder of His obligation to turn His face to His children, to acknowledge them and to love them as He had promised. Even the reference to their own naughtiness—the word is purposely applied here, because the comparison with children is so close at hand—is used for this purpose. They allude to their weakness and pardonable shortcomings with the inference: just because we are so defiant and wicked, Thou must forgive us and love us.[6] Even in hinting at that covenant they supported their pleading: did He not choose them, make them His people though He must have known their weaknesses, failings, and faults? Not only they, but God also has to justify Himself. After so many tortures and torments they had to suffer to sanctify His name, it was now His turn. He needed their forgiveness on Judgment Day.

[6] An excellent example of this unconscious attitude, the solemn prayer of Kol Nidre, was analytically explored by this writer in a chapter of *The Ritual* (Farrar, Straus and Cudahy, New York, 1940). Bernard Lazare points out that "to the Jewish mind the natural bad tendency is an extenuating circumstance which the sinner can successfully plead before God." (*Job's Dung Heap*, New York, 1948, p. 48.)

CHAPTER XXXI

HOW ODD OF THE JEWS . . .

PERHAPS this is the appropriate place to indicate that the Jewish attitude of suffering, of defiant and obstinate masochism that insists on justice being done, became one of the character traits of the Jewish people that has not been recognized by the psychologists of groups. It is to be expected that the expression of such a characteristic attitude will not be restricted to the relationship of a community to its God. The same behavior is certainly evident, although to my knowledge not noticed until now, in the relationship to other peoples, especially to the nations in whose center the Jews live. The complex of problems known under the name of the Jewish question will, in my view, not be solved as long as this aspect of the issue is not taken into account.

I am speaking of the Jewish problem as though it had to be solved by an effort of will of the Jews and their hosts. I do not believe that great moral issues can be solved in this manner. There is no glib answer nor formula for them. They are "solved" by hidden emotional forces within themselves. That is, they are "dissolved." Following unalterable laws, they progress in their own way and come to an organic close as a melody that unfolds with the inevitability determined by its first bars. Whatever will be the solution of the Jewish

problem, it lies in the line of the "elaboration" of the
theme—to continue the musical comparison—that the dis-
sonances have first to be dissolved from the side of the
other peoples.

Postively expressed, no "solution" to that problem is
possible without preceding acknowledgment of the spiritual
values that the civilization of the world owes to the Jews,
of the indebtedness of Western culture to ancient and
modern Judaism. No solution is imaginable without the
deeply regretful admission of the terrible cruelties inflicted
on the Jews who were made the scapegoats for the guilt of
all peoples. Only when that Rabbi Jehoshuah of Nazareth
will be seen as a great representative of His people and His
destiny as the embodiment of their tragedy can Israel make
peace with the world. Only when the Jewish people, who
conceal but maintain their pride, are given the honors due
to them from all mankind, when that prediction that they
will be a "light to the Gentiles" is acknowledged, will the
Jews renounce their "splendid isolation."

As long as this collective recognition is withheld, the
masses of the Jews will remain in their separation, isolated
and insulated, and keep up the silent claim that they are
the "Chosen People." I am certainly not the first to express
a view of this kind about the so-called "solution" of the
Jewish question. In Heinrich Heine's posthumous *Gedanken
und Einfälle,* written more than a hundred years ago, similar
thoughts are to be found.[1] Here are two instances: "If there
were no Jews any more and if people would know that
there is somewhere a single person of these people left, they
would travel a hundred hours to see him and to shake
hands with him," and more decidedly: "At the end, people

---

[1] Heinrich Heine, *Sämtliche Werke* (Ernst Elster), VII, p. 408.

will make amends to Israel for its sacrifices by recognition of the world, by glory and greatness."

There is more to say about the segregation of the Jews, first enforced from outside and later maintained with secret pride and defiance. But first a few more remarks about that initial rejection of Christianity, founded more on dark emotions, especially on an intensive reluctance, than on religious reasons. There was certainly a strong resistance against a doctrine that resembled the pagan myths of a young god who had died and was resurrected as Osiris and Dionysus. In other words, the uniqueness of the Jewish God could not be infringed upon. The assumption of a divine son or of another god besides Jahveh was intolerable to the pious Jew—and there were only pious Jews when Christ walked on the hills of Galilee.

But deeper and more decisive than this motivation for the rejection of Christianity were others that were unconscious. The pulling down of the severe laws filled the pious with the dark fear of temptation. In the heretic Nazarene they condemned their own temptation to throw off the yoke of the rituals and ceremonials of their religiousness. On the other hand an all-loving, reconciled God was too remote, too invulnerable, too unaffected by placation and aggression from their side. They would not be important to Him any more. The God of the old covenant is a father whose interest, shown in kindness or in wrath and vengeance, is concentrated on His children who can please Him or enrage Him. Better to arouse His wrath than His all-forgiving deluded love, whose remoteness makes Him independent of His children. In rejecting Christianity, the Jews unconsciously refused to accept a poor gesture of reconciliation from His side. They insisted on their rights, on their privilege to be treated as His chosen people. No mercy—justice! One can imagine Shylock as representative of his people in a wrangle not with Antonio, but with God, standing on his right and demanding that the law He had given should be administered to the letter of the Book. The Jews hold out on Him because their pride wants to keep Him within their power. Better to be important to Him even as objects of His wrath than looked upon by Him with kind indifference.

The "splendid isolation" of the Jews dates back to antiquity. Many reasons, some of them certainly not understood by us, are responsible for their separation or segregation. It cannot be doubted that it must have been to a great extent a determination to retain their religious and national identity in the middle of differing culture patterns, but the decisive factor was intense pride. It is obvious that the soil from which their belief in their superiority sprang was a meager and poor one. How did those primitive, miserable, and uncultivated Bedouin tribes, which are the ancestors of the Hebrews, arrive at the assumption that they were favored by Jahveh? It is perhaps correct, as Freud surmised, that their contact with the Egyptian civilization and especially the religious and moral education by the lawgiver Moses changed their original sense of inadequacy and inferiority into a feeling of superiority. Freud's hypothesis is not conclusive but worth testing because there is much in it indicating that the incentive for such a belief came originally from outside.

Since we are unprepared to answer that question we prefer to follow an independent line of investigation, founded on psychological considerations. We have to start from a point far removed from the subject matter of ancient history, from insights into emotional processes of neurotic patients. Many features of the endurance record of their history and their strange resilience remind the analyst of the psychology of "social" masochists. We have often observed that the initial phase of self-assertion in the recovery of these masochistic patients takes a paranoid form. This means that the patients think of themselves as superior and important persons and suspect that they are being envied, persecuted, exploited, or misused. This view is rarely as distinctly manifested as I defined it here. In most cases, considerable admixtures of masochism or alternations of masochistic and slightly paranoid attitudes are observed. Some analysts, especially Jule Nydes,[2] are inclined to conceive of those attitudes as two aspects of a struggle for power with an omnipotent will. In the masochistic attitude the patient tries to win love and to force the "omnipotent" person to serve him through suffering and submission. In the paranoid attitude, the need for love has become unconscious and would be despised as an expression of weakness. The aggression that has been repressed before is now self-righteously acted out. Here is the description of that transition Jule Nydes gives from his clinical experiences: "A meek plea turns into an arrogant demand; a cherished privilege into inalienable right. He no longer needs love, but boasts of his power to endure hatred in the reality of which he has an unshakable conviction. Whining placation may turn to fierce provocation which, if successful, may force a retreat to masochism or redouble efforts in the direction of paranoia."

Nydes thinks that for both attitudes reward and punishment are the only consequences. To both, all that happens is due "to the design of a benevolent or malevolent will," which they try to manipulate. The deep unconscious guilt

[2] The following paragraphs are the result of an exchange of ideas with J. Nydes.

(as distinguished from the show of guilt) that is central to both attitudes is an index to true grandiose feelings ("infantile omnipotence"). "Great guilt equals great power— power to hurt—power to provoke punishment—power by guile, by deceit, or by coercion to wrest a reward." Change is difficult mostly because the patients loathe to loose that sense of power that feeds both orientations.

I have quoted the experiences of Jule Nydes (who, by the way, is kind enough to acknowledge that his ideas are in essence an elaboration of thoughts developed in my *Masochism in Modern Man*) so extensively because the investigator who tries to obtain an unbiased view of the Jewish attitude toward God will find featurse similar to those described in the alternative phases of Jewish history. The main character is, of course, the conviction of being chosen by God, whether as carrier of His mission or as His scapegoat or both is not essential—this means a collective belief analogous to the paranoid idea of grandeur. Necessarily connected with this conviction is the belief in a special destiny for the people. The attitude of a "defiant masochism"—if the expression is allowed—tallies well with this largely unconscious assumption. Our final impression of the people's attitude to Jahveh is: How odd of the Jews to put on God the screws!

Their splendid isolation—the emphasis is on the adjective—evolves as a consequence of being the chosen people. It also secured the spiritual values, the contributions of that small group to civilization that were as splendid as their isolation. The Jews are among the nations decidedly not the collective counterpart of what is known as a "good mixer," but their function as ferment of civilization is still scarcely acknowledged. There is still everywhere against them that almost instinctive hatred fed from deeper sources,

still that accusation of God-murder. As the Old Mariner
the Jew could complain:

> Ah, well-a-day! What evil looks
> Had I from old and young!
> Instead of the cross, the Albatross
> About my neck was hung.

I hope it is well understood that these psychoanalytic
considerations do not pretend to present an explanation of
the obscure destiny of the Jewish people. They only want
to add some new or unacknowledged points of view, to
open a novel approach to a complex problem that can be
understood only by the combined research of historians,
sociologists, and psychologists. It would be presumptuous
of the psychoanalyst to expect a full explanation of the
many-sided Jewish problem from his science.

Our endeavor to answer Freud's question of why the
Jews did not participate in that confession of primeval
murder and its benefits that Christianity enjoyed was only
partly successful. We could contribute only a few undiscovered factors, more indicative than decisive, to the solution of the problem—either because it is too difficult to
solve with the means at our disposal or because it out-
reaches our intellectual power. Our line of investigation
was determined by the assumption that there were certain
definite psychological tendencies resisting the diminution
of guilt feeling by such a collective confession. In their refusal to accept the "salvation" and "redemption" Christianity offered to them, the Jews declared that primordial
crime indelible. They immortalized it. In condemning themselves to an existence of solitude and persecution, they
claimed at the same time that salvation has to come from
their people.

From their midst a quiet voice asks the other people the

same question that Jesus asked Paul on the way to Damascus, "Why persecutest thou me?" That zealous Pharisee went in his daydreams back to the sin of Adam in whose expiation the Lord died on the Cross. Without being aware of the real character of the original sin, Paul was on the right track in his regression to the primal past, in tracing the universal guilt feeling to its prehistoric sources. His answer was that of religion. Nineteen centuries later another Jew gave the world the scientific reconstruction of the origin of mankind's collective guilt feeling. Freud's discovery of the prehistoric reality of a primal parricide and its psychological evaluation present, so to speak, that confession in the terms of science. It does not give any promise of redemption or salvation. It does not pretend to bring glad tidings. It presents, however, unexpected insights whose significance will be even more thoroughly appreciated and understood in the third millennium after the birth of the Redeemer.

CHAPTER XXXII

HUBRIS

THE NARRATIVE of Genesis 3 was treated in this book as a primordial crime story and we attempted a *reconstruction du crime* as the French say. The weakest link in the chain of evidence was that of motive. A kind of internal evidence can perhaps be discovered on a detour. Even when we assume that the serpent part of the story is a later interpolation, the wise animal might give away some of the reasons why the Lord forbade the eating of the tree (Genesis 3:5): "For God doth know that in the day ye eat thereof, then your eyes shall be opened, and ye shall be as gods, knowing good and evil." The original text is almost certainly altered in those lines, but possibly something of the primary meaning is preserved. An indirect argument for this assumption is given by what God said later on: "Behold, the man is become as one of us to know good and evil: and now, lest he put forth his hand, and take also of the tree of life, and eat, and live for ever . . ." (Genesis 3:22).

The critical argumentation of the text of these two passages leads to the impression that their meaning is that Adam's real or implied motive for eating of the tree is to deprive God of something that is His prerogative. There was and still is a drawn-out discussion of what this something is: immortality, omniscience, or imnipotence, discernment of what is good or evil in a moral sense, or what is useful or harming in a practical direction. We would be inclined to answer: the magical power or, to use the term of Australian savages, mana.

But we are released from the necessity of giving such a special and definite answer by the interpretation of the myth at which we arrived. If the tree is the representative of the totem or primal god, eating of it would endow the eater with every superior quality, power, or ability the deity possesses. The motive for the primal crime or sin was, in short, to become God by such embodiment.[1]

At this point indignant objection will come from two opposite sides: the religious or believing person will rise in revolt against the plot of a biblical story as such. The outrage here implied can only be imagined against the gods or the fetishes of the heathen, but not against God-Father of Jewish and Christian faith, the Creator of the Universe. But this is precisely the view of the Jehovist or of the writers or compilers of the Genesis tale. It was the impossibility of the idea that God-Father could be murdered and eaten that made the distortion and secondary elaboration of the old tradition necessary. The camouflage of the Tree of Life is there to conceal the murder and devouring of God—not the god of some barbarous cannibalistic tribes, but the almighty Lord of Israel that had reached a peak of civilization.

The introduction of God-Father into the crime story will also arouse the indignation of atheists and agnostics. They

[1] We do not forget that the object of Christ's desire is the same. The gifted but confused Simone Weil (*The Notebooks of Simone Weil*, New York, 1956) constructed a contrast where an identity exists: "It is not by eating the fruit of a certain tree, as Adam thought, that one becomes the equal of God, but by going the way of the Cross."

too will reject the selection of such a singular victim of the crime. They feel like addressing Jahveh as Spinoza does in Voltaire's words: "Je crois, entre nous, que vous n'existez pas." It is easy enough to answer them: Yes, God-Father does not exist, but He did exist in primeval times. That means a despotic and overpowering father of the horde existed whose figure was much later immortalized in the shape of the primitive god. But with this reduction we have brought the myth back to earth again and to its very earthy original form. The motive for the primeval deed of the brother gang is the same as that of Australian natives who eat a white missionary to seize upon his envied and admired power.

But we are interested in another side of the problem. We see in Adam—we adopt this case for the anonymous sinner —the first criminal. Since "in Adam's Fall we sinned all," some of the dark potentialities of crime—of the same crime—must live in each of us. We are all tainted by our common, most distant ancestor. This is the doctrine of the Church. We believe in that article of faith according to that sentence that there is no salvation outside the Church ("Extra ecclesiam non est salus"). But even when we accept the lessons of biology, something of the nature of that primal man and criminal must still be alive somewhere in our heritage as his descendants just as in the dog the inherited features of the wolf are still observable.

There is another aspect of the same problem: the original sin—or crime—was certainly typical for crime in general and the psychology of the first offender must be informative with regard to character traits of all criminals. Are such character traits common to all criminals, especially to men inclined to murder and deeds of violence?

At the occasion of the discussion of Dostoevski's criminal

disposition, Freud remarked[2] that two features are significant for the criminal: limitless egotism and an especially
strong destructive tendency. There can be no doubt that the
constitutional intensity of destructive trends is characteristic
of the criminal. It seems to me that enormous selfishness,
although undeniably present, is less characteristic than
boundless vanity of a certain kind. Let us test this assumption in the case of the first crime. The brothers, expelled
from the primal horde, united against the father, assaulted
and killed him. In the eyes of his sons the father of the
horde was certainly a superman whose murder was as
unimaginable to them as the murder of God to us. Yet they
did it. They got away with that murder. That is to say, their
doubts and fears must have been swept away for some time
by the feeling that they were supermen themselves. They
were drunk with power. We know that the murderers were
in reality rather subhuman, not yet entirely Homo sapiens
as we know the species. But in their own minds—if this
expression is permitted—there was certainly a grandiose
confidence in themselves, a limitless conceit, a self-assurance
that knew no restriction.

The superman whom Nietzsche saw as the ideal of a distant future belongs thus to the remotest past of mankind.
The criminologists and the psychologists, interested in the
emotional life of murderers, tell us that such an inflated
ego, such hypertrophic self-confidence is characteristic of
many killers even today. It seems that the swollen, abundant
confidence in one's own power, a kind of extreme vanity or
conceited opinion of oneself, is to be found with many
types of violent and brutal criminals. At the fringes of our

[2] *Dostojewski und die Vatertötung,* Gesammelte Schriften, XII, p. 8.

thoughts the figure of Dostoevski's Raskolnikov with his idea of grandeur appears.

The idea of that unspeakable deed that we reconstructed as the hidden content of the Fall story, the murder and the eating of God-Father, presupposes an underlying pride or presumptuousness of such gigantic dimensions that such expressions as conceit, vanity, rebelliousness are insufficient and inappropriate. We really have no word for the basic hyperbolic emotion from which such a plan or action can spring. The word we search for is not always to be found in English dictionaries, but it was a term familiar to the ancient Greek: *hubris*. It is more than a semantic interest that makes us turn our attention to the meaning of that expression; our psychological interest is awakened. We would like to know not only what the word denotes, but what it meant emotionally to the Greeks of antiquity.

According to a new dictionary,[3] the word *hubris* means "wanton arrogance, or violence, arising from passion or recklessness; insolent disregard of moral laws or restraint." The scholars have defined *hubris* as[4] "the personification of overweening pride in which man, heedless of his mortal nature and losing all sense of measure, allows his skill, his power, and his good fortune to make him arrogant toward god; Nemesis." The inevitability of such final defeat is clearly presented in the Greek tragedies, and Milton also expresses this view with regard to Satan's fall:

> . . . who aspires must down as low
> As high he soar'd.
>   *Paradise Lost, IX, 169.*

[3] Webster, *New International Dictionary* (2d ed., Springfield, Mass.), 1956.

[4] Roscher, *Lexicon of Greek and Roman Mythology*, I, 2, 2767.

Hubris is the theme of Greek tragedy, especially of that of Aeschylus, and it is in connection with tragedy that the term is most discussed.[5] But the idea of *hubris* transcends the realm of the stage. It is an essential part of the religious and moral outlook of the Greeks, of the tragic atmosphere of Greek life. Aristoteles calls pride "the crown of the virtues," but the tragic poets stress the dangers of pride. At a certain period there grows up, as Miss Jane Harrison points out,[6] "the disastrous notion that between god and man there was a great gulf and that communion was no more possible. To attempt to pass the gulf was *hubris;* it was *the* sin against the gods."

The hero of the Greek tragedy suffers a cruel fate. The gods have inflicted a terrible penalty on him. Why he incurred it often remains mysterious or veiled. It seems he has consciously or unconsciously aroused the wrath of the gods, has committed some crime or at least done something that they—sometimes only one of them—consider deserving of severe punishment. The nature of this tragic guilt is not often explained or reveals itself only at the end. There is the chorus, several individual actors dressed alike, behaving in the same manner and speaking in unison. They warn the single and central figure, the tragic hero, remind him of the divine laws and of the power of the gods, try to prevent his rushing into hasty actions, express their sympathy for him, and mourn him when he becomes a victim of inevitable fate. Whatever are the original features of the oldest forms of the Greek tragedy, the part of the hero in classical times is clear: he is a criminal, sometimes a half-god, a king or

[5] From the literature on *hubris* only a few books will be mentioned here: Carlo del Grande, *Hybris* (Naples, 1904); Herbert I. Muller, *The Spirit of Tragedy* (New York, 1956); R. J. Werblowsky, *Lucifer and Prometheus* (London, 1942); Karl Kerenyi, *Prometheus* (Zurich, 1946).

[6] *Themis,* p. 468.

savior, against the gods. He has committed an outrage against the deities and has to suffer punishment for it.

The chorus leaves no doubt of what his essential guilt is: an extreme pride or presumptuousness, an extreme impudence or boldness—all that which the Greek expression *hubris* includes. His penalty is, of course, merited by the crime he has committed against the gods, whatever that may be, but the chorus condemns him for and vainly warns him of his overweening pride and of the impudent or immodest attitude he takes towards the deity. Although the attitude of the tragic hero is too proud and defiant, his unconquerable spirit appeared to the Greeks admirable. Aeschylus clearly takes the part of his *Prometheus Bound* against Zeus and agrees with his final utterance: "Behold me, I am wronged." It is not difficult to recognize in the tragic hero the representative figure of the parricidal son and in the chorus those of his brothers who, now in a hypocritical distortion, keep a distance from him as though they were not as guilty as he.[7]

The attitude of *hubris* is the same that is manifested in the original crime told in the Genesis narrative. Adam's revolt against Jahveh has its roots in that too high opinion of himself whose consequences God foresees in His omniscience ("Behold the man is become as one of us . . .").

Is there, besides the Fall story, nothing similar in the realm of Hebrew civilization? Certainly not in the form of tragedy or of the dramatic play. With the exception of the Purim festivals, there was no drama in ancient Israel. All performance of this kind was comprised in religious ritual. But there was another, more important reason for the lack

[7] Freud has expressed the guess that the hero of the tragedy was originally the primal father and the scene upon the stage re-enacts the prehistoric scene. *Totem and Taboo* (New York, 1950), p. 156.

of tragedy in Hebrew civilization, one that reaches deeper into the underground out of which the character of tragedy grows. Tragedy in general has the psychological premise of a fight between at least two parties or powers. Followed to its original source, the conflict is that between the gods and their creatures.

Even today tragedy is impossible without the supposition of a basic conflict, although we have replaced the deity by the impersonal power of destiny. But at the progressed state Hebrew religion had reached and with the sublimation of the god to the majesty of Jahveh, a rebellion against God as it was assumed in Greek tragedy was unimaginable. The idea of divinity had been elevated to heights beyond human reach and had become untouchable. The *basso continuo* of the Hebrew religion was in contrast to that of the Greek: "Walk humbly with thy God." In the late classical Greek tragedy the character of the crime has later on become difficult to define and has rather obtained the nature of a transgression of divine laws or commandments, but ancient Hebrew civilization excluded the possibility of an open break with Jahveh. The Biblical world is *"hubris*-free," as Werblowsky says.[8]

There are, however, enough traces of such an open conflict preserved in the tradition of Hebrew myths, besides the core of the Fall story as we reconstructed it. In Genesis we find the remnants of myths whose original shape must have been much more coarse and definite than it is now, the myth of another Fall, not of man, but of angels. There is the episode of the sons of God who saw "the daughters of men that they were fair; and they took them wives of all which they chose." Here are divine beings who are in revolt against Jahveh, of giants in rebellion in the midst of the

---

[8] R. J. Werblowsky, *Lucifer and Prometheus* (Zurich, 1952), p. 13.

Genesis narrative whose priestly scribes knew only a divinely transcendent deity. But also there is the adversary of Jahveh and his name is Lucifer. But his revolt is defeated: "How art thou fallen from heaven, O Lucifer, son of the morning! How art thou cut down to the ground, which didst weaken the nations!" (Isaiah 14:12).

Satan, leader of the angels, appears in full opposition to the Lord in the prologue to the Book of Job, which belongs to the postexilic literature. An attentive study of that work, if undertaken without preconceived ideas, leads to impressions and conclusions so daring that one should express them only with great caution. There is Job, who was "perfect and upright, and one that feared God, and eschewed evil." Satan suggests that the Lord put forth His hands and touch all that Job has, and Satan expects that Job will "curse thee to thy face." Whereupon the Lord told Satan, "All that he hath is in thy power." Job suffers when, as he supposes, the Lord strikes him again and again. He does not know why Jahveh inflicts so cruel a punishment upon him who has not sinned. The tragic hero curses the day of his birth and complains of life.

There are the three friends Eliphaz, Bildad, and Zophar, who "come to mourn with him and comfort him." They "lifted up their voice and wept; and they rent every one his mantle and sprinkled dust upon their heads toward heaven." They "sat down with him upon the ground . . . for they saw that his grief was very great." But after they listened to his complaints, each of them reproves him and wants to prove that he is unjust and unfair to God, speaks of His wisdom, and tries to console the sufferer. He argues with them and calls them "miserable comforters" who "heap words" upon him and shake their heads at him. He renews his complaints against the Lord and appeals to Him. At the end, Jahveh

appears and answers out of the whirlwind and challenges
Job to answer. God enumerates His works and Job humbly
submits himself to Him. He abhors himself and repents in
dust and ashes and the Lord restores him and his estate,
giving him twice as much as he had before.

Is our impression deceptive when we seem to recognize
the same great lines behind the scenes of the Job story as
they appear in the Greek tragedy? Are we misled and mistaken by a superficial resemblance of the situation? Here
is the tragic, suffering hero complaining and his friends
showing sympathy, comforting him, warning and reproving
him. Is it not a variation of the scene on the Greek stage,
with the figure of the hero, victim of a dark destiny, and
around him the chorus? But there is more to it than external
similarities: here is the figure of the lonely sufferer in opposition to the Lord and punished by Him for an enigmatic
crime—we should say for a crime he has not committed or
only unconsciously committed.

What is Job's sin? Many hundreds of books and papers
have been written on that subject. The kind of punishment
to which he is subjected, the answer of the Lord to his complaints and his submission give a clear answer: Job challenges the power and justice of God. The man in the land
of Ur is guilty of the same sin as the hero from Greece:
of intolerable pride and presumptuousness in the face of
God. The adversary expresses that unconscious sin in the
words, "Doth Job fear God for naught? Hast not thou
made an hedge about him, and about his house, and about
all that he hath on every side?" Satan is sure that Job will
curse the Lord, if He inflicts pain on him.

Job is guilty of *hubris* in the same way as the heroes of
the Greek tragedy and in reversal of the sequence sin-punish-
ment has to suffer the penalty for unconsciously defying the

Lord and for daring to consider himself equal to Him. He is stricken although he feels innocent and he is restored and re-established. It is a situation like that of Prometheus bound and released, like that of many heroes of the Greek tragedy. The form of presentation is different from that of the drama, but even in this direction in the almost uninterrupted shape of arguments, of dialogue and monologue the Hebrew epic approaches that of the plays of ancient Hellas. There is no doubt that here old Jewish literature comes closest to the character and the latent content of the Greek tragedy. Here is a bridge between two civilizations of antiquity founded on the common ground of basic human experiences.[9] Here is a manifestation of the solidarity of man: not of the brotherhood of love that appears in the idealistic and delusional dreams of contemporary statesmen, but of the spirit of the brotherhood of hate and rebellion against God—a late echo of revolt that propelled the primeval crime.

It is not unlikely that the great poet who wrote the Book of Job took his material from an old folk tale as Aeschylus borrowed his plot from an ancient myth. Myths were formed from the rich store of oral tradition and finally shaped into folk epics or plays as were those of Homer and of the Greek dramatists. The necessarily condensed form of this presentation does not allow us more than a side glance at the later development of myths. Freud answers the question of why the epic, as a literary form, disappeared: the conditions for its production do not exist any longer since the old myth

[9] After finishing this manuscript I became acquainted with the brilliant study, *The Book of Job as a Greek Tragedy*, by H. M. Kallen (New York, 1918). The scholar develops the hypothesis that the book of Job is a Greek tragedy in Hebrew, specifically modeled after Euripides. An earlier monograph by Dr. Bernard Hausner, *Job tragedya grecka* (Jahresbericht des K. K. zweiten Staatsgymnasium in Lemberg, 1913) was not accessible to me.

material is used up and later events are reported by historians who have replaced the epic poets.[10] In this sense the gospels and the apocrypral literature of Christianity are the last products of mythological imagination.

There are late offshoots, for instance the legend of the Wandering Jew, of that figure of the deathless old man who roams the earth, cursed with immortality. According to the legend, the shoemaker Ahasuerus watched the Saviour being led to Calvary and when Jesus, weary and faint, stopped to rest, shouted at Him: "Move on, move on!" Jesus looked at him and said: "I shall stand and rest, but you shall know no rest until Judgment Day!" From then on the Jew must wander on to the end of time. In another version, the doorman of Pilate who taunted Jesus was doomed to wander till the second coming of Christ.[11]

The legend appears first in a pamphlet published at Leyden, in 1602. It relates that Paulus von Eizen, Bishop of Schleswig, had met Ahasuerus at Hamburg, in 1542. It is obvious that the Wandering Jew personified the old Father-God, but the figure should also explain the fate of His worshipers who had to wander from one country to another. In the late literary usages of the legends (Goethe, Lenau, Robert Buchanan, Eugene Sue, Hijerman), the Eternal Jew appears sometimes as Jahveh, sometimes as Jesus Himself.

Anti-Semitic tendencies using ancient mythical material are also expressed in the published legend of the ritual murder of a Christian child at Passover spread in medieval times (Heine, *Der Rabbi von Bacharach*) and in the last ramification of an imagined conspiracy of the Jews (*The Protocol of Zion*) to conquer the world.

[10] *Moses and Monotheism*, p. 111.
[11] Joseph Gaer, *The Lore of The New Testament* (Boston, 1952), p. 213.

It seems to me that Freud was mistaken when he assumed that the old mythical material from which folk epics drew their plots was used up. Only the tributaries to the old stream had dried. The original flow is inexhaustible and is fed from deep, invisible sources. The old Greek tragedy was continued in the Christian Passion plays and traces of its primal situation can even be found in the suffering of Hamlet. But it was the novel that entered upon the inheritance of the epic. Strangely enough, perhaps the greatest of all novels has beneath all camouflage and modification essentially that old theme of the murder of the father by his sons. I mean, of course, *The Brothers Karamazov,* by Dostoevski. Here is the magnificent tale of a parricide of which all sons are consciously or unconsciously guilty. Here is the picture of that primeval crime, committed by the sons uniting against their begetter, the family tragedy of early prehistory transported into a Russian province of the last century. Dmitri, Ivan, Alyosha, Smerdyakow—here are the brothers, around the father, doomed to be killed by them. (There are perhaps remnants of some fantasies about the Christ figure in the shaping of Alyosha.) In Dostoevski's novel a very late descendant of that primal father figure is killed.

There is a continuation of the same epic flow in Melville's *Moby Dick.* The White Whale is (as Leviathan) a totemistic representative of God and Ahab's passionate hate against Him is that of Prometheus in the modern figure of a captain. Ahab's cry is: "Who's to doom, when the judge himself is dragged to the bar?" The crew of the Pequod takes in this interpretation the place of the brothers of the primal horde. By the way, is it accidental that Captain Ahab is at the end bound to the whale by the ropes of his harpoon as Prometheus is fixed on the rock and Christ on the Cross?

The old myth of the primordial parricide still lives on
and the shadow of the first father, murdered by his sons, is
cast over the ages as if he had become immortal. "Rest,
noble spirit, in thy grave unknown!"

After so long a digression it is difficult to find the way
back to our subject, modern man trapped in that squeeze
between the demands of his instinctual drives and the claims
of society that awaken his guilt feeling. Yet it is perhaps
easier than we thought to discover the connections between
that topic and the problem dealt with in *The Brothers
Karamazov*. There are different threads running from one
to the other. It surprised us that a sense of guilt is not only
aroused by knowing that one has done wrong—we would
prefer to call that reaction remorse—but also, and more so,
by the awareness of being tempted to do it without having
yielded to it. In the one case the person is afraid of losing
love and gaining punishment and social disapproval; in the
other, the individual is haunted by the shadow of the deed
he had fervently wished to commit.

In the former case, he is condemned by the community,
in the latter by a powerful voice in himself that attributes
to that shadow all the terrors of reality. You could say
that he is doomed if he does, and he is doomed, if he
does not. The brothers in Dostoevski's novel who have
not murdered their father feel as guilty as though they had
committed the crime and one of them, Ivan, accuses himself of it before an open court. But it may be more advantageous for the continuity of this essay to follow another
thread. The real murderer of his father, Smerdyakow, the
illegitimate son of Fyodor Pavlovitch Karamazov, betrayed
"a boundless vanity, and a wounded vanity too" and is
characterized as having "a strangely high opinion of himself." Here we find again that attitude the Greeks called

hubris, that mixture of arrogance, presumptuousness, and exaggerated pride.

It is this attitude to which the tragic guilt of the hero of the Attic drama is attributed. From it springs the incentive to rebellion and murder, to lawlessness and hateful transgressions of divine and civil laws. That same hidden spark was the incendiary for the catastrophic events whose reflections are preserved in the censured and distorted Genesis tales of the Fall of Man, of the Tower of Babel, and others. In the Greek tragedies and in the Biblical stories, this *hubris* is determined as presumptuousness responsible for the outrage against God or the gods and is restricted to the sinners or criminals. Greek and Hebrew moralists seem to agree that self-attributed absolute power corrupts absolutely. The doctrine of the original sin in its Augustinian form, generally accepted by Christianity, states that all mankind is tainted by the sin of Adam and proclaims that in all of us there is a disposition to the evil character responsible for that terrible deed. But it means that in all of us, besides the inclination to revolt against the deity and his commandments, is something of that exaggerated pride and hypertrophic vanity that makes us think of ourselves as godlike.

After removing all theological and ethical trimmings we face at this critical point an unexpected aspect of extraordinary impact for our psychological problems. Brushing away all religious veneer and looking at the question from the viewpoint of sober scientific research, is there, in reality, in all human beings a kind of innate overconfidence in their own power? Is there in man generally an overappreciation and overly high opinion of himself from which that attitude of *hubris* can develop as hypertrophic enlargement or pathological outgrowing? When we think of the helplessness and timidity of small children, of their dependency and of their need for protection, we cannot imagine that they have too much self-assurance. It is very likely, however, that the assumption of such a general disposition does not regard actions, but rather activity in thoughts: in other words, overevaluation of mental activities, fantasies, and wishes.

Psychoanalysis asserts that children have really a grandiose concept of the power of their own thoughts and learn only late to acknowledge the limitations set to their daydreams and wishes. A small boy or a small girl will at first believe that he or she can grasp the moon looking into the nursery. Such extraordinary belief in one's own mental processes is often unconsciously maintained and kept in spite of opposite rational views. In psychoanalysis of neurotic patients, especially in obsessional cases, we regularly encounter manifestations of that old belief in the omnipotence of their thoughts. Freud has shown how much of this superstitious confidence in one's own wishes is operating in the emotional life of savage and half-civilized peoples and what a decisive part it plays in the creation of their religious and social institutions. It is obvious that this belief is also extended to their fears and anxieties. Prehistoric man must have had an even higher degree of overevaluation of his thoughts and fantasies. We would call such an excessively high opinion of one's power "ideas of grandeur," if met in insane patients, for instance the paranoics. But we occasionally catch surprising impressions even of ourselves, as though our secret thoughts could direct the course of events, could decide the outcome, the failure or success of external occurrences.

The questions we now face are the following: Is that overly high opinion man has of himself and of his mental acts—mostly concealed also from himself—a factor in the emotional impasse from which he vainly searches for an escape? How far is the evolution of civilization responsible for the development of that attitude of abnormally enlarged pride? Finally, what, if anything, can be done to improve the human condition today as a corrective to bring man's self-evaluation to its appropriate proportions? All these questions are difficult if not impossible to answer, but the attempt has to be made, even though it is only because we do not want to appear to ourselves as moral cowards. At this critical moment of human civilization man cannot afford to avoid or circumvent these decisive questions.

CHAPTER XXXIII

MAN, THE MORAL CLIMBER

BEFORE WE even try to answer those questions, we would like to follow the history of human civilization in a telescopic manner from the beginning of Christianity to the present, from the age of Atonement to the age of Atom bombardment.

Christianity spread from the Jews to the Gentiles and gave the world, so to speak, a breathing spell. For a moment in the evolution of civilization that part of mankind that had accepted the Christian doctrine of Paul felt released from guilt. It was comparatively not more than a second in the history of the world, an intermission in the wrestling match between the two giants of innate drives and of the repressing powers. The guilt feeling, lifted by the sacrificial death of Christ who has atoned for the sins of all mankind, returned. The original sin had tainted all generations descending from Adam. And men had not stopped sinning, had not given up violence and aggression, bloodshed and murder. About four hundred fifty years ago an anonymous writer expresses his astonishment about that fact:

> Since Christ from sin us to release
> Hath suffered all His pain
> Why do we not then from them cease
> But still in sin remain?

And why, he could furthermore have wondered, do we still feel guilt even when we abstain from sin since Christ has redeemed us? Why do we who are saved sometimes suffer the tortures of the damned?

The human situation shows this picture: the individual is alternatively pulled from two sides. He is unhappy after he yielded to his inclination to aggression and he is oppressed by a sense of guilt when he resists it. People are caught in that trap between the instinctual gratification and the inner tension owing to repressed aggressiveness. In the intervals between eruptions of violence, wars, pograms, bloody persecutions, crusades, inquisitions, and gas chambers, an increasing discomfort and dissatisfaction pervaded our civilization. The essential mood of the secret life of man, concealed behind the technical progress, is quiet desperation. Suppression of instinctual urges is necessary for the maintenance of culture. Yes, one can say, civilization began in prehistoric times with such repression created by pressure from outside and later internalized. It seems that the lot of prehistoric man, who already was subjected to instinctual renunciations, was not a happy one. He had to suppress his desires and to suffer when he fulfilled the early requirements of primitive civilizations as does the child who is subjected to the process of education. Man could have expressed his bitterness as did the six-year-old boy, who complained to his mother:[1] "I'd no idea when I was born that I should have such a bad time."

Collective actions of most violent aggression periodically eased the tension. In a transport from the original object, from the despotic father of the primal horde, to the rulers of society and their subjects, the old struggle was continued,

[1] Reported by Alice Balint, *The Early Years of Life* (New York, 1954), p. 118.

changing its forms with the transformations of civilization. The house built over the body of the murdered head of the primeval family was divided in itself. The original deed is repeated in new forms:[2] "That which began in relation with the father ends in relation to the community." If civilization is "an inevitable course of development from the group of the family to the group of humanity as a whole," then an intensification of the sense of guilt is inextricably bound up with it. Religious wars, fought in the name of the Prince of Peace, were followed by bloody conflicts of the nations and these replaced and complemented by the struggles of classes. At the moment the great fight looms ahead between the capitalistic and the communistic system, both claiming to be the true democracy.

The progress of civilization reflected itself also in the improvement of weapons, the instruments of collective aggression and tools of mass destruction.[3] Nuclear weapons and atomic power are symbolic of this age of anxiety. It is very possible that our species will not wait for the "end of days," to use the theological term, or, to speak biologically, for its organic extinction. It is imaginable that the murderous instincts that are an innate inheritance of our species

[2] Freud, *Civilization and Its Discontents.* (London, 1949), p. 121.

[3] In a polemic dispute of Freud's view of an innate disposition to aggressiveness in man M. F. Montague declares that it is not human nature, but "human nurture that is the cause of human aggression." He is of the opinion that human nature is good and, if treated as such, leads to goodness. He does not doubt that the innate drives are never oriented to destruction and that such disturbances are mostly caused by cultural factors. He warns against falling into the error of attributing to innate nature what has been produced by those cultural agencies. ("Man and Human Nature," *The American Journal of Psychiatry,* II, 1955, p. 409.) The findings of prehistory, during which those "cultural agencies" scarcely produced aggression, and the insights of psychoanalysis regretfully but energetically contradict Montague's admirably optimistic conception of human nature.

may turn against ourselves and make an end to the fight. If the saving grace does not intervene, the homicidal passion of the masses has to result in suicide of mankind. Perhaps man is destined not to end with a bang, but with a whimper dying in an unheard explosion. Above the debris after the blast of the last atom bombs His voice will perhaps be heard as in one of Strindberg's plays, saying, "Es ist schade um die Menschen" (What a pity about man!) It is not impossible that the *leitmotif* of the sacred tree will linger on to the last days of mankind. A recent cartoon showed a Christmas tree whose branches were hung with hydrogen bombs.

We return to our questions. One of them, it seems to me, is the easiest to approach because there is a point of contact with the psychoanalytic assumption of an original state in which the infant, as the primitive or prehistoric man, over-appreciates the power of his thoughts. Does civilization increase or reduce this primal belief? It certainly lessens it: the child, as the savage, hesitatingly realizes and acknowledges the limitations of his power and concedes a part of it to spirits, ghosts, demons, and finally gods. There remains, however, enough of it in the child, although education to reality works on that superstition in order to diminish it. These same educational forces will compel primitive man to acknowledge the power of nature and of other restrictions of the surrounding world, of illness and death, of enemies, of earthquakes and glacial periods, and so on.

But besides and beyond those external factors progressive civilization compels him, first with the help of punishment and threats, to submit to the laws and orders of society. That is at first, and to great extent until now, done in the name of the tribal gods. The Psalms proclaim that the fear

of the Lord is the beginning of wisdom. With that fear not
only wisdom begins, but also many other qualities, results
of many prohibitions, renunciations of instinctual gratification, and privations, reluctantly accepted. There is no doubt
that the beginnings of civilization educated primitive man
to a gradual decrease of his belief in his own omnipotence.

Two factors are responsible that this education did not
reach its ideal goal—none does—but failed in certain directions. The first is the tenacity of that primitive belief or
conviction that when repressed found a secret refuge in
unconscious thinking and operated as an underground
movement. It grew and prospered in its hiding place, always
ready to break through to the surface. The second frustrat-
ing factor has its deep roots in the very character of civilization. It was unavoidable that the very civilizing process in
its later phases favored an increase in self-confidence and
a growing belief in the power of one's mental abilities. Did
not man learn to cope with the forces of nature and finally
to tame and to use them so that they were not his masters
any longer, but became his servants? And did not many
of his daydreams of conquest of the world become reality?

Not only individuals, but mankind itself has established
a superego. His imagined ability to live up to his own
moral demands filled man with the same satisfaction children feel when they are praised as good boys and girls who
behave themselves. But while man consciously prided himself on being virtuous, because he has become the lord of
creation, he had somewhere the uncomfortable feeling that
he was not the master of his soul. That unpleasant doubt
often emerged in the middle of his self-complacency. This
doubt had its origin in the dark awareness that something

was rotten in the inner state, in the recesses of the cellar areas of his emotional life.

We know that his growing discontent is due to that same civilization that has given such a boost to the ego of modern man. The contrast between his high ego demands and the increasing aggression within himself produced an obscure but distinct discomfort. The unconscious guilt feeling springing from aggressiveness and going hand in hand with the frustration of other strong desires is one of the main sources of that discontent felt in our civilization. Restrictions and privations in the area of sexuality are especially resented, yet they are claimed in the interest of society. The price man had to pay for his superiority and his pride was too high. Man maintained his exaggerated opinion of himself and of his singular, elevated, moral position in the world in spite of such lingering uneasiness. Another aspect of the consequences of human presumptuousness, favored by civilization, will soon become apparent.

We cannot hope to make even a small contribution to the answers to the other questions we put if we do not consider the kind of beings we men are, that is, without a concept of human nature. Philosophers, theologists, psychologists, and representatives of other sciences have had long debates about whether man is good or bad, that is, soberly speaking, moral or immoral in terms of our present standards. Such discussions awaken in the scientist a feeling of vivid uneasiness if he is invited to take part in them. No zoologist is asked to express his opinion about whether the stag beetle is good or bad.

If the psychoanalyst reluctantly expresses a view about such a questionable problem he can only state that man seen in a conventional sense is better and worse than he himself imagines. That means that in terms of depth psychology man has more, and much more intensive, asocial and antisocial impulses than he consciously perceives and that he has also some unconscious moral trends he never dreamed of. But those are platitudes for every psychoanalyst. Has he nothing else to add to such commonplace remarks on human nature? Does his experience not enable him to contribute something more penetrating? It is obvious that statements of such fundamental nature will always have a highly subjective character and cannot claim to be scientific in a sense that can be proved or verified. It is in this spirit that the following general remarks have to be taken.

When a person such as this writer has been occupied with the analytic study of men and women during forty-odd years he will not only obtain many specific psychological insights, but also necessarily arrive at some general psychological impressions of human nature. In the course of many years these impressions will coalesce and finally lead to certain conclusions. One cannot know whether they are correct or not, since their general character does not allow any test or evidence. There remains only the possibility of expressing them and of listening attentively to the views and voices of others, of better observers or of research workers who approach the problem equipped with more appropriate tools.

For once we have to spell things out crudely: man is a moral climber. Let us exlain what is meant by this expression with the help of the analogous expression used in another area. We call a person a social climber when he tries to rise to a social level much higher than his position and

circumstances would justify. Colloquially, the expression
has a critical or even derogatory note: it implies that the
person is overzealous in this attempt or uses every possible,
also ridiculous, means in his efforts to ascend to a higher
social place. The expression "moral climber" was introduced in my book *Masochism in Modern Man* in 1940. It
denotes analogously a person who tries to live beyond his
moral standard and makes energetic, sometimes even desperate efforts to mount to a moral position that is too high,
compared with his means and abilities.

In this sense man is in my view a moral climber. The limi-
tation set by his biological and psychological make-up as
well as by the external conditions of his life are such that his
moral goals ought to be very modest. Considering his poor
endowment and his archaic inheritance as well as the many
handicaps from outside, the aims he can reach are necessarily restricted. Granted that there is also a trend in him
to strive for higher moral standards, he is not made to
become an angel nor a moral superhuman. You can play
only with the cards you have. Man's place in nature and
nature's place in man determine his kind of existence and
stature, an infinitesimal span and a quick episode on this
little planet, which is itself not more than a speck of the
dust of the Universe. As a matter of biological and psychological fact he is not as far removed from the animals
as he imagines. All the technical progress has not given him
a different fundamental constitution and no effort of his will
enables him to overcome the disadvantages connected with
it. He can daydream that he will penetrate the stratosphere.
He will perhaps succeed, but he is at home on this
poor planet.

The dynamics of civilization made it unavoidable that

man's moral demands on himself surpassed the state of his actual position, that he has overreached himself. Ethics and religion have propelled and forced him so far ahead that he has overshot the mark. Christianity decrees that he ought to love even his enemy, a humanly impossible goal. When you want to hit the doorknob of the room with your revolver, you have to aim a little higher, but when you aim too high you will not hit the target. Robert Browning said that "a man's reach should exceed his grasp, or what's a Heaven for?" The poet's question can be sincerely answered: We do not know. We doubt that this is its purpose. To tell the truth, we even doubt its existence. We do know, however, that the danger to man is overreaching.

We spoke earlier of *hubris,* of the sense of power and superiority of the Greek hero, of his claim to be exempted from the ordinary laws that govern average man. Here is the other side of the presumptuousness or conceit of that Greek hero: the tragic figure of the moral climber who imagines that he can ascend heights neither allowed nor allotted to him. The fateful consequence of man's too high opinion of himself is that in despair about not reaching perfection man is inclined to reverse the course and become as evil as possible. The highest ethical ideals can well live in wicked men, yet their presence and pressure can and sometimes do make man more wicked.

Our experience in analytic practice confirms again and again that there are secret alliances in which violent impulses and aggressive tendencies are joining hands with high moral demands. Worse cruelties and massacres, pogroms and mass murder were committed in religious or national zeal, in the name of a sacred cause, than by uninhibited, undiluted sadistic drives. The reason and ambition of man, all his refinement and technical capabilities were put into the service of the most ferocious, savage, bloodthirsty and brutal drives, sanctioned and sanctified by religion. Mephisto discussing man's nature throws it in Jahveh's teeth:

> Ein wenig besser würd er leben
> Hätt'st Du ihm nicht das Himmelreich gegeben
> Er nennt's Vernunft und braucht's allein
> Nur tierischer als jedes Tier zu sein.

> He'd have got on better, Lord, had you not let
> Him have that merest glimpse of heavenly light
> Which he calls reason, using it at best
> Only to grow more bestial than the beasts.

Thus speaks in grim sarcasm the Prince of Darkness who in another scene writes into the album of a student "You will be as God, knowing good and bad." He very appropriately refers to the advice of the Serpent in the Bible:

> Follow the ancient text and heed my coz, the snake,
> With all your likeness to God you'd sometime tremble
>   and quake.

We live in an age in which not only preachers from the pulpit, but also psychologists from their armchairs and even psychoanalysts admonish us that we have to renounce aggression and hate and that we have to love the neighbor and the neighbor's neighbor and the enemy. Though these new apostles speak with the tongues of men and of angels, and have a program of charity, they are become as sounding brass band. Yes, in the name of such all-embracing Christian charity we are warned that this is the only means to prevent the extermination of our species ("Love or perish").

Such a psychological do-it-yourself prescription is in

accordance with our "American vision,"[4] but leaves man's innate aggressiveness out of account. These moral counselors of mankind intensify and enforce just those presumptuously overidealistic and proud, vain, and conceited concepts. They are unconsciously sponsors of those tendencies of man, the moral climber, that lead to the great catastrophes of history. If history teaches anything, if man can learn anything from the evolution of his species, it is that he is an animal that can be tamed or civilized, as he calls it, only to a certain very modest extent. Such a realistic self-evaluation contradicts, alas, the popular belief that man becomes better every day, in every way.

The repeated and urgent pleading for Christian love and the expectation that men can be made into kind, noble, and virtuous beings are equally foolish and futile. The most enlightened minds of mankind have tried to reduce man's optimistic and exaggerated expectations and to diminish the excessive moral demands on himself. Such a more casual concept of man's nature is not identical with humbleness. It is rather a courageous and realistic attitude of self-acceptance.

[4] Joseph Adelson of Bennington College characterized the American vision an optimistic one "which is captured by the idea of infinite possibility" ("Freud in America," *The American Psychologist,* Summer, 1956). "The key antithesis" is between Freud's view, which emphasizes the limitations imposed on man by his nature and "the American emphasis on perfectibility that leads to a belief in extreme human plasticity." Lionel Trilling acknowledges the same contrast in his essay on Freud's last book, which shows his "ultimate tragic courage in acquiescence to fate" (*Gathering of Fugitives,* Boston, 1956). Recently Walter Weisskopf justly pointed out that the approach of new American social thought, for instance the concepts of Riesman and Fromm, stands in sharp contrast to Freud's attitude: "However, Freudian irrationalism, dualism and pessimism are incompatible with the American optimistic belief in the rational, progressive perfectibility of man and society." ("The Socialization of Psychoanalysis in Contemporary America," *Psychoanalysis,* 1956, 4.)

Three hundred years ago Blaise Pascal warned in his *Pensées* that whoever wants to become an angel ends by becoming a beast ("Qui veut faire l'ange, fait la bête").

Anatole France, following the trail of Goethe in this direction, asserts that his Abbé Jerome Croignard would direction, asserts that his Abbé Jerome Croignard would not have signed a single line of the Declaration of the Rights of Man "because of the excessively iniquitous distinction which is established in it between man and gorilla." The Abbé Croignard considered pride the source of the greatest evils and the only vice against human nature. He believed that man makes himself unhappy by that exaggerated feeling he has of himself and that he, if he could obtain a more humble and more realistic idea of his nature, would be gentler towards others and himself.[5] Anatole France, in *Le Jardin d'Epicure,* states that Robespierre was an optimist who believed in virtue and adds: "Statesmen of this temperament do most harm. If one wishes to govern men, one must not lose sight of the fact that they are michievous monkeys. This is the only condition upon which one can be a human and benevolent politician. The folly of the Revolution was its desire to found the government of virtue on earth. When one wants to make men good and wise, free and noble, one necessarily arrives at the wish to kill them all. Robespierre believed in virtue; he introduced a government of terror. Marat, who also believed in virtue, ordered that two hundred thousand heads be chopped off." If Anatole France had lived long enough he would have found a confirmation

---

[5] "Il semble bien, en effet, que les hommes se rendent malheureux par le sentiment exaggeré qu'ils ont d'euet de leur semblables et qui, s'ils se faisaient une idée plus humble et plus vraie de leur nature humaine, ils seraient plus doux d'autruis et plus doux à eux-mêmes." Anatole France, *Les Opinions de Mr. Jerome Croignard.*

of his views in the fact that Hitler, who believed men ought to be heroic, ordered that a few million people be killed in gas chambers and concentration camps.

The sage of the Béchellerie was a very old man when the first World War approached its end. He did not believe in a future era of peace and thought that the future was a very convenient place in which to put our utopias. He told a beautiful lady who visited France at the Béchellerie and who had remarked that he had a very poor opinion of man:[6] "Did you not realize that the greatest cruelties, the most horrible massacres are inspired by the idea that man is good and virtuous? The small demagogic speakers and would-be physicians who caused the revolutionary mass-murder and who drowned France in blood wished exactly to restore the primitive goodness, the virtue of Eden of man. They lacked that benevolence, that tolerance that only the certainty of human infirmities secures. Those doubtful visionaries wanted to make truth govern on earth and to offer justice for all. They exterminated a great number of people in order to let the few who survived live in a sort of promised land. If I on the contrary have a poor idea of men, it is because I love them and feel sorry for them."

The ardent love of virtue is as murderous as a fanatic hate of vice. Mankind has several times experienced a reign of terror of virtue and justice. An observer who is wise and sober and loves man can only wish that we all might arrive at a more modest concept of our innate nature. If man is taken down a few pegs in his moral climbing and if he gives up the idea of his own grandiosity and perfectibility, there is perhaps a little hope that he will survive.

We observe in analytic treatment that a lowering of self-

[6] Nicolas Ségur, *Dernières Conversations avec Anatole France* (Paris, 1927), p. 35.

imposed moral demands, a reduction of the claims of a too
severe superego and a reasonable measure of self-acceptance combined with the acknowledgment of one's limitations, bring about a decrease of individual unconscious guilt
feeling. It is not unlikely that such a reduction of guilt feeling could have a similar beneficial effect in the collective
treatment of pathological mankind. It is perhaps too optimistic to hope that the diminution of universal guilt feeling
could check the outbreak of the world aggression that
would result in the extermination of man. Our recommenda-
tion for a considerable reduction of exaggerated moral
demands and of man's too high opinion of himself might
come a few hours too late—too close to the time that the
H bombs begin to fall. Maybe it resembles those remedies
of folk medicine that are advised after the illness has too far
progressed, instead of being applied to prevent it. The observer has occasion to recognize such similar confusion of
therapy with prophylaxis in the frequent hindsights of our
American politicians. It looks at this moment as though
mankind had missed the bus. But such an impression is
perhaps too pessimistic and others see a silver lining on the
dark cloud threatening human civilization.

Religion is far from telling nothing but the truth, and
it is farther from telling the whole truth. There is, however,
some truth in the Fall myth that warns man he should not
think of himself as godlike. A German proverb says that
trees do not grow into heaven. We would add, with the
exception of the giant world trees in various ancient mythologies. But those are really gods, totemistic tree gods.

We look back at the evolution of civilization that began
with man's first disobedience and with Adam's eating the
fruit of the forbidden tree. The opening scene of Frazer's
Golden Bough occurs to us. The landscape is the sacred

grove and sanctuary of Diana of the Wood, near the Lake of Aricia. "In this sacred grove there grew a certain tree round which at any time of the day and probably far into the night, a grim figure might be seen to prowl. In his hand he carried a drawn sword, and he kept peering warily about him as if at every instant he expected to be beset by an enemy. He was a priest and a murderer, and the man for whom he looked was sooner or later to murder him and to hold the priesthood in his stead. Such was the rule of the sanctuary." And such, we would like to add, is the picture in depth of man. If wishes were horses, some of them would pull the hearse of our near relatives and dear friends. We are all potential murderers.

POSTSCRIPT

THE OUTLINE of this book emerged when this author was twenty-five years old. He read its final draft when he approached his seventieth year. His main interest in the subject matter is still the psychological, as once in the spring of life. We learn what man is by his history and the remnants of his prehistory.

The main part of this book is a reconstruction of an important part of this prehistory, dragged from the deep amnesia of mankind by the analysis of its most significant myths. The discovery that I made as a young analyst and that was presented in the form of an interpretation of the Fall story and of the Passion was not through my merit. It was a stroke of luck, comparable to the felicitous finding of a valuable object that was before all eyes on the main street and remained unobserved and passed by. It was facilitated by the fact that I had not acquired that "frame rigidity" that is one of the characteristic features of modern research and that I did not dwell in prefabricated thought houses.

A single isolated fact, an insignificant and neglected detail, became for me a fascinating lead around which I built my construction. All evidence stands on the issue of this single fact. If the issue of this decisive small thing fails, all the evidence fails with it.

I do not doubt that there are many errors, uncertainties,

and gaps in the content and in the presentation of my thesis, but I believe that this new interpretation of the Fall myth and the Christ tale, the heart of the matter, is in its essential features correct. I sometimes rushed in where scholars fear to tread and the result of such daring must be many mistakes. One can in sincere modesty well admit such errors and inaccuracies and yet state the conviction that one has discovered something that had remained unrecognized until now. It is on this note that I bring to its close this inquiry into the sense of guilt which haunts our civilization.